Praise for Emotionally Intelligent Leadership: Facilitation and Activity Guide

"A remarkable collection of contributors have come together to create this guide. Each module is clearly laid out by experienced practitioners, making the already accessible emotionally intelligent leadership model a real pleasure to work with."

—*Rian J. Satterwhite, Center for Student Leadership, Kennesaw State University*

"Student life professionals everywhere will want to make the *EIL Facilitation and Activity Guide* part of their regular leadership training. The guide allows practitioners to explore EIL with students through various activities, discussion questions and reflection that encourage students to put EIL into action."

—*Shelley K. Bannish, director of student life and involvement, Centralia College*

"In classrooms, co-curricular settings, or other environments, professionals involved with leadership development or student life will find these activities easily manageable and relatable to most any scenario that a person could develop in their own life. Shankman, Allen, and company have brought a very important piece to the emotionally intelligent leadership discussion by making it *tangible*."

—*Dr. Denny Bubrig, assistant dean of students, Bowling Green State University*

"Provides groundbreaking leadership training that emphasizes the role emotional intelligence plays in the development of student leaders."

—*Ceci Brinker, director of student life, Eastern Illinois University, and Katey Beverlin, assistant director of student activities/coordinator of Greek life, Augustana College*

"Offers creative and applicable modules on emotionally intelligent leadership. It is a definite resource for anyone working with and educating student leaders."

—*Anne H. Arseneau, associate director of student activities, College of William & Mary*

Emotionally Intelligent Leadership for Students

Facilitation and Activity Guide

Marcy Levy Shankman & Scott J. Allen

EDITORS

JB JOSSEY-BASS™
STUDENT LEADERSHIP

The Jossey-Bass Higher and Adult Education Series

Copyright © 2010 Marcy Levy Shankman and Scott J. Allen. All rights reserved.

Published by Jossey-Bass

A Wiley Imprint

989 Market Street, San Francisco, CA 94103–1741—www.josseybass.com

Readers should be aware that Internet Web sites offered as citations and/or sources for further information may have changed or disappeared between the time this was written and when it is read.

Limit of Liability/Disclaimer of Warranty: While the publisher and author have used their best efforts in preparing this book, they make no representations or warranties with respect to the accuracy or completeness of the contents of this book and specifically disclaim any implied warranties of merchantability or fitness for a particular purpose. No warranty may be created or extended by sales representatives or written sales materials. The advice and strategies contained herein may not be suitable for your situation. You should consult with a professional where appropriate. Neither the publisher nor author shall be liable for any loss of profit or any other commercial damages, including but not limited to special, incidental, consequential, or other damages.

Jossey-Bass books and products are available through most bookstores. To contact Jossey-Bass directly call our Customer Care Department within the U.S. at 800–956–7739, outside the U.S. at 317–572–3986, or fax 317–572–4002.

Jossey-Bass also publishes its books in a variety of electronic formats. Some content that appears in print may not be available in electronic books.

Library of Congress Cataloging-in-Publication Data

　　Emotionally intelligent leadership for students : facilitation and activity guide / Marcy Levy Shankman and Scott J. Allen, editors.

　　　　p.　cm. — (The Jossey-Bass higher and adult education series)

　　Includes bibliographical references.

　　ISBN 978-0-470-61575-1 (pbk.)

　　　1. Educational leadership.　2. Teacher effectiveness.　I. Shankman, Marcy Levy.　II. Allen, Scott J., 1972-

　LB2346.E47 2010

　371.2001'9—dc22

2010009692

Printed in the United States of America

FIRST EDITION

PB Printing　　　10 9 8 7 6 5 4 3 2 1

CONTENTS

PREFACE

When we sat down to write the book *Emotionally Intelligent Leadership: A Guide for College Students*, we began by discussing the purpose of the book. Although some authors may come to a project with different goals, we came with a shared vision. We intended to write the book as a vehicle for sharing our ideas with as broad an audience as possible. We wanted to introduce emotionally intelligent leadership (EIL) to students, professionals working with students, faculty, and others who engage with students throughout their college experience.

Simply put, we believe this subject has the potential to make a difference in student leadership development. For students, EIL provides a lens to view themselves and enhance their capacity to make a difference on campus and in their community. For those working with students, EIL provides a framework for supervision, advising, teaching, mentoring, coaching—the application potential is wide open.

In some ways, we think about EIL as the baseball diamond in the movie *Field of Dreams*—"If you build it, they will come." Leadership is available to all of us—and to all students who desire to enhance their skills. Student organizations, residence halls, project teams, workplaces, the larger campus community — all are potential practice fields for those interested in making a difference in the lives of others. And we think EIL provides students with one way to embark on a future full of amazing possibilities.

So here we are, on the next step of our journey—and, we hope, of yours. From the outset, even while we were writing the book, we envisioned a suite of EIL resources. These resources provide direct, hands-on learning experiences for students and professionals alike. The suite consists of five separate but inter-related resources:

- *Emotionally Intelligent Leadership: A Guide for College Students*
- *Emotionally Intelligent Leadership for Students: Inventory*
- *Emotionally Intelligent Leadership for Students: Facilitation and Activity Guide*
- *Emotionally Intelligent Leadership for Students: Student Workbook*
- *Emotionally Intelligent Leadership for Students: Development Guide*

✦ Emotionally Intelligent Leadership: A Guide for College Students

Emotionally Intelligent Leadership: A Guide for College Students is a groundbreaking book that combines the concepts of emotional intelligence (EI) and leadership in one model: emotionally intelligent leadership (EIL). This important resource offers students a practical guide for developing their EIL capacities and emphasizes that leadership is a learnable skill that is based on developing healthy and effective relationships. Step by step, we outline the EIL model of three facets (consciousness of context, consciousness of self, and consciousness of others) and explore the twenty-one capacities that define emotionally intelligent leadership.

✦ The Inventory

One of the greatest challenges in leadership development is translating theory into practice—how do the big ideas about leadership make sense to us as individuals so that we can behave differently? Talking about leadership is one thing—integrating ideas about leadership into our thoughts and actions is another. Assessments serve many purposes along this line—making an abstract concept real, translating theory into practice, and finding meaningful connections between ideas and ourselves. The *Inventory* is our contribution to the field of assessment.

The *Inventory* offers a formative learning experience. While some leadership assessments are diagnostic or predictive in nature, the *Inventory* is an opportunity for individuals to explore their experiences in leadership with a focus on learning one's strengths and limitations based on past behaviors. At the same time, the *Inventory* propels students' thinking into the future with a focus on self-improvement and leadership development. Results include an enhanced understanding of EIL and its application, identification of perceived strengths and limitations, and a plan for further development.

A free downloadable *Inventory Facilitator's Guide* is available (see p. viii); it also appears as an appendix to this *Facilitation and Activity Guide*.

✦ The Facilitation and Activity Guide

The *Facilitation and Activity Guide* is written for leadership educators and practitioners, campus-based professionals, faculty, and anyone interested in guiding students through hands-on learning opportunities that deepen their understanding of emotionally intelligent leadership. The *Facilitation and Activity Guide* is organized in a similar fashion to *Emotionally Intelligent Leadership: A Guide for College Students*, with at least one chapter (module) dedicated to each of the three facets (consciousness of context, consciousness of self, consciousness of others) and the twenty-one capacities of EIL. Each module provides everything that a facilitator needs to know to prepare and facilitate the learning experience (generally forty-five to sixty minutes in length). The modules are written with specific directions, talking points, and discussion questions. When supplemental materials are needed, they are listed at the outset. This resource includes the worksheets, also found in the *Student Workbook*, that the students may utilize during the course of the learning experience. Finally, the *Facilitation and Activity Guide* includes a facilitation plan, suggested program designs, and syllabi in the appendices.

✦ The Student Workbook

Recognizing the need for students to actively engage in their learning, the *Student Workbook* supports and complements the material covered in the *Facilitation and Activity Guide* and the *Inventory*. The *Student Workbook* includes handouts, learning activities, case studies, questions for reflection, and additional resources for further learning. Each chapter of the *Student Workbook* follows the flow of *Emotionally Intelligent Leadership: A Guide for College Students* and the *Facilitation and Activity Guide*. Students may also use the *Student Workbook* as a follow-up to the EIL Inventory.

✦ The Development Guide

The *EIL Development Guide* provides students with hundreds of ideas for improvement. The *Development Guide* offers the reader a description of each capacity and a detailed description of what it looks like to others when an individual is over- or underusing each capacity. In addition, we identify dozens of films, online resources, learning opportunities, books, student quotes, and reflection questions for each of the twenty-one capacities. An individual interested in developing their skills will have a strong foundation in the material and the guidance needed to begin this work.

Eleanor Roosevelt said "living and learning go hand in hand" (Gerber, 2002, p. 256). We believe that this notion extends to leadership—we all have the potential to lead. It's up to us to do it. We hope these resources help students further discover the leadership potential within them. And we hope these materials empower those working with students—to help them guide students in their development, and perhaps, along the way, learn more about leadership for themselves. We certainly have.

Marcy Levy Shankman, Ph.D.
Scott J. Allen, Ph.D.

REFERENCE

Gerber, R. (2002). *Leadership the Eleanor Roosevelt way: Timeless strategies from the first lady of courage*. New York: Portfolio.

ACKNOWLEDGMENTS

From the outset, we have placed a high value on genuinely engaging in open dialogue and creative thinking. Not only does this approach bring out our best, but it also allows us to tap into the minds and talents of a wide range of colleagues and students. Approaching our work in this way has resulted in a resource far more powerful and inspiring.

This *Facilitation and Activity Guide* demonstrates the power of collaborative work. Our contributors eagerly engaged in developing the modules that comprise the *Guide*. The authors are all practitioners in leadership development—in higher education, the nonprofit sector, and business. Collectively, they've created an incredibly accessible resource that makes active learning a reality for our students. Thanks to:

Ginny Carroll, principal, inGINuity

Les Cook, Ed.D., vice president for student affairs, Michigan Technological University

Lucy Shaffer Croft, Ed.D., assistant vice president for student affairs, University of North Florida

Jill Davidson, director of children and day camping services, The Mandel Jewish Community Center of Cleveland

Jon Dooley, Ph.D., senior associate dean of student development, Marquette University

Tara Edberg, assistant director for leadership programs, University of Iowa

Darin Eich, Ph.D., leadership facilitator and consultant, ProgramInnovation.com and CollegeMotivation.com

Paige Haber, instructor, Department of Leadership Studies, University of San Diego

Mike Hayes, executive director of campus life, Washington University in St. Louis

Amy Kautz, coordinator for resident student learning, University of South Carolina

Gabrielle Lucke, director, Training and Educational Programs, Office of Institutional Diversity and Equity, Dartmouth College

Gary Manka, director for student government advising, training and operations, University of South Florida

Jim Meehan, law student, University of Akron

Anthony Middlebrooks, Ph.D., assistant professor, Organizational and Community Leadership, School of Urban Affairs and Public Policy University of Delaware

Susana Muñoz, Ph.D., postdoctoral research associate, Department of Educational Leadership & Policy Studies, Iowa State University

Cathy Onion, assistant professor, Western Illinois University

Henry C. Parkinson III, Ed.D., director of student development and campus center, Fitchburg State College, and leadership consultant for LTE Consulting, Inc.

Adam Peck, Ph.D., dean of student affairs, Stephen F. Austin State University

Mary Peterson, executive director, Sigma Lambda Gamma and Sigma Lambda Beta

Tracy Purinton, associate director, MIT Leadership Center

Darbi Roberts, student development coordinator, Carnegie Mellon University in Qatar

Sabrina Ryan, coordinator of Greek programs, Case Western Reserve University

Wes Schaub, director of Greek life, Case Western Reserve University

John Shertzer, vice president, Leadership Ventures

Karyn Nishimura Sneath, owner, nPower

Sarah Spengler, principal, Grace Partners, LLC

Diana Wilson, advanced program coordinator, Center for Early Childhood Studies, Pima Community College/University of Arizona Undergraduate Community of Practice

David Zamansky, assistant director of the Memorial Union, Programming and Leadership, University of New Hampshire

We also appreciate the feedback of Josh Merkle, graduate assistant, John Carroll University.

ABOUT THE AUTHORS

Marcy Levy Shankman, Ph. D., has been training and consulting in leadership development and organizational effectiveness since 1998. She is principal of MLS Consulting LLC, which she founded in 2001, and enjoys working with a wide range of clients, from small direct service agencies to national voluntary associations, from local high schools to large public universities. Marcy facilitates strategic planning and visioning initiatives, organizational change and development projects, as well as leadership training and coaching. Marcy has spoken to various groups in the local nonprofit community as well as conferences and campuses across the country. Her focus is on helping students, young and experienced professionals, faculty, and staff consider ways to enhance their own leadership development.

Marcy also teaches as a Presidential Fellow for the SAGES program of Case Western Reserve University and as an instructor in the David Brain Leadership Program of Baldwin-Wallace College. Prior to establishing her training and consulting practice, Marcy held professional positions with the Indiana University Center on Philanthropy, the Hillel Foundation at the George Washington University, and the Office of Orientation Services at the University of Iowa.

Marcy actively volunteers with her alma mater The College of William and Mary, her local school district, the learning committee of her synagogue, and the Organizational Assessment Committee of the United Way of Greater Cleveland.

Marcy lives in Shaker Heights, Ohio, with her husband and two children.

Scott J. Allen, Ph.D., is an assistant professor of management at John Carroll University, where he teaches leadership and management skills. In 2005, Scott formed the Center for Leader Development (www.centerforleaderdevelopment.com), a website that provides resources, tools, and services to businesses, organizations, and schools seeking to build leadership capacity in their employees, members, or students.

Scott is published in the *Encyclopedia of Leadership* and completed a chapter for the China Executive Leadership Academy Pudong, entitled "A Review on Leadership Education and Development Outside China." He is also a contributing author of the book *Leadership: The Key Concepts* (Routledge, 2007). In addition, his work is featured in a number of academic journals, such as the *Journal of Leadership Educators*, *Advances in Developing Human Resources*, *Leadership Review*, *The OD Journal*, *SAM Advanced Management Journal*, *International Leadership Journal*, *Journal of Leadership Studies* and *Leadership Excellence*.

In addition to his writing and work in the classroom, Scott consults, facilitates workshops, and leads retreats across industries. Scott is involved in the International Leadership Association and serves on the board of trustees of Beta Theta Pi Fraternity. Since 2007, he has served as a Sam Walton Fellow for Students in Free Enterprise (SIFE).

Scott resides in Chagrin Falls, Ohio, with his wife and three children.

FACILITATION NOTES

The following modules have been developed with the intention that they are facilitated learning experiences. Recognizing that people learn in many different ways, each module facilitates learning in various ways. Although each module does not follow a formulaic approach to the matter, the modules do seek to mix the delivery of information with experiential learning opportunities. Each module has a defined set of learning objectives that are accomplished through the delivery of the suggested activities, exercises, reflections, and short lectures. Worksheets that are referenced in the modules are contained in the companion resource, *Emotionally Intelligent Leadership for Students: Student Workbook*. The *Student Workbook* follows the same order as this *Facilitation and Activity Guide*, with page numbers stated in each module: (Activity #X, SW). Additional material presented in the *Student Workbook* supplements the facilitated modules and deepens the learning for students.

The table of contents lists the modules in the order they are presented in *Emotionally Intelligent Leadership: A Guide for College Students* (Shankman & Allen, 2008). We hope you will use this *Guide* as a way to translate the ideas presented in the book into active learning experiences, as part of a class, co-curricular leadership development opportunity or as a follow-up to the *Inventory*.

The modules themselves can be facilitated in any order. This is one way this resource provides you, the facilitator, with maximum flexibility. Each module is a self-contained learning experience. The modules do not assume that students have read the book; however, if students *have* read the book, these modules provide an opportunity for a deeper exploration of the topic at hand. Similarly, the modules are not geared to a specific type of participant, nor does the *Guide* assume leadership experience. The depth to which participants go depends on your facilitation and the knowledge and experience that participants bring to the learning environment.

Before you facilitate a module, be sure you've reviewed the capacity carefully and are familiar with the content. Each module should start with a brief overview of emotionally intelligent leadership. Appendix A: EIL Overview offers a synopsis of the model of emotionally intelligent leadership. Feel free to review this material in a manner that suits your session and facilitation style. Each module contains reference points to worksheets in the *Student Workbook*: (Activity #X, SW). You will also see direct cues for when to allow time for students to complete the work and when you should put material on a flipchart (abbreviated as "FCH"). If you want to put the suggested material into a Powerpoint presentation, or some similar program, feel free to do so.

Additional resources provided in this *Guide* include Appendix B: Facilitation Plan, which contains a series of questions to consider that relate to the three phases of effective facilitation: preparation, facilitation, and follow-up. In Appendix C: Suggested Program Designs you will find suggestions from leadership educators for ways to integrate these modules into either curricular or co-curricular settings.

The most important decision that you as a facilitator need to make is how to encourage student growth and development in relation to each given topic. Consider the following questions prior to facilitating your chosen module(s):

- *How do you hope your students will benefit from this leadership development experience? Do your learning goals align with the stated objectives of the selected modules?* Be sure you are clear about why you have selected a particular module and that the learning objectives make sense in relation to your audience, your setting, and the purpose for which you are facilitating the module.

- *Have you created a learning environment that is conducive to the module you've selected?* These modules are most effective when the learning environment encourages student participation, validates student voice, and supports students in their individual learning. Regardless of whether students experience the module as part of an intact learning experience (a leadership class or retreat) or as a one-time experience (a workshop as part of a conference), it's important to think in advance about how the environment will support the stated learning objectives of the module(s).

- *How have you prepared to facilitate the module?* Are you familiar with the written instructions as well as the flow of the module? Do you have a set of talking points that situate the module in your particular context? Be sure to take the time to read through the module. Become familiar and comfortable with the instructions and the information you will share. Have a clear understanding of how this material and the activities relate to the learning objectives and the setting in which you are facilitating the module. References to the specific chapter in *Emotionally Intelligent Leadership: A Guide for College Students* are included for each module so that you can explicitly connect the activities with book content.

- *Have you practiced the module with a group prior to going "live" with your audience?* Your participants will benefit greatly if they are not experiencing your first attempt at facilitating the module. We strongly recommend practicing each module prior to conducting it. This can be accomplished by approaching colleagues, friends, family members and co-facilitators to help you prepare. By doing so, you will ensure that you and the participants have a better experience with each of the activities.

- *How well do you know your audience?* These modules are written to provide learning opportunities for students who are interested in leadership. The modules do not assume a leadership position or role is held by the students. If you are working with a group of established leaders who hold specific positions, be sure to tailor your comments accordingly. Similarly, if you are working with a group of emerging leaders, avoid falling into traditional assumptions associated with leadership (for example, holding a formal position or having a title). If you have a mixed audience, take advantage of the opportunity to speak broadly about the selected topic as it relates to leadership—after all, the focus of these modules is both *leadership* development and *leader* development. Finally, be in tune with how the audience will respond to the activity. Will they be energized by it? Will they think it's too "soft"? Know your audience and, if possible, run the module by others to see whether they think it is a good fit for the group.

- *How will you prepare students for the learning experience provided for by the module?* According to Meier (2000), a successful learning experience begins with adequate preparation of the learner. Although each module includes a brief introduction, it's assumed that you have prepared the students for a positive learning experience. Consider the following suggestions in anticipation of facilitating each EIL module:
  - Create a positive physical, emotional, and social environment so that the students feel safe and comfortable.
  - Offer clear and meaningful goals as well as benefits for the students. The stated learning objectives of each module can help you do this.
  - Stimulate curiosity among the students to increase the likelihood that they will actively engage in the learning.
  - Do not allow yourself or one member of the audience to dominate the conversation.

Addressing these issues prior to facilitating your chosen module(s) will lead to a more successful learning experience.

One of the most common mistakes facilitators make with off-the-shelf training materials is to skip the preparation stage. The modules are written to maximize the facilitator's time by clearly listing required materials, important preparation steps, facilitation tips, and learning objectives. Although the material can be presented verbatim as suggested in the modules, the most powerful learning experiences are those that benefit from appropriate preparation. Take the time to consider and create the desired learning environment, the goals for this particular leadership development and learning experience, and how to make the most of the allotted time. When you have taken these steps, students are sure to benefit from the learning and leadership development experience.

Finally, remember that learning is about the learners. We suggest following the 80/20 rule—when you are facilitating these modules, students should speak 80 percent of the time. Your role is to facilitate the learning, not dominate it. The experiential nature of these modules necessitates their involvement. As such, manage your time carefully with your short presentations of material or stories. Likewise, if you're asking for volunteers to share their thoughts, be sure to monitor the time and suggest that they keep their responses clear and concise.

REFERENCES

Meier, D. (2000). *The accelerated learning handbook: A creative guide to designing and delivering faster, more effective training programs*. New York: McGraw-Hill.

Shankman, M. L., & Allen, S. J. (2008). *Emotionally intelligent leadership: A guide for college students*. San Francisco: Jossey-Bass.

MODULE 1

Consciousness of Context
Marcy Levy Shankman and Scott J. Allen

✦ Focus of Module

Consciousness of context means thinking intentionally about the environment of a leadership situation. The larger system, or environment, has notable influence on an individual's ability to lead. Similarly, the situation and setting in which leadership occurs are important factors for consideration. Aspects of the environment directly affect the psychological and interpersonal dynamics of any human interaction. Being conscious of the context entails recognizing a variety of environmental factors such as community traditions and customs, the political environment, and even small group dynamics.

Primary Activities

Students will engage in a quick activity to alter their physical environment, learn about what context means, and interpret quotes from other students about the importance of context and how it influences leadership.

✦ Learning Objectives and Resources

- To provide a hands-on experience that introduces students to the importance of the physical environment
- To offer basic information about the facet, consciousness of context
- To identify key internal and external factors that may influence leadership

Total Time
Forty-five minutes

Supplies
Quotes on Context (one copy)
Pens, pencils (one per participant)
Watch or clock (one for the facilitator)
Copy of *Emotionally Intelligent Leadership: A Guide for College Students*

✦ Facilitator Preparation Notes

Read Part One, Consciousness of Context, in *Emotionally Intelligent Leadership: A Guide for College Students* and answer the reflection questions for yourself. (Refer to Appendix A for an overview of the EIL model.) Prepare introductory comments based on your reading.

Be sure the room selected has movable seats; otherwise the initial activity cannot be used.

Prepare an example from your own experience that illuminates the setting and situation of a leadership experience. You will share this during the short presentation on consciousness of context.

Download *Quotes on Context* (see p. viii) and cut so that each quote is separate from the others. Determine how many quotes you want to distribute for discussion—for example, one or two per group. Consider sharing with participants that these quotes come directly from college students who were surveyed as part of the research for *Emotionally Intelligent Leadership: A Guide for College Students*.

← Facilitator Tips

After the initial instruction is given to "improve the seating arrangement," do not provide further instruction.

Context is a concept that is difficult for many people to grasp. When describing *consciousness of context* during the module, consider supplementing the talking points in the module with phrases from the Focus of Module, presented at the outset.

REFERENCES

Fiedler, F. E. (1996). Research on leadership selection and training: One view of the future. *Administrative Science Quarterly, 41*, 241–250.

Shankman, M. L., & Allen, S. J. (2008). *Emotionally intelligent leadership: A guide for college students*. San Francisco: Jossey-Bass.

✦ Introduction

Ten minutes

Announce to the group that they have two minutes to improve their seating arrangement. Look at the time and tell them to begin. If asked for clarification, repeat the initial instruction verbatim. *(Allow two minutes.)*

Have participants sit in their "new" seats. Ask the following questions:

- Who thinks they have successfully improved their seating arrangement? Ask for a couple of participants to explain why.
- Who does not believe they have improved their seating arrangement? Ask for a couple of participants to explain why.
- What might have helped you improve your process? Allow for one or two comments; then add the following points if participants do not offer them as important factors:
  - Having a clear objective—defining what a better "seating arrangement" means
  - Planning before acting
  - Identifying a "leader"
  - Soliciting input from everyone
  - Being sure that all participants are clear about what is being done and why
- What aspects of the arrangement have been changed?
  - What makes a difference to you in terms of how you sit? (For example, facing each other in a circle.)
  - What matters most to you in terms of where you sit? (For example, "I like to be in the front row.") How did this affect how you participated in the activity?

✦ Consciousness of Context

Ten minutes

Begin with a quick review of Appendix A: EIL Overview. Ask participants to focus on the definition of *consciousness of context*. Ask for a few responses to the following question: Why is consciousness of context important for emotionally intelligent leadership?

Acknowledge participants' responses. Use the following talking points to introduce what is meant by *consciousness of context*.

- Fred Fiedler is a leadership scholar and researcher who was one of the first to introduce the importance of context in considering leadership effectiveness. He defined it as the environment that the leader and followers work in (Fiedler, 1996).
- Context = setting + situation (Shankman & Allen, 2008)
  - The *setting* refers to the structure of the organization: a business, sports team, or any organization or group (formal or informal) in which leadership occurs. The setting is often a stable entity.
  - The *situation* includes the many different forces on a particular time and place: for example, individual personalities, organizational politics, perhaps even the tensions or challenges within the group. Situations are dynamic.
  - Each new context requires a different set of knowledge, skills, and abilities on the part of leaders and followers.

Provide an example from your own experience that illuminates the concept of setting and situation.

✦ Activity

Twenty minutes

Divide participants into groups of four or five. Distribute *Quotes on Context* (one or two per group). Ask participants to discuss whether they agree with the quote(s) and in what ways their own experience does or does not align with the passage. Encourage participants to give specific examples as they talk about their own experiences. *(Allow ten minutes.)*

Bring the whole group together and ask the following questions or use questions of your own to facilitate this discussion.

- What did you identify as the primary external factors (outside of the organization/group) that impact leadership?
- What did you identify as the primary internal factors (within the organization/group) that impact leadership?
- In what ways do these quotes help you describe or define the "politics" of an organization?
- In general, how do you manage forces that are out of your control?
- What strategies or steps do you take to consider the context of the organization?

✦ Wrap Up

Five minutes

Share personal observations of the challenges of being aware of the context.

Conclude with the idea that our context is always around us. We don't have to look far to find it—we just have to look at our environment differently. To close, offer the following quote:

The real voyage of discovery consists not in seeking new landscapes, but in having new eyes. —Marcel Proust (1871–1922), French author

Quotes on Context

An environment that I feel comfortable in is a huge factor in my ability to lead. If I feel that I am in the kind of place where I can say what I want and take charge, then I am more likely to lead. However, if a teacher, advisor, or another student is imposing or not inviting, I often have the feeling that I want to just sit back and not be noticed.

When external forces make a team's work seem more relevant, it's easier to inspire group members and feel as though I'm impacting what is happening in a positive manner.

The environment only impacts me when other things are happening—as in, if I am busy, it causes a lot of stress and tension when leading a group.

The environment and especially the attitudes of the people you lead have a definite effect on your ability to lead.

The environment has a total effect on how I lead. I am a better leader in a positive environment rather than a negative environment. If the overall environment of a group is hostile, it is very difficult for a leader to impact a group. Whereas if the group is more open to new people and trying new things, then the group is much easier to impact.

(Continued)

The environment has a large impact on how effectively a group can operate. If a group is willing to participate and has a high energy level, then I feel more compelled to have a similar attitude. If a group doesn't show interest, though, it sometimes seems better just to give up.

The environment can completely dictate whether or not you are able to lead a group of people. To be a successful leader, you must have the attention of your followers and clearly express yourself—this is difficult to do in a distracting environment.

The environment plays a factor when it comes to space, resources, and outside factors that may distract or aggravate the group . . . The thing about environment, though, is that there are many ways to grasp it. It could mean the literal environment (e.g., the weather) that comes into play when trying to work with or lead a group or an organization. If the weather is a distraction then groups do not work as efficiently and diligently. Now if it is the emotional environment, I think that this is a more important factor when affecting and impacting an organization. If people do not feel emotionally comfortable or stable they are less likely to trust others, and the end result is not successful.

Environment can either make or break leadership ability. If you are working around others in an environment where they fully support your duties, you will succeed many times over. If you are constantly battling for credibility, it will start to feel troublesome or hopeless.

I think that the environmental impacts are dually faceted. The first facet is the staff, administration, advisors. They can play a big role, and whether or not they like it, they can have a lot of influence over students. Their attitudes and opinions will mold the behavior of a group. The other facet is the nature of the host institution. In a school where the majority of students are supported in their endeavors, you will see more successful leaders. A school that does not encourage student-run programming will have a negative effect on student life.

I feel that sometimes the environment is one that you create, and sometimes it is created by others. If I am placed in a position to lead, I would hope that it would be one where everyone's ideas can be expressed.

The environment describes the mood, almost to what I want to call the "integrity" of the organization or group. If it's a positive environment, that's great, but when it lacks support and communication, there is room for error and even failure.

If you are in an environment that is hostile or work with people you don't get along with, then you can't focus on your work and as a result your organization's efficiency suffers. Also, an environment where you do not get feedback from your superiors leaves you wondering if you are doing a good job. Effective communication, supportive or critical, is essential.

MODULE 2

Environmental Awareness
Anthony Middlebrooks

✦ Focus of Module

Environmental awareness entails thinking intentionally about the environment of a leadership situation. The larger system, or environment, directly influences an individual's ability to lead. Aspects of the environment affect the psychological and interpersonal dynamics of any human interaction. Emotionally intelligent leaders are in tune with a variety of factors such as community traditions and customs, the political environment, and major institutions (e.g., religion, government). Demonstrating environmental awareness means having the ability to observe these dynamics and factors present in the environment as they occur. Being aware of one's environment enables a person to use this knowledge to determine a course of action with greater perspective and insight.

Primary Activities

Students will engage in personal reflection as well as a large group activity. This large group activity provides an opportunity to experience how decisions are affected by that person's

11

environment and the ways those decisions affect the possibility for future decisions.

✦ Learning Objectives and Resources

- To identify desired future goals on an individual basis
- To increase students' awareness of the full range of decision options and how time plays a role in decision making
- To explore the implications of how one's environment influences choices and potential future decisions

Total Time

Sixty minutes

Supplies

Strung-Out Decisions worksheet (one per participant)

One ball of brightly colored string or yarn

One pair of scissors

Audiovisual support to show video clip if desired

Copy of *Emotionally Intelligent Leadership: A Guide for College Students*

✦ Facilitator Preparation Notes

Read Chapter Two, Environmental Awareness, in *Emotionally Intelligent Leadership: A Guide for College Students* (Shankman & Allen, 2008). (Refer to Appendix A for an overview of the EIL model.) Prepare introductory comments based on your reading.

Identify an outgoing, talkative participant who will serve as the primary volunteer. This person is ideally someone who has a variety of ideas about his or her future.

At the start of the activity, position the chairs so that a single empty chair sits at one end facing an open parting of all other occupied chairs (picture the parted Red Sea with the empty chair at one end, positioned as if to move down the aisle).

Optional: To illustrate the new "way of seeing" as described at the end of the session, consider the following:

Incorporate the scene from the movie *The Matrix* when Keanu Reeves' character Neo begins to "see" the world as the computer code that forms it (the scene begins with the fight in the subway toward the end of the movie) or any number of scenes from *The Pursuit of Happyness*. Another film clip that could be used comes from Charles and Ray Eames' short film *Powers of Ten*, which provides an incredible illustration of awareness by first zooming out from a picture by distances in powers of ten until the viewpoint has drawn back into the universe, then zooming into the picture down to the molecular level.

A non-film-based option is to use either *Zoom* or *Re-Zoom*, two books that do the same thing as the short film *Powers of Ten* through photographs in succeeding pages.

✦ Facilitator Tips

Begin the activity with the ball of yarn in your hands.

*Very important! The strings used in the activity represent decision paths into the future. Your role as facilitator is to position the strings from a single participant to various points, based on the kind of idea shared:

- Some decision options remain open for life (for example, to learn the guitar). Hand the opposite end of the string to audience participants far away across the room.
- Some decisions need to be made by a certain age (for example, to travel to places that require strength and endurance to

reach, have children, go to medical school). Hand the opposite end of the string to audience members a modest distance away based on the "distance" to that certain age.

- Others are more limited by time (for example, to become a concert pianist, make an Olympic team, be a fashion model). Hand the opposite end of the string to audience participants parallel with or close to the participant in the chair.

Obviously these judgments are open to exceptions, but for the purpose of this activity, assert that the general practice does impose these limitations. For example, for most individuals, the possibility of being a fashion model ends in their twenties.

REFERENCES

Banyai, I. (1998). *Zoom*. New York: Puffin.

Banyai, I. (1998). *Re-Zoom*. New York: Puffin.

Shankman, M. L., & Allen, S. J. (2008). *Emotionally intelligent leadership: A guide for college students*. San Francisco: Jossey-Bass.

← Introduction

Ten minutes

Begin with a quick review of Appendix A: EIL Overview. Ask participants to focus on the definition of *environmental awareness*. Ask for a few responses to the following question: "Why is environmental awareness important for emotionally intelligent leadership?"

Acknowledge participants' responses. Offer that this session will help participants better understand one important component of environmental awareness—the relationship between time and decision making.

Ask students to complete task #1 (all columns) of *Strung-Out Decisions* (Activity #1, SW). (*Allow three to four minutes. If more time allows, have participants share with a partner.*)

Identify an outgoing, talkative participant, preferably one about to begin a transition of some sort (for example, a new job or graduation). Ask that participant to sit in the single empty chair.

Share the following observation: In leadership, and in life, we face many decisions—more than we realize, with more options than we realize. Quite often our awareness of the full range of decision options and implications is limited, largely because we have a limited awareness of our context *in* and *over* time. Time is one important component of the environment. This exercise illustrates the temporal facet of context by actually showing what decision making would look like if you could *see it*.

← The Decision

Fifteen minutes

Ask the participant in the chair about his or her future plans—what does the participant want to do, achieve, and so on? Follow with: Well, here, today, you have a decision to make: what do you want to do with your life, with your future?

Hand the end of the string to the participant in the chair. Explain that for every decision option, we're going to roll out a string into the future. (Demonstrate unrolling the ball of yarn.)

As the speaker provides ideas and answers about the future, a string for each answer is first handed to the participant in the chair, and then the ball of yarn is unrolled out to another participant in the group, where it is cut and the newly-cut end is handed to the audience participant. (Recall that other participants are sitting out in front and on both sides of the participant in the chair. Be sure that for decision options that may end soon, the end of the string handed to an audience participant is parallel or close to the participant in the chair; for decision options that remain open for life, extend the string to audience participants far away or across the room.)

Ask participants holding the other ends of the strings to remember which decision option they represent as they continue to hold their string.

As the generation of the ideas slows, ask the group to suggest other ideas and allow the participant in the chair the option to use them or not.

Once twelve to twenty strings are stretched out, pause and ask the participants to look carefully and reflect for a moment on what they are observing. Go around the room and have participants holding opposite ends of the string state the decision option that their string represents.

The room should end up with a fanned-out array of strings emanating from the participant in the chair, with that person holding one end of all the strings and many individual audience participants each holding the other end of a single string.

✦ Making a Decision

Fifteen minutes

To the person in the chair holding all the strings, say the following:

> Now it is time to make a decision. The definition of "decide" originates from the Old French *de caedere*, meaning "to cut off," as in cutting off disputes with the stroke of a sword—certainly one way to decide something! You, however [at this point produce a pair of scissors], can "cut off" options with scissors. Be mindful—for the purposes of this exercise, once you cut off an option, it is cut for good.

Prompt the decision maker to cut two or three strings, one at a time. Ask the participant to talk about the reasoning behind cutting off each decision option. After a few initial cuts, ask the person to move with the chair away from those holding the remaining strings, about five or six feet.

Explain that time has passed, so the person in the chair is getting older (five to ten years). Some strings held by participants nearby may become taut or pulled out of their hands entirely—this demonstrates how, over time, decisions may be made by *not* deciding, simply because the time has passed. Thus those options close due to time.

Repeat this process—cut a few strings, move farther away—until only a single string remains, representing the person's decision. Typically the process becomes rather challenging as the remaining decision options diminish.

✦ The Debrief

Ten minutes

First, ask the person in the chair making the decisions (and cuts) about his or her thoughts and feelings throughout the process.

Now open the discussion to the full group, soliciting general observations. Offer that an important capacity of emotionally intelligent leadership is environmental awareness—defined as "thinking intentionally about the environment of a leadership situation" (Shankman & Allen, 2008, p. 15). Ask what this activity illustrated about environmental awareness, context, leadership, and/or decision making.

Share a selection of the following points, and ask the relevant questions, if they are overlooked by participants:

- Note the many, many decision options you have available—likely many more than you can "see." Ask: What can you do better to see those options?
- Context shifts ever so slightly as time passes and decisions are made.
- With those changes come changes in the available options (the strings). Picture the fan of strings disappearing and reappearing, becoming slightly different, with every passing moment. That is the reality of your decision options and your dynamic environment.
- You can follow more than one string for a time, but the more you focus on multiple strings, the more diffuse your actions become. Pursuit of a single string will alter the available options as you move into the future. Ask participants: what are the advantages and disadvantages of focusing on a single string versus more than one?
- As you move forward in time, some decision options are no longer available. Thus you have decided by not deciding and letting time pass.
- What are the implications and applications of this activity, given that your context contains many more options than you initially recognize? Given that your context has a dynamic and temporal dimension?

← Wrap Up

Ten minutes

Conclude by asking participants to return to *Strung-Out Decision* (Activity #1, SW) and complete tasks #2 and #3.

If time allows, show a film clip (for example, *The Matrix* or *The Pursuit of Happyness*) or book (*Zoom* or *Re-Zoom*) to emphasize the importance of learning how to "see" a new way.

Strung-Out Decisions

Emotionally intelligent leadership includes being aware of your context, in the present and the future. Having a greater understanding of where actions will lead enables you to more effectively influence others toward a vision. Understanding the full array of options for action reveals the broad spectrum of relevant emotions, in both yourself and others. As you watch the activity, consider your own context, the specific decisions you face, and the relevant emotions that each decision option entails.

1. Identify an important decision that you are currently facing:

2. For the decision you identify in item #1, brainstorm as many decision options as possible. Determine when that particular decision option will or may expire; for example, at what point will it be too late to pursue that option? Fill in your decision options in accordance with the relevant time frame noted and describe the emotions you feel in relation to each decision option.

(Continued)

Decision options: **How you feel:**

Now or never:

Ending next month:

Ending next year:

In five years:

In ten years:

Never ending . . .

3. Share your ideas with a partner and brainstorm five to ten
   more decision options. Challenge yourself to move beyond
   the most obvious decision options to see the full array, even if
   some of those options appear impractical at first glance.

MODULE 3

Group Savvy 1: Diagnosing Organizational Culture

Ginny Carroll

✦ Focus of Module

Group savvy is about interpreting the situation and/or networks of an organization. Every group has written and/or unwritten rules, ways of operating, customs and rituals, power dynamics, internal politics, inherent values, and so forth. Emotionally intelligent leaders know how to diagnose and interpret these dynamics. Demonstrating group savvy enables one to have a direct influence on the work of the group.

Primary Activities

Students first learn, through a short presentation, what group savvy entails; they then apply strategies for diagnosing organizational culture to a group with which they are familiar.

✦ Learning Objectives and Resources

- To explore the definition and dynamics of group savvy, including organizational politics
- To practice the skills of identifying key elements of a group's culture
- To learn how organizational awareness enhances one's ability to demonstrate group savvy

Total time

Sixty minutes

Supplies

Diagnosing Organizational Culture worksheet (one per participant)

Organizational Awareness: Reading Social and Political Currents worksheet (one per participant)

Flipchart, markers, easel

Copy of *Emotionally Intelligent Leadership: A Guide for College Students*

✦ Facilitator Preparation Notes

Read Chapter Three, Group Savvy, in *Emotionally Intelligent Leadership: A Guide for College Students* (Shankman & Allen, 2008). (Refer to Appendix A for an overview of the EIL model.) Prepare introductory comments based on your reading.

Decide ahead of time whether you will use a flipchart (FCH) to present information or Microsoft PowerPoint or other presentation software. Prepare the following flipchart pages or slides before the session begins:

1. Group savvy is about:
   ". . . interpreting the situation and/or networks of an organization. Every group has written and/or unwritten rules,

ways of operating, customs and rituals, power dynamics, internal politics, inherent values, and so forth.
Emotionally intelligent leaders know how to diagnose
and interpret these dynamics. Demonstrating group
savvy enables one to have a direct influence on the
work of the group."—Shankman and Allen

2. Politics

"It's hidden, but . . . full of life. It's where deals are cut,
where reputations are ruined, where policies are dropped,
where the guilty are promoted, where the innocent are
convicted, and where the undiscussable is discussed.
Every organization has a shadow aspect, hidden but alive.
Once we realize it is there, we can harness that energy
and use it to defuse the bad . . ."—Stephen Denning

3. "Man is by nature a political animal."—Aristotle

4. Studies have revealed that organizational politics
   - Increase conflict in the workplace
   - Affect the health of individuals
   - Increase people's stress, strain, and anxiety
   - Negatively affect performance
   - Lead to organizational withdrawal (for example, turn-
     over, inability to attract volunteers or new hires, and so
     on) (Gentry and Leslie, 2007)

Prepare a personal story of your own about an example of
witnessing the negative effects of politics for sharing during the
section on politics. Plan to speak on the example for only two or
three minutes.

☩ Facilitator Tips

Be prepared for participants to need clarification that politics
in organizations is your focus, not politics in the larger arena of
policy and government.

REFERENCES

Denning, S. (2004). *Squirrel, Inc: A fable of leadership through storytelling*. San Francisco: Jossey-Bass.

Driskill, G., & Brenton, A. L. (2005). *Organizational culture in action: A cultural analysis workbook*. Thousand Oaks, CA: Sage.

Gentry, W. A., & Leslie, J. B. (2007, July). *CCL webinar: Gaining clarity about political organizations: Dispelling the negativity of organizational politics*. http://www.ccl.org/leadership/community/clarityWebinar.aspx.

Goleman, D. (1998). *Working with emotional intelligence*. New York: Bantam Books.

Shankman, M. L., & Allen, S. J. (2008). *Emotionally intelligent leadership: A guide for college students*. San Francisco: Jossey-Bass.

⬥ Introduction

Five minutes

Begin with a quick review of Appendix A: EIL Overview. Ask participants to focus on the definition of group savvy. Ask for a few responses to the following question: Why is group savvy important for emotionally intelligent leadership?

Acknowledge participants' responses. Offer that one way to think about group savvy is that it integrates all the capacities of emotionally intelligent leadership. Explain that when you are aware of yourself and others, especially in terms of building positive relationships; then you will be astute in how you demonstrate group savvy.

Share that it is important to understand that group savvy is all about how to navigate the inner workings and networks of an organization. This is a unique capability that is difficult to teach and more often learned with many years of practice and intentionality. Once you know how to pay attention to this invisible web of relationships—which many refer to as politics—you will begin to use the capacity of group savvy.

Return to the definition of group savvy (FCH). Add that group savvy helps you learn both the politics and values of an organization or group. Offer that today, the first step is to understand what is meant by "organizational politics."

⬥ The Shadow Aspect

Fifteen minutes

Refer to the quote on politics (FCH) and then share:

In his book *Squirrel, Inc.*, Stephen Denning defines politics as "the shadow side of the organization. It's hidden, but pulsing, throbbing, moving, and full of life. It's where deals are cut, where reputations are ruined, where policies are dropped, where the guilty are promoted, where the innocent are convicted, and where the undiscussable is discussed. Every organization has a shadow aspect, hidden but alive. Once we realize it is there, we can harness that energy and use it to defuse the bad . . ."

Ask participants for their thoughts related to the quote. After a few comments, lead a discussion using the following questions, along with any of your own.

- Beyond this definition, how would you describe group politics?
- Would anyone like to share an experience with politics in a student organization?
- Are politics considered good or bad for an organization? Why?

Provide transition from this discussion to the next with the quote from Aristotle (FCH).

← Outcome of Politics

Ten minutes

Review what studies have revealed about organizational politics (Gentry, 2007) (FCH).

- Increase conflict in the workplace
- Affect the health of individuals
- Increase people's stress, strain, and anxiety
- Negatively affect performance
- Lead to organizational withdrawal (for example, turnover as people quit, inability to attract volunteers or new hires, people's refusal to take leadership positions, and so on)

Ask for comments related to this information.

Ask whether anyone would like to share an example of witnessing the negative effects of politics in an organization. Invite participants to share a *short* personal story, as appropriate.

Point out how important it is for leaders within an organization to pay attention to these dynamics. Leaders (and followers) involving themselves in detrimental politics can be devastating to an organization (and the individual).

✦ Diagnosing Culture

Twenty minutes

Offer that group savvy represents a set of skills developed through experience. Encourage participants to use their time whenever possible to practice this capacity. For example, during a meeting (of a campus organization, a volunteer group, a team, and so on), begin to pay attention in different ways. In the book *Organizational Culture in Action: A Cultural Analysis Workbook* (Driskill & Brenton, 2005), the authors infer that diagnosing an organization's culture is at the core of group savvy.

Ask participants to identify an organization that they belong to or work for that they would like to use to practice their ability to diagnose the culture.

Instruct participants to jot down their thoughts about the organization they've chosen on *Diagnosing Organizational Culture* (Activity #1, SW). Have participants work alone or with one other person who also belongs to that organization. (*Allow ten minutes.*)

Ask for a volunteer to share his or her responses and lead a discussion on how the elements they have identified do or do not affect their ability to lead the group. What does all the data mean for an individual trying to lead the group?

✦ Organizational Awareness

Five minutes

Daniel Goleman, who helped popularize emotional intelligence, describes group savvy as *organizational awareness*

(Activity #2, SW). In his groundbreaking book *Working with Emotional Intelligence* (1998), he describes the ability as "being able to read social and political currents" in an organization.

Point out that Goleman describes the characteristics of someone with this capacity and then describes the human dynamics a person should pay attention to in a group setting.

Offer that this information can help everyone think more deeply about the intricacies involved with this EIL capacity. Ask for one or two volunteers to share how group savvy could help them become more successful personally or inspire the people around them to be successful.

✦ Wrap Up

Five minutes

Remind participants that group savvy is the ability to effectively understand others in a group and to use that knowledge to influence them to act for the good of the organization. Conclude with the following points:

- Organizational success relies upon people with an unwavering commitment to the organization's purpose and accomplishment.
- Organizational life (in business, government, and so on) is composed of people, and people often succumb to behavioral tendencies that corrupt teams, create silos, and breed dysfunctional politics. This may lead to a focus on gaining power, advancing personal agendas, or protecting one's own turf.
- When we focus on building group savvy, and we understand its importance, we focus on the forces that shape views and actions in productive ways, leading organizations toward success rather than failure.

Diagnosing Organizational Culture

Learning to recognize and understand an organization from Driskill and Brenton's (2005) *four categories of elements of group culture* will enhance your ability to figure out what's affecting the culture of a group.

Choose an organization that you belong to and record your answers to the following questions.

Name of organization:

_____

1. What are the symbolic elements? Aspects that represent something of value: logos, web pages, mission statement, organizational stories, slang used by members, formal speeches, and so on. Describe these for your organization:

2. What are the role elements? The two main roles that help in understanding a group's culture: the heroes (people within the organization whom everyone admires) and the villains (members who work against the grain). Who fills these roles for your organization?

(Continued)

3. What are the interactive elements? The rituals, group norms (written/unwritten rules), accepted behaviors, and communication styles demonstrated by groups members and by the group itself. Describe these for your organization:

4. What are the context elements? The important role that place and time play in an organization. An organization's culture is affected by its history, location, and space (both physical space and the context in which the organization exists in relation to its external environment). Describe these for your organization:

Reference

Driskill, G., & Brenton, A. L. (2005). *Organizational culture in action: A cultural analysis workbook*. Thousand Oaks, CA: Sage.

Reading Social and Political Currents

People who excel at this capacity of group savvy pay attention to:

Political Savvy

"The ability to read political realities is vital to the behind-the-scenes networking and coalition building that allows someone to wield influence—no matter what their role" (Goleman, 1998, p. 160).

The Invisible Nervous System

"Every organization has its own invisible nervous system of connection and influence" (Goleman, 1998, p. 160). Some people are oblivious to this, whereas others have it fully on their radar screens.

Personal Bias

Understanding the influence of one's own assumptions and knowing how to objectively read situations is a distinguishing skill of organizational awareness. Minimizing the distortions based on personal biases allows people to respond more effectively.

Organizational Climate

Empathizing at the organizational level means being attuned to the climate and culture of the organization. "The inevitable politics of organization life creates competing coalitions and power struggles" (Goleman, 1998, p. 162). Understanding this dynamic and identifying relevant underlying issues enables one to better address what really matters to decision makers.

Disdain or Disinterest

A lack of interest in or disdain for organizational politics is a liability. Those "who lack political astuteness more often blunder in, trying to mobilize others to their cause

(Continued)

because their attempts at influence are misdirected or inept" (Goleman, 1998, p. 162).

Political Animals

Some people thrive on organizational politics. Their primary focus is pursuing their own interests and goals. They study "the invisible web of power" (Goleman, 1998, p. 162). Political animals are weakened by their self-interest and tend to ignore information that might be useful to them, thus creating blind spots.

How well do each of these manifest themselves in your organization(s)? Which ones are you in tune with and where could you improve?

Reference

Goleman, D. (1998). *Working with emotional intelligence.* New York: Bantam Books.

Group Savvy 2: Identifying Group Savvy

Jim Meehan

⟜ Focus of Module

Group savvy is about interpreting the situation and/or networks of an organization. Every group has written and/or unwritten rules, ways of operating, customs and rituals, power dynamics, internal politics, inherent values, and so forth. Emotionally intelligent leaders know how to diagnose and interpret these dynamics. Demonstrating group savvy enables one to have a direct influence on the work of the group.

Primary Activities

Students learn through storytelling about what group savvy entails, then work in small groups to identify examples through popular films.

✦ Learning Objectives and Resources

- To reflect on experiences of group dynamics and the difficulties involved with learning how to fit in
- To identify core elements of group savvy, including personal examples and experiences
- To enhance understanding of how to demonstrate group savvy through analysis and learning how to ask key questions

Total Time

Forty-five minutes

Supplies

Group Savvy, A Summary worksheet (one per participant)

Group Savvy at the Movies worksheet (one per participant)

Flipchart, markers, easel

Pens, pencils (one per participant)

Copy of *Emotionally Intelligent Leadership: A Guide for College Students*

✦ Facilitator Preparation Notes

Read Chapter Three, Group Savvy, in *Emotionally Intelligent Leadership: A Guide for College Students* (Shankman & Allen, 2008). (Refer to Appendix A for an overview of the EIL model.) Prepare introductory comments based on your reading.

Prepare a flipchart page with the following quote:

"Coming together is a beginning. Keeping together is progress. Working together is success."—Henry Ford

Prepare a short personal story about a time when you were new to a group. This will relate to the Story-Time exercise.

✦ Facilitator Tips

Run through the module once as if you were a member of the audience. This will help you develop answers to some of the questions you will be asking. Use these answers as examples to generate conversation in the event that you are presenting to an unresponsive or a particularly lackadaisical audience.

During the *Story-Time* exercise, consider dividing participants into pairs or triads when you ask them to think of a time when they struggled to fit in. This may facilitate a greater level of sharing and participation.

During the introduction, consider asking participants to read the *Group Savvy, A Summary* worksheet silently before you discuss, or read it together out loud by asking for volunteers from the audience.

REFERENCES

Driskill, G., & Brenton, A. L. (2005). *Organizational culture in action: A cultural analysis workbook*. Thousand Oaks, CA: Sage.

Shankman, M. L., & Allen, S. J. (2008). *Emotionally intelligent leadership: A guide for college students*. San Francisco: Jossey-Bass.

✦ Introduction

Five minutes

Begin with a quick review of Appendix A: EIL Overview. Ask participants to focus on the definition of group savvy. Review the information provided in *Group Savvy: A Summary* (Module 4, SW).

Ask for any questions or comments, then offer the Henry Ford quote on the flipchart (FCH): "Coming together is a beginning. Keeping together is progress. Working together is success."

Ask participants why they believe Ford said, "Keeping together is progress." Encourage them to ground their answers in the context of what they have just read about group savvy.

After two or three responses, feel free to share your opinion and/or transition to the next segment.

✦ Story-Time

Fifteen minutes

Ask participants to think about a time when they were new to a group and struggled to fit in. Start with a short example of your own to give them time to think of their experiences. Discuss how you did or did not use group savvy and what the results were. Involve participants in this discussion by asking what elements of group savvy would have helped in the given situation.

Ask a participant to share a story of a time when he or she was new to a group. Ask others to comment on how group savvy might have been demonstrated in the situation just mentioned. Then follow up with the actual storyteller about what the person could have done differently.

✦ Group Savvy at the Movies

Twenty minutes

Divide participants into groups of three or four and ask them to think of movies with characters who exemplify or struggle with the capacity of group savvy. Ask students to complete *Group Savvy at the Movies* (Activity #3, SW).

Be sure that participants record their thoughts on the worksheet. If some groups seem at a loss for such a movie, suggest any of the following: *Rudy, Pirates of the Caribbean, Avatar, Shrek, Harry Potter, The Chronicles of Narnia,* or *Iron Man.* (Allow 10 minutes.)

Reconvene the large group and ask each group to share some or all of their examples.

✦ Wrap Up

Five minutes

Conclude by asking participants to suggest questions they can ask members in their group to help them better understand group savvy. As questions are offered, follow with the question "How will the responses you get to your question advance your understanding of the group?"

After two or three questions and responses, consider the following discussion questions to enhance greater awareness of group savvy (Shankman & Allen, 2008):

- Who is leading the meeting? How would you describe his or her interactions with the group?
- What would make the leader of the meeting more successful or influential?
- Who are the followers or contributors in the meeting? How would you describe their level of engagement or

involvement? (apathetic or motivated, subservient or independent, and so on)

- Would you say there is "something going on" that isn't being
addressed? How do you sense this? What needs to happen to
bring out this under-the-surface issue?

Group Savvy, A Summary

How does the capacity of group savvy fit into the larger picture of EIL?

Group savvy is a capacity of consciousness of context, along with environmental awareness. Although closely related to environmental awareness, group savvy focuses on the deeper levels of context in a group, such as the ways the internal politics of an organization affect decisions.

What are the primary characteristics involved in demonstrating group savvy?

Although there are several components of group savvy, reading between the lines, identifying the power players in a group, and knowing how to be an effective member without being told what to do are some of the most important ones.

Why is group savvy an essential capacity of EIL?

Identifying the underlying forces guiding an association of people can enhance your ability to make informed decisions within it. This greater knowledge of the dynamics and inner workings will likely improve your chances of, and effectiveness in, contributing to the group.

What are the critical components of group savvy?

Driskill and Brenton (2005) identify four categories of elements that help you demonstrate group savvy:

Symbolic elements: Those representing the larger values of a group such as its web page and the slang used by members

Role elements: Those that differentiate between the group's heroes (those whom many admire) and its villains (those whom most see as the rebels)

Interactive elements: The behaviors of the group, like ritual and communication styles, that will reveal broader meanings upon further group savvy analysis

Context elements: Those that define the environment and the purpose of the group, such as its physical space and its shared visions

(Continued)

When should one rely on group savvy?

Ideally, group savvy will produce the greatest benefits as you gain experience within a group. Therefore, group savvy might best be acquired and employed on a gradual basis, helping you to navigate your journey toward finding a niche in the group. Asking relevant questions facilitates one's use of group savvy.

References

Driskill, G., & Brenton, A. L. (2005). *Organizational culture in action: A cultural analysis workbook.* Thousand Oaks, CA: Sage.

Shankman, M. L., & Allen, S. J. (2008). *Emotionally intelligent leadership: A guide for college students.* San Francisco: Jossey-Bass.

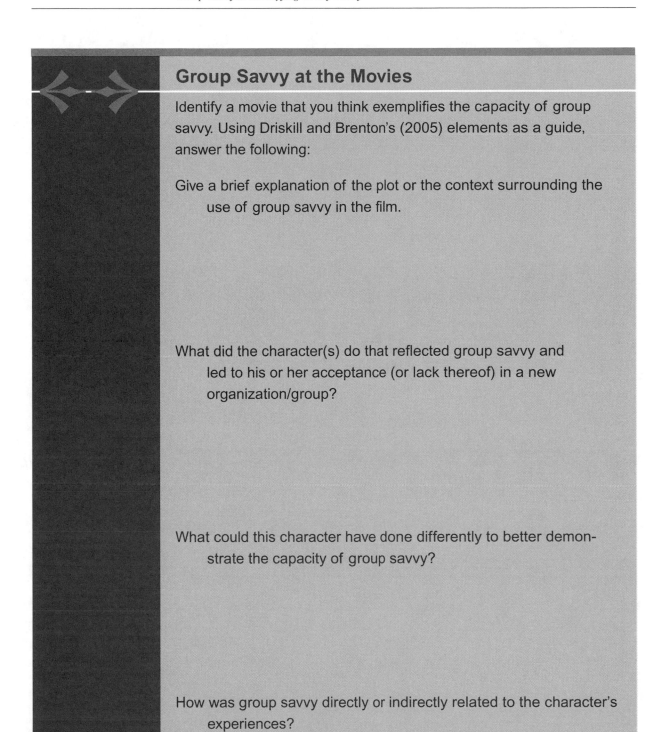

Group Savvy at the Movies

Identify a movie that you think exemplifies the capacity of group savvy. Using Driskill and Brenton's (2005) elements as a guide, answer the following:

Give a brief explanation of the plot or the context surrounding the use of group savvy in the film.

What did the character(s) do that reflected group savvy and led to his or her acceptance (or lack thereof) in a new organization/group?

What could this character have done differently to better demonstrate the capacity of group savvy?

How was group savvy directly or indirectly related to the character's experiences?

MODULE 5

Consciousness of Self

Marcy Levy Shankman and Scott J. Allen

⟵ Focus of Module

Consciousness of self is obviously all about your identity, your priorities, your values, your strengths, your goals, and so on. As Helgeson (2001) found in her research, people need to clearly understand themselves and what they have to offer to determine the best way for them to contribute and make a difference. If you are not working to better understand your motives, values, and inner workings, who will? Not only will this introspection result in some answers, but the *process* itself is also critical. For instance, when was the last time you had fun? Who were you with? What were you doing? Did you feel motivated? Having an awareness of these and other factors can help you create *more* happiness. The more you know about the values, activities, people, organizations, topics, and environments that energize you, the better equipped you will be to place yourself in situations that will bring out your best.

Primary Activities

> Students begin by talking about themselves, then engage in two activities that elicit thoughts and dialogue about a time when they successfully accomplished a task and the strengths they offered.

✦ Learning Objectives and Resources

- To practice self-reflective thinking and writing
- To explore skills and emotions related to completing a task successfully
- To identify personal strengths that contribute to completing a task

Total Time

Forty-five minutes

Supplies

Getting It Done worksheet (one per participant)

Assorted colors of wrapped hard candies (fruit-flavored, mints, and so on)

Bowl for candy

Pens, pencils (one per participant)

Flipchart, markers, easel

Copy of *Emotionally Intelligent Leadership: A Guide for College Students*

✦ Facilitator Preparation Notes

> Read Part Two, Consciousness of Self, in *Emotionally Intelligent Leadership: A Guide for College Students* (Shankman & Allen,

2008). Be sure you are familiar with the concepts so the session flows naturally. Prepare introductory comments based on your reading.

Purchase a variety of candies to increase the likelihood that each participant will select at least one piece.

✦ Facilitator Tips

Feel free to alter the topics associated with the different colored candies to fit the group's culture or reason for coming together; for example:

- Blue candy—a favorite song or group
- Red candy—a favorite childhood game
- Yellow candy—the best movie seen recently
- Green candy—preferred comfort food or meal
- Purple candy—a desired location for a trip
- Orange candy—a favorite winter or summer activity
- Striped candy—a favorite book

If participants ask if they can have more than one piece of candy, say "yes"—that way they will share more about themselves.

REFERENCES

Helgeson, S. (2001). *Thriving in 24/7: Six strategies for taming the new world of work*. New York: The Free Press.

Shankman, M. L. & Allen, S. J. (2008). *Emotionally intelligent leadership: A guide for college students*. San Francisco: Jossey-Bass.

✦ Introduction

Five minutes

Pass around the bowl and ask participants to help themselves to some candy. Once everyone has selected their candy, introduce yourself and share your responses to the following, based on which candy was selected (assign all the colors in your assortment; these are examples):

- Blue candy—a favorite song or group
- Red candy—a favorite childhood game
- Yellow candy—the best movie seen recently
- Green candy—preferred comfort food or meal
- Purple candy—a desired location for a trip
- Orange candy—a favorite winter or summer activity
- Striped candy—a favorite book

Thank everyone for their introduction.

Provide a brief review of Appendix A: EIL Overview. Ask participants to focus on the definition of consciousness of self. Ask for a few responses to the following question: Why is consciousness of self important for emotionally intelligent leadership?

Acknowledge participants' responses. Offer that this session will provide many opportunities for participants to demonstrate consciousness of self.

✦ Getting It Done

Twenty-five minutes

Ask participants to divide into groups of three. Instruct participants to think about a time when they were successful at something that was important to them. This may have been getting a good grade in a class, accomplishing a goal, playing on a team, or starting a new project. Ask participants to write their thoughts about the experience in *Getting It Done* (Activity #1, SW). (*Allow one to two minutes.*)

Next, instruct participants to share their experience in their small groups while focusing on the following (*allow fifteen minutes*):

- What they did
- What they did well to succeed
- How they felt before, during, and after the experience

Ask participants to reconvene as a large group. Solicit volunteers to share examples of emotions felt and when they felt them. Record answers on the flipchart (FCH).

Ask participants what themes they heard. Suggest that often, when we engage in work that is important to us, we're more likely to feel a wider range of emotions than if the work was not important to us. This often yields a higher level of stress, intensity, satisfaction, and/or frustration. Add personal observations, if time allows.

✦ What I Like About Me

Ten minutes

Have participants pair up. Ask them to review what they wrote about their successful experience and talk to their partner about what they *did* to make this happen. The structure for this sharing is as follows:

- One partner talks for three minutes, without interruption.
- The only time the listener gets to speak is if the speaker says anything to diminish or minimize his or her accomplishment. Then the listener will say "I object" or some other

phrase that challenges the speaker's negative self-talk. The speaker then needs to rephrase what he or she said.

- After three minutes, switch roles, following the same directions.

Announce the beginning of Round 1. After three minutes, announce that it is time for partners to switch roles. After three minutes, announce that time is up.

✦ Wrap Up

Five minutes

Ask participants to comment on which was harder to talk about—emotions or skills (for example, what they did to bring about their success). Solicit a few responses for both areas.

Offer that it is often difficult to take the time to reflect on our accomplishments and identify what we did and felt throughout the experience. Ask why it is useful to take this time.

Conclude with the idea that the more they learn about themselves, the more likely they will feel content with the tasks they must complete. When they are aware of their strengths, they have the fundamental base for knowing how to align their strengths so that they can complete tasks successfully.

Getting It Done

Think about a time recently when you were successful at accomplishing something that was important to you (for example, doing well in a class or accomplishing a task). Describe that accomplishment here:

What did you do well to experience this success? Be specific. How did you feel ...

- Before the experience?

- During the experience?

- After the experience?

What do you want to remember from this experience?

(*Continued*)

What strengths do you want to draw from in the future?

1. _____

2. _____

3. _____

MODULE 6

Emotional Self-Perception 1: Identifying Emotions
Wes Schaub

✦ Focus of Module

In essence, emotional self-perception is about identifying your emotions and reactions and their impact on you. Emotional self-perception means that individuals are acutely aware of their feelings (in real time). In addition, emotional self-perception means understanding how these feelings lead to behaviors. Having emotional self-perception also means that emotionally intelligent leaders have a choice as to how they respond. This capacity enables one to differentiate between the emotions felt and the actions taken. In most situations, both healthy and unhealthy responses are available.

Primary Activities

Students will create a shared vocabulary of emotions as well as practice different strategies for naming and discerning emotions.

✦ Learning Objectives and Resources

- To develop a broader range of descriptive terms to name emotions
- To learn strategies for enhancing emotional self-perception
- To practice the process of differentiating between emotions and knowing how to name stronger emotions

Total Time

Sixty minutes

Supplies

Name Your Emotions worksheet (one per participant)

Emotional Log worksheet (one per participant)

Stronger Emotions worksheet (one per participant)

Daydream Diary worksheet (one per participant)

Pens, pencils (one per participant)

Flipchart, markers, easel

Audiovisual support to show video clip of *Freedom Writers*, if desired

Copy of *Emotionally Intelligent Leadership: A Guide for College Students*

✦ Facilitator Preparation Notes

Read Chapter Four, Emotional Self-Perception, in *Emotionally Intelligent Leadership: A Guide for College Students* (Shankman & Allen, 2008). (Refer to Appendix A for an overview of the EIL model.) Prepare introductory comments based on your reading.

Prepare a flipchart with two columns, one titled Love, the other Fear—just as the worksheet is structured.

Find a short (two to three minutes) clip that shows a situation involving a variety of individuals where a range of emotions is evident for the *Emotional Log* activity. This clip could be from a television show, a movie, or YouTube. For example, show the scene from *Freedom Writers* when students attend the Museum of Tolerance.

Prepare another flipchart with the following questions about the clip:

- What did you think about this clip?
- What emotions do you associate with those thoughts?
- Did this concern something that had been on your mind already?

Try the various activities yourself prior to facilitating this session.

✦ Facilitator Tips

Many questions are posed in the introduction; decide ahead of time whether you want these to be rhetorical questions or have time for participants to respond to them. If you want participants to engage in dialogue, feel free to have the conversation happen in a large group, a small group (roughly five participants to a group), or pairs. This decision is best made in the context of the time available and the anticipated group dynamics.

For the *Name Your Emotions* activity, spend five minutes on the introduction and the rest of the time on the group activity.

Some of the activities described in the module are meant for participants to do after they leave the session.

Optional: When finished with completing the Love/Fear lists, announce that you will make a copy to share with everyone.

REFERENCE

Shankman, M. L., & Allen, S. J. (2008). *Emotionally intelligent leadership: A guide for college students*. San Francisco: Jossey-Bass.

✦ Introduction

Fifteen minutes

Welcome participants and share the following:

Sam is driving to work when all of a sudden someone who is texting while driving cuts in front of him, causing Sam to slam on his brakes and barely avoid crashing his car.

Ask participants to call out words or phrases that describe how they might feel in this situation.

Ask whether they might be angry or frustrated. Then share that, in this instance, Sam gets angry. "That jerk just cut me off," he thinks. "Who does he think he is?" Sam's anger affects his entire day.

Ask participants to raise their hands if they've ever been in a situation like this. (Pause). Invite students to think for a second about the other driver and then ask, What do you think the other driver is thinking about the situation?

Offer that the other driver likely isn't thinking much about the incident. The other driver may be so caught up in his or her own situation that he or she does not even know Sam was cut off. How often are we in the position of the other driver, when we cause a major problem for someone else and don't even realize it?

Here's another way to think about how our emotional reactions are tied to our individual experiences and perspective. When good things happen to us, we tend to own those feelings. For example, when you get an A on a test, what might you think?

- "I aced that test."
- "I am the best."
- "I knew I could do it."

What might you think about the same test if you don't do so well?

- "That test was too hard."
- "That professor is the worst teacher."
- "I didn't have enough time to prepare."

When bad things happen, we often externalize the blame to other people or circumstances. We divert the responsibility away from ourselves. When we give away that responsibility, we become a victim of the circumstance.

Our emotions are ours—they belong to us. If we are ignorant of this, we might be unaware of how we are reacting in certain situations. Understanding our emotions makes them work for us rather than against us. If we can learn to understand and manage our emotions, we can have much more control over our own lives.

Ask participants to think of a time when they spent the entire day thinking about how terrible or tough an upcoming event or activity was going to be (for example, a speech for class or a conversation with a roommate). Ask them to try to remember what they were feeling and what the outcome was.

Share that sometimes we create self-fulfilling prophecies— we think the outcome will be terrible, so we experience that outcome. What if we went into the same situation thinking a different set of thoughts—what might we learn from this upcoming experience? How can this experience help me? How might it help someone else? Would the outcome be different?

← Indentifying Your Emotions

Fifteen minutes

Provide a quick review of Appendix A: EIL Overview. Ask participants to focus on the definition of emotional self-perception.

Share that emotions control much of what we do and are reliable indicators of what is happening in our lives. To understand our emotions, however, it is important to accurately identify them. Confusion arises from using broad terms to describe how you feel. You might say you are mad, but in reality you are *frustrated* or *impatient* or *worried*.

One paradigm for understanding our emotions is that love and fear are the two most basic emotions. In fact, many of our feelings stem from either love or fear. Refer to *Name Your Emotions* (Activity #1, SW).

Ask participants to write down as many emotions as they can under the two headings, starting with the emotions closest to love and fear at the top and working to the bottom. They should try to record all of the emotions they can think of in the two columns. (*Allow three to five minutes.*)

Bring the group back together as a whole, and ask each person to name an emotion for the love column until they have all exhausted their lists. Record their responses on a flipchart. Repeat for the fear column. Look at both lists and ask whether there are other emotions to add to either column.

✦ Create an Emotion Log

Fifteen minutes

Observe that these two lists are pretty comprehensive and cover a wide range of emotions.

Point out that some of us may think it is in our best interest to control our emotions. In fact, at times, it isn't wise to try to change or control our emotions. We may distract ourselves or hide the feelings for a while, but the emotion will come back. When our minds are idle, we tend to go back to the situations that triggered the emotions and think about them again and again. This can influence our entire day.

To that end, understanding and managing how we feel emotionally is a valuable tool. It can be helpful to log our daily emotional activity on the *Emotional Log* (Activity #2, SW). Refer participants to the worksheet and explain that keeping a journal of feelings for two days enhances our awareness and emotional self-perception.

Suggest to participants that they be explicit in describing their emotions. Think about the list generated from *Name Your Emotions* (Activity #1, SW). In the *Emotional Log*, broad emotion categories (like happy or sad) are to be avoided. Make sure you write the full spectrum of emotions. For stronger emotional situations, note some further information:

- What triggered the emotion?
- What are my senses telling me?
- What is it that I want from the situation?
- What judgments or conclusion have I made, and are they accurate?
- What is the emotion trying to tell me?

Now ask participants to practice this process by watching a video clip (from a TV show, YouTube, or a movie like *Freedom Writers*).

After the clip, have participants complete an entry in *Stronger Emotions* (Activity #3, SW). After a couple of minutes, talk about the clip, using the questions just listed.

Remind participants that keeping a personal emotional log is a powerful learning experience that helps us develop emotional self-perception.

✦ Daydream Diary

Ten minutes

Reiterate that we tend to own our more pleasurable feelings, and we often externalize the troubling ones. According to research, holding onto negative feelings over time can affect our relationships and eventually our health (Whetten & Cameron, 2006). Learning to release troubling feelings that serve no purpose in an effective way is a helpful skill. Without this ability, these negative feelings tend to creep back into our thoughts and affect our daily routine. How might we know we aren't effectively dealing with our emotions? Solicit one or two comments.

Offer the following idea: One way to better manage the whole range of your emotions is to track your daydreams. When your mind wanders, hold those thoughts and write them down in a journal. This process can help you track how your thoughts affect your moods and responses. For instance, sometimes you get so used to thinking or feeling a certain way, you may not be conscious of it. This happens for all of us. These thoughts end up affecting our attitudes, behaviors, reactions, and perceptions.

Tell the group: get comfortable, close your eyes, and imagine a time you served on a team that you are really proud of. Think about the experience you had with one another. Think about the conversations, the location, and other factors that contributed to this positive memory. (*Allow three to five minutes.*)

Have the group open their eyes and bring them back together. Give them a second to adjust, then ask them to write down what they thought about while thinking about the team experience. Have them list, on the back of one of their worksheets, the thoughts and emotions they had while doing the activity. Ask them to consider the following questions (FCH):

- What did you think about?
- What emotions do you associate with those thoughts?
- Was this something on your mind already?

Present these suggestions: If your emotional reaction is strong, look at the situation as a third person might. If you are involved in a highly emotional situation, step back and imagine the same situation happening to someone else. How did that other person handle it—the same, differently? This will help you look at the situation more rationally and logically.

Offer that if participants complete the *Daydream Diary* (Activity #4, SW) over the course of a week, they'll make some amazing discoveries.

✦ Wrap Up

Five minutes

Suggest that another way to work on our emotional self-perception is to talk about our emotions with someone. Talk about your experiences. Talk not just about the events, but also about the feelings associated with the story. What's exciting? What's challenging? What gives you energy? What tires you out? What are the different emotions you experience, given these different reactions and experiences?

Conclude with the idea that emotional self-perception leads us to recognizing our emotions more effectively and learning how to release them. When releasing an emotion, it is important to concentrate on the emotion—not the person or situation. Focus solely on the emotion and how you feel. You'll be amazed at what you discover about yourself.

REFERENCE

Whetten, D. A., & Cameron, K. S. (2006). *Developing management skills* (7th ed.). Upper Saddle River, NJ: Prentice Hall.

Name Your Emotions

Write as many emotions as you can under the two headings;
place the emotions closest to love and fear at the top and work
to the bottom. Circle those that you experience on a daily basis.

Love	Fear
_____	_____
_____	_____
_____	_____
_____	_____
_____	_____
_____	_____
_____	_____
_____	_____
_____	_____
_____	_____
_____	_____
_____	_____
_____	_____
_____	_____
_____	_____

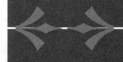

Emotional Log

Based on the list created in the previous activity, keep a journal of your feelings over the next two days. Be specific in naming the emotion. Avoid broad emotional categories like happy or sad; be as specific as possible, like *elated* or *despondent*. Make sure you include both positive and negative emotions.

Date/Time _____ Emotion_____

Associated Behavior _____

Date/Time _____ Emotion_____

Associated Behavior _____

Date/Time _____ Emotion_____

Associated Behavior _____

Date/Time _____ Emotion_____

Associated Behavior _____

Date/Time _____ Emotion_____

Associated Behavior _____

Date/Time _____ Emotion_____

Associated Behavior _____

Date/Time _____ Emotion_____

Associated Behavior _____

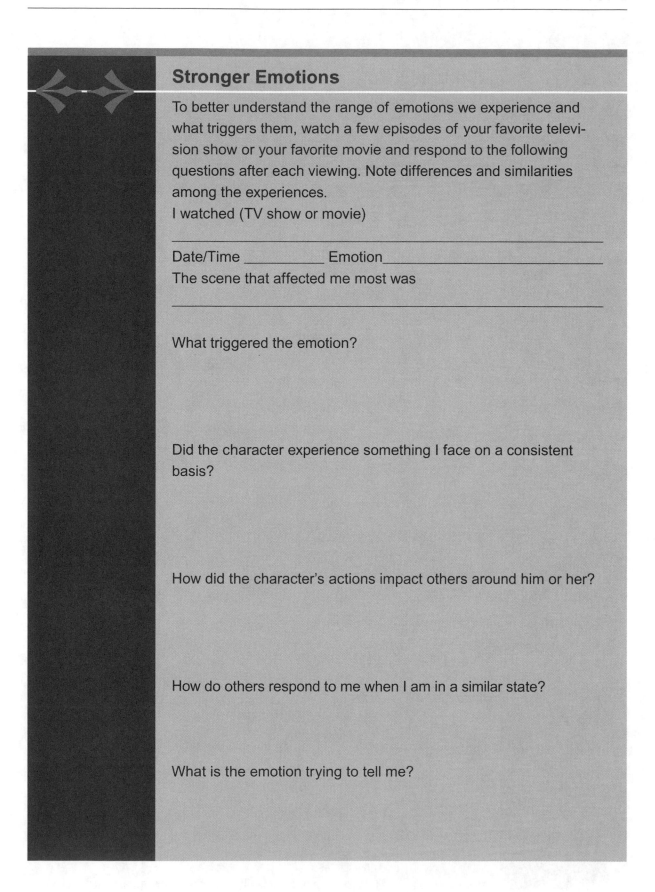

Stronger Emotions

To better understand the range of emotions we experience and what triggers them, watch a few episodes of your favorite television show or your favorite movie and respond to the following questions after each viewing. Note differences and similarities among the experiences.

I watched (TV show or movie)

_____

Date/Time _____ Emotion_____
The scene that affected me most was

_____

What triggered the emotion?

Did the character experience something I face on a consistent basis?

How did the character's actions impact others around him or her?

How do others respond to me when I am in a similar state?

What is the emotion trying to tell me?

I watched (TV show or movie)

_____

Date/Time _____ Emotion_____
The scene that affected me most was

_____

What triggered the emotion?

Did the character experience something I face on a consistent basis?

How did the character's actions impact others around him or her?

How do others respond to me when I am in a similar state?

What is the emotion trying to tell me?

Daydream Diary

Learning to release negative feelings in an effective way is a helpful skill. One way to better manage the whole range of your emotions is to track your daydreams. When your mind wanders, hold those thoughts and write them down here. This process can help you track how your subconscious thoughts affect your moods and responses.

Daydream Situation:_____
Why are you thinking about the daydream?

What emotions or feelings do you associate with the daydream?

What is the best way for you to attend to this emotion?

If the daydream relates to a problem, what is the ideal solution?

How do you get there?

Daydream Situation: _____

Why are you thinking about the daydream?

What emotions or feelings do you associate with the daydream?

What is the best way for you to attend to this emotion?

If the daydream relates to a problem, what is the ideal solution?

How do you get there?

Emotional Self-Perception 2: Scavenger Hunt

Jill Davidson

⭐ Focus of Module

In essence, emotional self-perception is about identifying your emotions and reactions and their impact on you. Emotional self-perception means that individuals are acutely aware of their feelings (in real time). In addition, emotional self-perception means understanding how these feelings lead to behaviors. Having emotional self-perception also means that emotionally intelligent leaders have a choice as to how they respond. This capacity enables one to differentiate between the emotions felt and the actions taken. In most situations, both healthy and unhealthy responses are available.

Primary Activities

At the beginning, participants take part in a personal scavenger hunt; this activity leads to opportunities for self-reflection and dialogue about reactions, the power of emotions, and how to derive lessons for self-awareness from personal experience.

❧ Learning Objectives and Resources

- To experience the connection between activities and the range of emotional reactions they evoke
- To explore personal reactions for greater self-understanding
- To develop greater emotional literacy to enhance effectiveness and awareness

Total Time

Fifty minutes

Supplies

Personal Scavenger Hunt Reflection worksheet (one per participant)

Emotion Words worksheet (one per participant)

Pens, pencils

Flipchart, markers, easel

❧ Facilitator Preparation Notes

Read Chapter Four, Emotional Self-Perception, in *Emotionally Intelligent Leadership: A Guide for College Students* (Shankman & Allen, 2008). (Refer to Appendix A for an overview of the EIL model.) Prepare introductory comments based on your reading.

Download the *Emotion Words* and *Personal Scavenger Hunt* worksheets (see page viii).

Be sure the room is big enough to accommodate the personal scavenger hunt. You will need a room that allows participants to sit either in parallel lines on the floor or in chairs. See instructions in the module.

Develop an item list for the personal scavenger hunt; include items that participants will likely have on their "person"—like a sock, pen, earring, driver's license, cell phone—and be sure to also list a few uncommon items. Be sure you identify enough items to have the activity last ten minutes.

On the flipchart, write these directions in advance and conceal the page until needed:

1. Describe a time when you were not aware of your emotions and how this affected you and/or others in a negative way.
2. Describe a time when you were aware of your emotions and you intentionally used this information to be more effective.

Develop your own story in response to these directions (to be used if no participants volunteer a story).

✦ Facilitator Tips

Read Chapter Four, Emotional Self-Perception, in *Emotionally Intelligent Leadership*. (Refer to Appendix A for an overview of the EIL model.) Prepare introductory comments based on your reading.

A personal scavenger hunt is a nontraditional hunt in which members of a team have to find items the facilitator chooses, based purely on what they have with them. Each team has a runner—the one person on the team designated to stand up and run to the finish line with the items. When a team member finds an item, he or she must remain seated and pass the item through teammates to the runner. The first runner to the finish line with the item gets a point.

This activity can be high-energy, so some groups may find it difficult to switch gears to the self-reflection phase. It may be beneficial to have the participants each find a quiet space in the room when it is time for self-reflection, rather than having them remain in their groups.

When you're leading the personal scavenger hunt, participants won't necessarily know why they are playing the game. This is intentional: you want them to perform an activity and afterward examine their awareness of their emotions. How the game is played is not that important—what matters is that the participants have an activity on which to base their learning for the rest of the session.

Be aware that some participants may feel uncomfortable divulging private personal feelings. Try not to push participants if they are not willing to open up.

REFERENCE

Shankman, M. L., & Allen, S. J. (2008). *Emotionally intelligent leadership: A guide for college students*. San Francisco: Jossey-Bass.

✦ Personal Scavenger Hunt

Ten minutes

Begin by assigning participants to teams of five to ten. Try to divide the participants up so that they are not with people they know very well. Ask them to sit together as you share the following instructions:

As a team, you have to find a variety of items that I call off my list, based solely on what team members have with them.

Before I begin calling out items, each team will choose a runner—a person designated to stand up and take the items to the finish line, which is where I am standing. The runner will sit at the head of the line.

The rest of the team members will sit in a straight line behind their runner, with the team lines parallel to each other.

When a team member finds an item, stay seated and pass the item up through your teammates to the runner.

The first runner to the finish line with the item gets a point.

Begin play. Call out each item, one at a time. Note the winner of each listed item and ask runners to return to their teams and return the items to their owners. After everyone is seated and the item is returned to the owner, call out the next item. Continue until you have finished all items or the allotted ten minutes expires. Announce the winning team.

✦ Examining Your Own Self-Perception

Five minutes

Pass out pens or pencils. Ask participants to spend a minute reflecting on the *Emotion Words* list. After a few minutes of completing the reflection privately, create teams of two (or some teams of three if necessary) and spend two to three minutes talking about the questions on *Personal Scavenger Hunt Reflection*.

✦ Debrief After Personal Scavenger Hunt

Ten minutes

Lead a discussion of how participants felt while they played the game and how their emotions affected them. Questions should be driven from the group discussion. Consider the following questions to stimulate a productive exchange; other questions should flow naturally from participants' actual experiences.

- When I assigned groups, how did you feel?
- If you were apprehensive because you didn't know anyone, did that distract you from listening to the rules, or did it make you pay closer attention?

- If you felt relieved that you were with a good friend, did that make you more excited about the game or more easily distracted?
- Were there any items that made you uncomfortable? If so, did you have a physical reaction to that discomfort that you can describe?
- If you were a runner, how did you feel when you were picked? How did that affect your game play?
- If you wanted to be a runner and you weren't picked, how did you feel? How did that affect your game play?

Feel free to add any other questions as appropriate.

✦ Self-Reflection

Ten minutes

Ask participants to turn over the *Reflection* sheet and write about the two situations listed (FCH). Emphasize that any participants who are uncomfortable sharing their situations with the whole group do not have to do so. This is an opportunity primarily for self-reflection.

1. Describe a time when you were not aware of your emotions and how this affected you and/or others in a negative way.
2. Describe a time when you were aware of your emotions and you intentionally used this information to be more effective.

✦ Pair and Share

Ten minutes

Ask participants to find a partner to talk with. Ask pairs to share, at their own comfort level, about either a situation they wrote about *or* what it was like to reflect on these situations.

Encourage participants to share at their comfort level, while also challenging them to talk about what they've reflected on. Although sharing a specific experience may be too much, most of us can talk about what it is like to think about those situations (in terms of both our feelings and our thoughts related to these two different situations). (*Allow six or seven minutes.*)

Bring the whole group back together and ask who is willing to share what they just discussed with their partner. The facilitator can choose to ask follow-up questions to stimulate additional thoughts and interpretations from other participants.

✦ Wrap Up

Five minutes

Conclude by suggesting how important it is to be aware of our own emotions. Doing so increases our effectiveness, enhances our ability to examine our ineffectiveness, and improves our relationships. Encourage participants to take the *Emotion Words* list and keep it as a reminder of emotional self-perception.

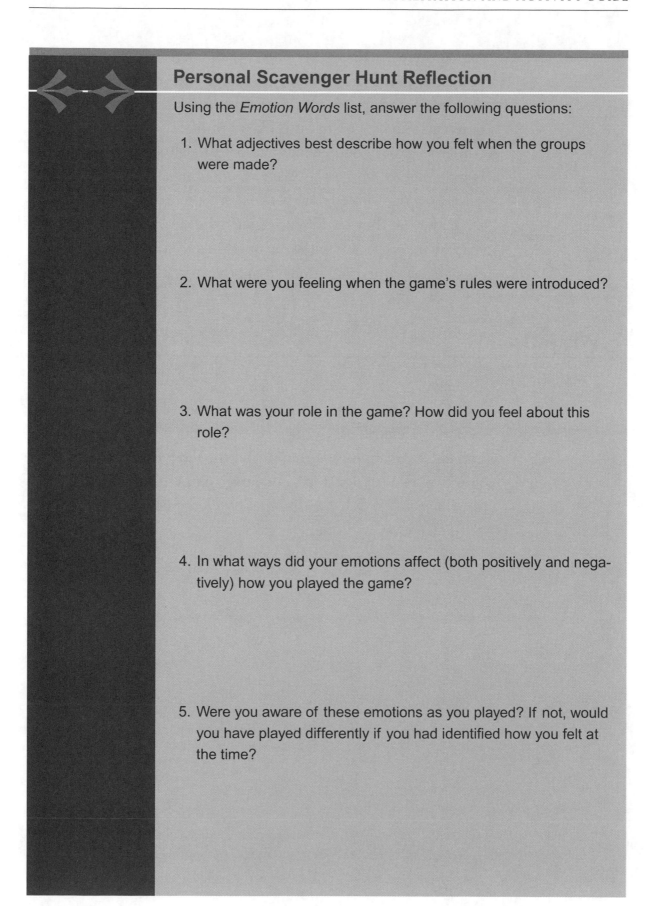

Personal Scavenger Hunt Reflection

Using the *Emotion Words* list, answer the following questions:

1. What adjectives best describe how you felt when the groups were made?

2. What were you feeling when the game's rules were introduced?

3. What was your role in the game? How did you feel about this role?

4. In what ways did your emotions affect (both positively and negatively) how you played the game?

5. Were you aware of these emotions as you played? If not, would you have played differently if you had identified how you felt at the time?

Emotion Words

Abandoned	Calm	Ecstatic	Level-Headed	Restless
Absurd	Capable	Embarrassed	Macho	Restrained
Accepted	Censored	Emphatic	Mature	Remorseful
Accepting	Challenged	Energized	Meditative	Sad
Accommodating	Cheerful	Entertained	Merry	Satisfied
Addicted	Childish	Enthralled	Methodical	Scared
Adequate	Cocky	Evaluated	Misinterpreted	Serious
Admired	Committed	Exasperated	Misunderstood	Silly
Admiring	Compelled	Excited	Mocked	Singled Out
Adored	Competent	Extroverted	Motivated	Smart
Afraid	Competitive	Fascinated	Needed	Sociable
Aggressive	Composed	Fidgety	Needy	Sophomoric
Alert	Compromising	Freaked Out	Nervous	Startled
Alienated	Condescending	Frightened	Nosy	Stifled
Alone	Confident	Frustrated	Obligated	Submissive
Ambiguous	Confused	Giddy	Obnoxious	Surprised
Ambivalent	Considerate	Guarded	Obsessed	Sympathetic
Ambushed	Considered	Happy	Optimistic	Talkative
Angry	Consumed	High-Spirited	Organized	Tenacious
Animated	Contemptuous	Horrified	Out of Place	Tender
Anxious	Contented	Humiliated	Patient	Thwarted
Apathetic	Craving	Idealistic	Patronized	Timid
Appreciated	Criticized	Ignored	Pessimistic	Tired
Apprehensive	Cynical	Immobilized	Pitiful	Trapped
Argumentative	Delighted	Impaired	Possessive	Troubled
Ashamed	Demolished	Inattentive	Powerless	Undeserving
Astounded	Demoralized	Incapable	Preoccupied	Undesirable
At ease	Determined	Independent	Pressured	Unfocused
Attacked	Discouraged	Insecure	Private	Unmotivated
Autonomous	Disillusioned	Intimidated	Proud	Unstoppable
Awed	Disjointed	Isolated	Purposeful	Useless
Awkward	Displeased	Jealous	Pushy	Validated
Badgered	Disrespected	Joyful	Put Down	Violent
Baffled	Distracted	Judgmental	Puzzled	Weary
Belittled	Distrustful	Jumpy	Raging	Welcomed
Bewildered	Doubtful	Keen	Relaxed	Whimsical
Blurry	Dumb	Kind	Reluctant	Withdrawn
Bored	Eager	Left Out	Respected	
Bowled Over	Earnest	Lenient	Responsible	

MODULE 8

Honest Self–Understanding 1: Declare Yourself

Amy Kautz

⤙ Focus of Module

Honest self-understanding is about being aware of your own strengths and limitations. Honest self-understanding means celebrating and honoring one's strengths and talents while acknowledging and addressing one's limitations. Honest self-understanding means accepting the good and bad about one's personality, abilities, and ideas. When emotionally intelligent leaders demonstrate honest self-understanding, they embody a foundational capacity of effective leadership—the ability to see a more holistic self and understand how this impacts their leadership.

Primary Activities

Participants create a self-portrait of their individual strengths, challenges, hopes, and fears, and then post these for others to see. This activity of reflection and self-disclosure is followed by a public speaking opportunity wherein participants introduce themselves as if they were their best friend.

✦ Learning Objectives and Resources

- To reflect on and publicly declare individual strengths, challenges, hopes, and fears
- To discover connections with other participants in relation to strengths, challenges, hopes, and fears
- To practice presenting oneself in a positive light through public speaking

Total Time

Forty-five to sixty minutes (depending on discussion)

Supplies

Newsprint/butcher/craft/easel/flipchart paper (one per participant)

Markers (at least one per participant)

Tape

Copy of *Emotionally Intelligent Leadership: A Guide for College Students*

✦ Facilitator Preparation Notes

Read Chapter Five, Honest Self-Understanding, in *Emotionally Intelligent Leadership: A Guide for College Students* (Shankman & Allen, 2008). (Refer to Appendix A for an overview of the EIL model.) Prepare introductory comments based on your reading.

Complete the reflection questions for yourself.

Think of at least one example of a personal strength, challenge, hope, and fear to share with participants.

Prepare a "best friend introduction" to share with participants as an example.

◆ Facilitator Tips

Anticipate that the activity will require participants to move around the space and minimal touching of others is involved.

The activity may run longer or shorter depending on the number of participants. If there are more than twenty participants, consider dividing the group into smaller rotating groups.

If time is an issue, omit the *Best Friend Introduction*. It is not as powerful a teaching tool as the *Head and Shoulders* activity.

The *Head and Shoulders* activity is also a great get-to-know-you activity for a new group.

REFERENCE

Shankman, M. L., & Allen, S. J. (2008). *Emotionally intelligent leadership: A guide for college students*. San Francisco: Jossey-Bass.

⤷ Introduction

Five minutes

Begin by introducing yourself and sharing that the focus of this session is honest self-understanding. Review the highlights of the chapter on honest self-understanding and have a brief discussion of topics with participants. Here are a few suggested topics:

- Celebrating the good and bad about your personality, abilities, and ideas
- Reflection and its importance
- Benefits of journaling or blogging

⤷ Head and Shoulders

Twenty-five to thirty minutes

Distribute paper, markers, and tape to participants.

Ask participants to partner with the person next to them to draw an outline of each other's head and shoulders on the paper with the marker. (*Allow two to three minutes.*)

Ask participants to work on their own to fill in the outline with their personal thoughts about their own strengths, challenges, hopes, and fears. Demonstrate what this looks like by sharing an example of each about yourself. Encourage participants to be as creative as they want as long as other participants can understand what they are saying, so both pictures and words are acceptable. (*Allow eight to ten minutes.*)

As participants finish, ask them to hang their papers on the wall. Once all are finished, instruct participants to rotate around the room to view all the other outlines, and note in their minds which characteristics they identify with. (*Allow eight to ten minutes.*)

Once everyone has rotated to all the outlines or time is up, consider the following questions:

- What were some of the common themes you noticed as you walked around?
- What did you have in common with other participants?
- What is unique about you?
- What surprised you about this activity?
- How might you continue this thinking by blogging, tweeting, or journaling? What would be the advantage to doing that?

✦ Best Friend Introduction

Ten to fifteen minutes

Ask participants to now introduce themselves from the perspective of their best friend. In their introductions, participants should focus on personality, abilities, and when they tend to most often show emotion.

Give your own example to start, then go around to all participants.

If time allows, ask participants to find a partner and discuss what their friends know and don't know about them, as well as how they've asked their friends for help or feedback.

✦ Wrap Up

Five to ten minutes

Wrap up the session by asking participants any of the following:

- What did you learn today about honest self-understanding?

- What did you learn today about yourself?
- How can you use the information you learned through the activity when leading others?

Share final thoughts to bring the session to a conclusion.

MODULE 9

Honest Self-Understanding 2: Look in the Mirror

Lucy Croft

✦ Focus of Module

Honest self-understanding is about being aware of your own strengths and limitations. Honest self-understanding means celebrating and honoring one's strengths and talents while acknowledging and addressing one's limitations. Honest self-understanding means accepting the good and bad about one's personality, abilities, and ideas. When emotionally intelligent leaders demonstrate honest self-understanding, they embody a foundational capacity of effective leadership—the ability to see a more holistic self and understand how this impacts their leadership.

Primary Activities

Participants create a personal mini-collage reflecting their individual strengths, develop a motto, and receive feedback from other participants about how they are perceived.

✦ Learning Objectives and Resources

- To express personal observations on identity and self-image
- To identify personal strengths and limitations
- To practice self-disclosure skills and how to give and receive feedback

Total Time

Sixty minutes

Supplies

The Mirror and Its Reflection worksheet (one per participant)

CD player for music (or iPod), soundtrack to Disney's *Mulan*, or another reflective song (such as Sting's "Brand New Day" or a calm instrumental)

Mirror (one per participant)

Markers, pens, pencils

Old magazines

Inspirational quotes and pictures

Glue

Clear tape

Scissors

Index cards

Blank refrigerator magnets (one per participant; instructions follow)

Cardstock (one per participant)

Copy of *Emotionally Intelligent Leadership: A Guide for College Students*

✦ Facilitator Preparation Notes

Read Chapter Five, Honest Self-Understanding, in *Emotionally Intelligent Leadership: A Guide for College Students* (Shankman & Allen, 2008). (Refer to Appendix A for an overview of the EIL model.) Prepare introductory comments based on your reading.

Create a sample personal mini-collage on cardstock to share with the group.

Develop a brief example of when and how you first discovered a strength and a limitation.

Create blank refrigerator magnets in advance of the workshop (one per participant) by gluing a magnet strip onto the back of a business card size (two-inch by three-and-a-half-inch) piece of cardstock.

Create a sample of the refrigerator magnet with your motto; for example,

> The flower that blooms in adversity is the most rare and beautiful of all.—Mulan

✦ Facilitator Tips

This module is designed to provoke deep discussion about strengths and limitations and encourage self-disclosure. Some participants may find it difficult to self-disclose, so you will need to model appropriate self-disclosure through the sharing of personal stories and examples.

Familiarize yourself with the story of Mulan for the first activity, *Know Thyself: Sharing with Others*. Review the lyrics of the song "Reflections" from *Mulan*, when Mulan looks into a mirror and observes that she's not the image of an ideal bride or daughter, and she muses about who she really is. You may want to prepare some notes on how to describe the content of the song.

> In the story, "Mulan disguises herself as a man to serve in the army in her father's place. While serving, she is recognized as a courageous soldier and offered a government post. She turns down the position in favor of going home and living a peaceful life with her family. After she returns home, she puts back on her lady's clothes—and shocks her fellow soldiers, who didn't know she was a woman during the time on the battlefield. The story was expanded into a novel during the late Ming (AD 1368-1644) Dynasty." (http://mybestchina.com/People_200408.html)

REFERENCES

Armstrong, T. (1999). *7 kinds of smart* (revised and updated). New York: Penguin Putnam.

McKay, M., & Fanning, P. (2000). *Self-esteem: A proven program of cognitive techniques for assessing, improving, and maintaining your self-esteem.* New York: MJF Books.

People (August 2004). http://mybestchina.com/People_200408.html.

Shankman, M. L., & Allen, S. J. (2008). *Emotionally intelligent leadership: A guide for college students.* San Francisco: Jossey Bass.

Spence, N. (2001). *Life medicine: Wisdom for extraordinary living.* Kula Press.

✦ Introduction

Five minutes

Begin by sharing that honest self-understanding means we celebrate and honor our strengths and talents while acknowledging our limitations. Knowing who we are means accepting the good and the bad about our personality, abilities, and ideas.

Share with participants that when we possess honest self-understanding, we are more likely to demonstrate effective leadership, develop robust relationships, and have healthy self-esteem.

Offer that this session will focus on establishing honest self-understanding. We will be exploring moments in our lives that have made us the people we are today. We will engage in a number of self-reflection and peer reflection exercises. Conclude that we will leave this session with a list of specific skills that are important to us as well as a personal statement reflecting our abilities.

✦ Know Thyself: Sharing with Others

Twenty minutes

Pass out a mirror and a piece of cardstock paper to each participant. Ask participants to look in the mirror beyond their physical appearance and complete *The Mirror and Its Reflection* (Activity #2, SW). Play "Reflections" from *Mulan* or another reflective song—when the song is finished, ask participants to stop writing.

Explain to participants that they will now create a collage that represents the different aspects that they just wrote about. Encourage participants to use whatever art supplies they would like, using the piece of cardstock as a foundation. (*Allow seven to eight minutes.*)

Ask participants to create small groups of three and have each participant share his or her collage. Encourage them to look for connections as they share their collages. (*Allow 5-7 minutes.*) If time allows, have participants ask one follow-up question of the person sharing.

After small group sharing, reconvene as a large group. Consider the following questions:

- What were some common themes in your group?
- What was the energy level when people were sharing?
- Was it difficult or easy to develop this collage?
  In what ways?
- Was it easy or difficult to share your collage with others? In what ways?

Conclude by sharing the verse from the song "Reflections" from *Mulan* when Mulan looks into a mirror and observes that she's not the image of an ideal bride or daughter, and she muses about who she really is.

Ask participants how the song lyrics connect with this module—for example, when you can honestly see your reflection, you can be honest with yourself and others.

✦ Seek Feedback

Twenty minutes

As Dorothy Corkille Briggs, author of *Celebrate Yourself*, explains:

> Your self-image—who you think you are—is literally a package you put together from how others have seen and treated you and from your conclusions as you compared yourself to others. By focusing on the inner core of your personal aliveness, vitality, and creativity, you can escape the prison of a negative self-image and find freedom in a much broader and expansive sense of "I am." (Armstrong, 1999, p. 133)

Pass out index cards and ask participants to draw a horizontal line across the card, dividing it in half lengthwise. Offer the following instructions:

> You're going to be given a chance to think about your strengths and limitations; then you'll have a chance to share some of these thoughts. (Pause)
>
> On the top half of the card, write down three strengths and when and how you discovered them. (Give a personal example, if appropriate.)
>
> On the bottom half of the card, write down three of your limitations and when and how you discovered them.

Once all participants have completed their cards, ask participants to find a partner whom they don't know well. Ask them to each share one or two strengths and when and how they discovered them. *(Allow two to three minutes.)*

Now, ask participants to share one limitation and when and how they discovered this limitation, then give their partner constructive feedback on how to manage this limitation. *(Allow three to four minutes.)*

Ask participants to find a new partner and repeat the process. *(Allow six to eight minutes.)*

Reconvene as a large group and ask for a few examples of suggestions related to managing limitations. Ask for one or two examples of lessons learned from taking this time to identify and talk about strengths and limitations.

Follow up with the idea that we have the potential to make the best out of a difficult situation. If we're serious about developing our leadership potential, we have to understand that it isn't easy, even if we have the best intentions. Our limitations may set us back. Understanding our limitations and identifying others who can help is a wonderful attribute. Effective leadership incorporates knowing one's limits as well as both when and how to tap into the strengths of others for the betterment of the group or common good.

✦ Personal Motto

Ten minutes

Suggest that many times, when we take the time to think deeply about ourselves, we benefit in that moment. The challenge is to figure out how to keep those ideas fresh in our minds. This next activity will help us take a small step in that direction.

Explain that with the supplies you have laid out, participants will now have a chance to choose a personal motto that they can transcribe onto a refrigerator magnet. Distribute the blank magnets. As participants are getting their supplies, suggest that the magnet can serve as a daily reminder of something they believe in strongly. The "motto" can be a quote, song lyrics, a favorite saying, or a phrase that best represents participants' true self. Share your own motto as an example, then have participants develop theirs. Encourage participants to share their ideas with one another, especially if they feel stuck. (*Allow five to six minutes.*)

In the large group, ask the following questions:

- What made it difficult or easy for you to create a personal motto?
- In what ways might this motto assist you to be honest with yourself?

Encourage participants to post their motto (on a refrigerator, bathroom mirror, and so on) as a daily reminder. Remember the power of daily reinforcement: hearing is believing, so telling themselves to remain true to who they are will translate into heightened honest self-understanding.

✦ Wrap Up

Five minutes

Close by referring to the book *Life Medicine* by Dr. Nancy Spence (2001), when Marsha Sinetar defines "right livelihood" as doing the best at what we do best. It is a conscious choice in correcting undesirable outcomes and maturing to make better choices in the future.

> And so it is that, as we weigh the yes/no possibilities of our choices, we learn about our strengths and weaknesses and become more willing to pay the price of each choice. Each choice we make consciously adds positively to our sense of ourselves and makes us trust ourselves more because we learn how to live up to our own inner standards and goals . . . (p. 36)

The Mirror and Its Reflection

Take a few minutes to respond to the following questions:

What makes me happy?

What challenges me?

What are my core values?

What do I stand for?

What motivates me?

When do I feel I most alive?

Find two people to share these thoughts with and get their reactions to your ideas.

Person 1: _____

Person 2: _____

MODULE 10

Healthy Self-Esteem
Sabrina Ryan

✦ Focus of Module

Having a balanced sense of self is the basis for healthy self-esteem. Emotionally intelligent leaders possess a high level of self-worth, are confident in their abilities, and are willing to stand up for what they believe in. They are also balanced by a sense of humility and the ability to create space for the opinions, perspectives, and thoughts of others. Singh (2006) found that psychologists identify high self-esteem as "the most important trait" of a person who is happy, healthy, and successful (p. 81). Healthy self-esteem therefore means recognizing your own self-worth, believing in your abilities, knowing yourself well enough to stand up for what you believe in, and being strong when you feel challenged. The "healthy" part means that you hold yourself in check—that you have some humility. You accept yourself, your strengths and your limitations, without arrogance or self-deprecation. This humility helps you have a balanced sense of self.

Primary Activities

Participants complete a self-assessment, reflect on how others perceive them, and engage in an activity to see how they and others work in certain contexts.

← Learning Objectives and Resources

- To translate the concept of self-esteem into tangible ideas
- To acknowledge the perceptions of others and how that relates to healthy self-esteem
- To explore how our environment influences our ability to work with others

Total Time

Sixty minutes

Supplies

Self-Guided Tour worksheet (one per participant)

Healthy Self-Enhancers worksheet (one per participant)

Others' Perceptions of You worksheet (one per participant)

Striking Resemblance worksheet (one per participant)

Reflection worksheet (one per participant)

Pens, pencils (one per participant)

Tape

Laptop/projector/screen for video (optional)

Reflective or background music to play during reflection time (optional)

Copy of *Emotionally Intelligent Leadership: A Guide for College Students*

← Facilitator Preparation Notes

Read Chapter Six, Healthy Self-Esteem, in *Emotionally Intelligent Leadership: A Guide for College Students* (Shankman & Allen, 2008). (Refer to Appendix A for an overview of the EIL model.) Prepare introductory comments based on your reading.

Decide whether you will use video or music as part of this module. If so, prepare accordingly.

If you want to use video, select all or parts of the following:

- Dove Self-Esteem Fund (http://www.youtube .com/watch?v=7rSjh52fGTg)
- Body Image and Self-Esteem (www.youtube .com/watch?v=gC9g-1MJdE4&feature=related)

Consider whether you want to enlarge the *Striking Resemblance* worksheet for all to see. If so, see page viii for download information.

← Facilitator Tips

This activity requires extensive writing and reflection, which may be challenging for participants. Also, this module may be difficult for some participants because of its focus on personal information and observation.

Review the module and change or add as you see fit, based on the participants or group dynamics, to increase your potential for success in this discussion.

The activity may go longer or shorter depending on the number of participants.

For an intact group, the final activity can have deep meaning for the participants, as they can learn more about who they are working with and how they will respond in different situations. If this is the case, feel free to encourage small group conversations for this deeper understanding, as time allows.

REFERENCES

Shankman, M. L., & Allen, S. J. (2008). *Emotionally intelligent leadership: A guide for college students*. San Francisco: Jossey-Bass.

Singh, D. (2006). *Emotional intelligence at work: A professional guide* (3rd ed.). New Delhi, India: Response Books.

✦ Introduction

Five minutes

Introduce yourself. If there is time, ask participants to introduce themselves, state what career paths they would like to go into, and share one accomplishment they take pride in.

Introduce the point that healthy self-esteem is one of the twenty-one capacities of emotionally intelligent leadership. Share with participants that there will be reflection and self-assessment in this module and that all should respect each other's responses to the activities.

Explain that this session is divided into the three facets of EIL—consciousness of context, consciousness of self, and conscious of others. These three facets affect how we understand ourselves. With better awareness of these facets, we are better prepared to assess our self-esteem and identify opportunities for development. Likewise, we are better at understanding how others view us and how we may act or react in different contexts.

✦ Consciousness of Self

Fifteen minutes

Ask participants to complete the *Self-Guided Tour* (Activity #1, SW) on their own. As participants finish, ask them to read *Healthy Self-Enhancers* (Activity #1, SW) on their own and play music, if desired. (*Allow five minutes.*)

Ask participants for their thoughts, now that they've completed the reflection. After a couple of comments, share that often, through discussions like this, we learn that others may be struggling with similar challenges. Ask for responses to one or two of the following questions. (*Allow three to five minutes.*)

- Who is willing to share a challenge that they're struggling with?
- How do the questions on the *Self-Guided Tour* relate to leadership?
- How does healthy self-esteem factor into the leadership equation?

Next, ask participants to consider how perceptions affect our self-esteem. Suggest that our own self-perception may be different from how others think of us.

Optional: Demonstrate how perceptions can be deceiving and how they may affect our self-esteem by showing either or both of the following video clips:

- Dove Self-Esteem Fund
- Body Image and Self-Esteem

After watching the videos, ask for a few initial reactions, thoughts, or feelings.

Transition to how perceptions are not just about how we see ourselves; how others view us and how we view others also affects our self-esteem.

☚ Consciousness of Others

Fifteen minutes

Ask participants to respond to the first question on *Others' Perceptions of You* (Activity #2, SW), "Who are you at the present time?" Write a list of at least ten adjectives and/or nouns that you would use to describe yourself right now. (*Allow five minutes.*)

Now ask participants to complete the chart. (*Allow five minutes.*)

- How do you think others perceive you? Write down at least five different people with at least one perception of you. Consider:

- Family members and friends, including boyfriend or girlfriend
- Coaches, professors, advisors, mentors, supervisors

Ask participants to partner and discuss one or two of the following questions. Choose the ones you would like to ask, or offer your own.

- Compare and contrast the columns. How do they differ?
- In what ways do you agree with what other people want you to be?
- Do you think this has to do with your reflection or view of yourself? Why or why not?

✦ Consciousness of Context

Fifteen minutes

Explain that consciousness of context describes our ability to understand the environment in which leaders and followers work. Share that the following activity will ask questions about how you react or act in different environments. You will use *Striking Resemblance* (Activity #3, SW).

Explain that this activity will require you and others to work in certain contexts. Explain to participants that the room is divided into corners. Each corner represents an animal. The expression "behaving like an animal" will take on a whole new meaning for them!

Give each corner of the room an animal assignment and tell the participants that after you read the question, they will move to the corner of the room assigned to the animal that they most closely identify with. *Note:* If this is an intact group (student organization, club, chapter, or class), encourage participants to notice who is in the corner with them so that they know who they will be working with and how they react or act in different situations.

After the last question, ask the following questions:

- What surprised you about this activity?
- What did you learn about others' reactions to different situations?
- What did you learn about your own reactions to different situations?

✦ Wrap Up

Ten minutes

Ask participants to complete *Reflection* (Activity #4, SW). (*Allow five minutes.*)

Have participants share their responses, if they would like, and, specifically, action steps.

Ask for final thoughts on the concept of healthy self-esteem and how it relates to the three facets of emotionally intelligent leadership (consciousness of context, consciousness of self, and consciousness of others).

Thank participants for their time, attention, and respect. Remind them that achieving healthy self-esteem is a lifelong process and fluctuates based on new experiences and interactions throughout life.

Self-Guided Tour

Circle the answer that best describes you. There are no right or wrong answers.

Caution: You may find you are responding to the questions in terms of how you would ideally like to be. Resist that temptation and answer, instead, from a place of complete self-honesty.

1. When you make a mistake do you tend to …
   a. Feel ashamed and embarrassed?
   b. Say "Who me? I never make mistakes." But if I did make one, I would immediately correct it and hope no one was watching.
   c. Have no fear owning up to it in public and be open to receiving help from others in fixing it?

2. On average, when you look at yourself in the mirror what do you believe you see?
   a. Someone who is attractive and confident.
   b. Someone who is average and often unsure about what to do in life.
   c. Someone who is ugly and insecure.

3. When you are dealing with a problem in your life, what do you tend to do?
   a. Blame everyone or anything that I think caused the situation. It's rarely my fault.
   b. Complain and vent to anyone willing to listen but rarely address my personal responsibility for the issue.
   c. Take responsibility for my thoughts, words, and actions because if I take ownership, I am not a victim to the situation.

4. If my wants and needs are different from those of others I am likely to …
   a. Give up and give in. I'd accommodate.
   b. Say, "My way or the highway!" I argue until I get my way.
   c. Try to avoid them altogether. Why bother trying to get my needs on the table? Mine aren't important, and neither are theirs.
   d. Create a win/win solution.

(Continued)

5. When you think about the greater purpose of your life what do you tend to think?

    a. I feel like I am drifting. I am ashamed to admit it, but I don't know what I should be doing or even where to start.

    b. I have a general picture of what I want to do and what I am capable of creating for my life.

    c. I am on course with my purpose, and know I am capable of creating whatever my heart desires for my life.

6. When I make a commitment to myself I often tend to …

    a. Break it before the end of the hour. I am terrible at following up on my self-goals.

    b. Do it with hesitation and fear because I so desperately hate disappointment.

    c. Stick to it with conviction and await the rewards that I believe will come from it.

7. When you talk to yourself (you know, that little voice in your head) what does it tend to sound like?

    a. Critical and negative. I often put myself down and beat myself up emotionally.

    b. Fairly confident and supportive, but I still have those days when my self-talk holds back my true greatness.

    c. Extremely confident and helpful. I have learned to become my own best friend and weed out my limiting thoughts from the empowering ones.

8. How do you often react to what other people say about you?

    a. I take things personally, and if I think someone is saying something negative about me I take it too much to heart.

    b. I get defensive and often respond with an equal, if not greater, negative reaction to them.

    c. I value what others have to say about me—but honestly—I know who I am, and other peoples' opinions have no bearing on my self-worth.

(Adapted from and reproduced with approval from the National Association of Self-Esteem.)

Healthy Self-Enhancers

The following thoughts correspond to the questions in the Self-Guided Tour.

1. It is quite "normal," and human, to not enjoy making mistakes! That is why we often feel embarrassed, deny their existence, and/or blame others for our errors. We believe that the best way is to admit your mistakes, learn from them, and take corrective action. After all, a mistake is a mistake—no more, no less.

2. We live in a society that emphasizes glamour and sex appeal. That is why most of us strive to achieve external beauty, but oftentimes we lose our uniqueness in the process. If we can accept the things we'd like to change without badmouthing or beating up on ourselves, we've come a long way toward self-acceptance.

3. Taking responsibility for your own thoughts, words, and actions is more easily said than done. However, we believe the quality of your well-being is directly proportional to how much self-responsibility you are willing to take. When we blame others or outside events for our position or condition in life we lock ourselves into a prison of pain. There truly is freedom in taking ownership for how we respond to what happens to us in life.

4. Your wants, needs, and self-worth are as important as those of anyone else. However, that doesn't mean others will automatically respect them. If you silence your own voice, others will not know what you want or need. It's up to you to claim your needs as important and learn how to respectfully assert yourself. With practice, you'll be amazed at how this will become second nature.

5. Have you ever wondered "Why am I here?" or "What am I supposed to do in life?" If so, you're in very good company. This is one of the most fundamental life decisions you can make. Your purpose is about what you plan to achieve and the kind of person you want to be. Your character and your habits will lead you to be healthier, happier, and more successful. What are you

(Continued)

good at? What do you really enjoy? These are two good places to look when you're trying to decide your direction. Your life has the potential to be so much more than you might imagine. The most important thing is that your life has meaning for you.

6. If you've ever heard the phrase "your word is your bond," you'll understand why honoring commitments is an aspect of healthy self-esteem. A commitment is a pledge, and a pledge is a guarantee. When you make a commitment to yourself or others you're putting your integrity on the line. As you learn to demonstrate that you can be counted on to do what you say, you build your self-esteem and your credibility at the same time. That way you and others will know that "you walk your talk."

7. If you're like most people you say things to yourself you wouldn't tolerate coming from another person. Negative self-talk scares us out of taking positive risks so we can avoid failure. Here's how you can start to build positive, self-empowering inner dialogues. First, recognize your negative self-talk. Next, interrupt the pattern; tell yourself "Erase that. Here's what I really mean!" The last step is to give yourself a positive instruc-tion, like "I can do this. I'm up to the task," or "Let's try it on for size." The more you replace your negative self-talk with positive self-talk, the more your self-esteem and self-confidence will grow.

8. When you put more weight on your own judgment than on others' it's easier to keep their words in perspective without becoming defensive. Your strong sense of self-worth allows you to maintain your power and still hear what others have to say without feeling bad about yourself.

The finest things in life are neither costly nor hard to find. They are waiting right within you.
—Japanese proverb

Reference

National Association of Self-Esteem, http://www.self-esteem-nase.org/rate.php. (Reproduced with approval from the National Association of Self-Esteem.)

Others' Perceptions of You

List at least ten adjectives and/or nouns that you would use to describe yourself right now.

Now think about how others perceive you.

List people who know you well; consider family, friends, coworkers, peers, and so on	How does he or she perceive you?	How does your perception differ from the person you identified?

Striking Resemblance

Responding to the following statements will help you think more deeply about yourself. Using the animal descriptions on the next page, complete the sentence, then write why you chose that description.

- When I find that tasks aren't getting done in the time I would like to see them done, I behave most like:

- I am the "most successful" as:

- When I am angry, I act like:

- When things are sailing along nicely, I behave most like:

- When I disagree with my friends, I behave most like:

- When I am in charge of a project, I behave most like:

- When I am working in a team environment, I behave most like:

- When I work alone, I behave most like:

- When I am happy, I am:

- When I disagree with the direction in which an organization is heading, I behave like:

- When I feel at my worst, I behave like:

- When I see a goal clearly and am inspired to head toward it, I behave most like:

Animal Descriptions

Monkey: Fun-loving, full of jokes most of the time, loves to make people laugh, rarely serious

Donkey: Strong-willed, hard-headed, rarely jokes, may be a jerk at times, may not have a reason for behaving like this

Ostrich: Shy and quiet, rarely speaks in a large group, does a lot of internal processing

Lion: Loud, strong-willed, takes charge, speaks out

See page viii for download information.

Reflection

Consciousness of Self

1. How would you describe your self-esteem?

2. What's healthy about your self-esteem?

3. What are your opportunities for improvement?

Consciousness of Others

1. How does your self-esteem influence your relationships?

2. What's healthy about your self-esteem in relation to others?

3. What are your opportunities for improvement?

Consciousness of Context

1. How does your environment influence your self-esteem?

2. How does your environment promote a healthy level of self-esteem?

3. How does your environment interfere with developing a healthy level of self-esteem?

MODULE 11

Emotional Self-Control
Amy Kautz

✦ Focus of Module

Emotional self-control entails consciously moderating both our emotions and our reactions. Although feeling emotions and being aware of them is part of this, so too is regulating them. Emotional self-control is about both awareness (being conscious of feelings) and action (managing emotions and knowing when and how to show them). Recognizing feelings, understanding how and when to demonstrate those feelings appropriately, and taking responsibility for our emotions (versus being victims of them) are critical components of this capacity.

Primary Activities

Participants watch video clips to enhance their understanding of what happens when people do not demonstrate emotional self-control; they then reflect on their own triggers for negative reactions and learn how to manage strong emotional reactions.

✦ Learning Objectives and Resources

- To enhance participants' understanding of the components of emotional self-control
- To explore the implications of not demonstrating emotional self-control
- To identify personal "hot buttons" or triggers for strong, negative emotions

Total Time

Forty-five minutes

Supplies

Emotional Worst-Case Scenario worksheet (one per participant)

Access to Internet (to view video clips) and/or videos or DVDs

Audiovisual to support video/DVDs and/or viewing clips from the Internet

Copy of *Emotionally Intelligent Leadership: A Guide for College Students*

✦ Facilitator Preparation Notes

Read Chapter Seven, Emotional Self-Control, in *Emotionally Intelligent Leadership: A Guide for College Students* (Shankman & Allen, 2008). (Refer to Appendix A for an overview of the EIL model.) Prepare introductory comments based on your reading.

Be prepared to tell a story (one to two minutes) about a time when you lacked emotional self-control and discuss how it affected your ability to lead others.

Complete the *Emotional Worst-Case Scenario* worksheet yourself.

Locate and select YouTube clips or movie clips (suggestions follow). Choose sections of videos clips to showcase poor emotional self control.

1. Angry German Kid: http://www.youtube.com/watch?v=PbcctWbC8Q0

   This does not need to be translated to get the point across; just be aware that many expletives are contained in the outbursts. The focus of his rage is in a game not loading on his computer, then frustration over not being able to do what he wants with the game.

2. Tom Cruise on *Oprah*: http://www.youtube.com/watch?v=ezlClilZJSw

   In the first few minutes of this clip, Oprah is trying to ask Tom about Katie and he responds by jumping up on the couch, physically demonstrating his emotions.

3. *Lost World* Trailer: http://www.youtube.com/watch?v=DbYvkRCO3iI

   The first fifty-five seconds are the best clip, which is the Matt Lauer interview.

4. John McEnroe: http://www.youtube.com/watch?v=ekQ_Ja02gTY&NR=1

   John McEnroe, at Wimbledon, expresses his opinions of the judge's abilities to make a call.

5. Almost any *Punk'd* video.

6. *Billy Madison*: Any number of scenes when Adam Sandler's character loses composure—just be careful to preview for language and appropriate content.

7. *Anger Management*: Any number of scenes when Adam Sandler's character loses control of his emotions.

8. Any episode of MTV's *The Real World*.

☚ Facilitator Tips

Review the YouTube videos and movie clips in advance and decide which ones (and how much) you want to show.

Anticipate that after watching the videos participants' discussion may veer away from the topic of EIL capacities. Be prepared to redirect discussion with questions.

REFERENCE

Shankman, M. L., & Allen, S. J. (2008). *Emotionally intelligent leadership: A guide for college students*. San Francisco: Jossey-Bass.

✦ Introduction

Five minutes

Begin with a quick review of Appendix A: EIL Overview. Consider covering the following areas from this chapter in *Emotionally Intelligent Leadership: A Guide for College Students:*

- Consciousness of feelings
- Actions
- Reactions
- Stress
- Hot buttons

Tell a brief story about a time when you lacked emotional self-control, and discuss how it affected your ability to lead others.

✦ Lacking Self-Control

Twenty minutes

Explain that you are going to show a few video clips that showcase some examples of poor emotional self-control. Share with participants that after each clip, you will discuss the clip, so while they watch the video, they should be prepared to discuss what they saw and answer some questions. Emphasize that they should focus their attention and comments on this idea of emotional self-control.

Be sure to offer the following:

> These videos may be of staged or fictitious events. These clips are offered for the purpose of discussion. It is meant to be educational and not hurtful to the people involved in the clips.

After each clip, consider the following questions:

- What happened in the clip?
- How did you feel watching the clip? Try to move beyond the "funny" to "what if that happened to me?"

Follow-up questions (if needed):

- Did you feel embarrassed? In what way?
- Could you empathize with anyone in the clip?
- How do you think the people in the clip might feel about themselves as they watch?
- What moment(s) in the clip could have gone differently?
- What was the impact on those around them?

➤ Emotional Worst-Case Scenario

Fifteen minutes

Ask each participant to fill out the *Emotional Worst-Case Scenario* worksheet (Activity #1, SW) individually. (*Allow five minutes.*)

Ask participants to partner and discuss their answers. (*Allow five minutes.*)

Next, ask the group to share strategies that could help in the future.

➤ Wrap Up

Five minutes

Conclude by asking participants:

- What did you learn today about emotional self-control?
- What will you do in the future when someone pushes your "hot button"?
- How does a lack of emotional self-control impact leadership?

Share personal observations on the topics discussed, and make any relevant comments to wrap up the session.

Emotional Worst-Case Scenario

Describe in detail a recent situation (within the last few weeks if possible) in which you lost your temper (an example of an "emotional worst-case scenario").

1. What was it about?

2. Where did it happen?

3. Who did it involve?

4. Who witnessed it?

5. When did it happen?

6. What did you say?

7. What were the reactions of others?

8. What else of importance do you recall?

(Continued)

9. How did you feel during the scenario?
What were your physical reactions (e.g., sweating, teeth clenching, upset stomach)?

What thoughts (such as "seeing red," extreme emotions, nothing) were going through your head during the scenario?

10. How did you feel after the scenario was over?
Physical reactions?

Thoughts?

11. Looking back, can you see a trigger or hot button that may have led to this "Emotional Worst-Case Scenario"?

12. Identify ways you can act or react differently in the future. Look at your physical and emotional triggers. How can you stop, change, or reframe your reaction to the situation?

Two important aspects of emotional self-control are recognizing how stress affects us and being aware of our hot buttons.
—Shankman and Allen (2008, p. 43)

MODULE 12

Authenticity
Darbi Roberts

✦ Focus of Module

Authenticity is about being transparent and trustworthy. It is a complex concept that emphasizes the importance of living in a way in which your words match your actions and vice versa. This is no small order. Being authentic means, in part, that emotionally intelligent leaders follow through on commitments and present themselves and their motives in an open and honest manner. This may sound simple, but it is not. You must know yourself well enough to know what you can honestly commit to and then follow through on this promise. Authenticity is also about being true to your values, feelings, and ideas. Often the hardest part about being authentic is in your actions—do you do what you say you will do? How well do your actions align with your words?

Primary Activities

Participants work in small groups to analyze case studies about authenticity; they then work on developing their own understanding of how to be more authentic in their lives.

121

✦ Learning Objectives and Resources

- To explore the concept of authenticity as a critical capacity for leadership
- To identify antecedents, actions, and outcomes of an authentic life
- To develop a personal commitment to being authentic

Total Time

Sixty minutes

Supplies

My Life Is My Message biographies (one per small group)

What Is My Message? worksheet (one per participant)

Flipchart, markers, easel

Pens, pencils (one per participant)

Copy of *Emotionally Intelligent Leadership: A Guide for College Students*

✦ Facilitator Preparation

Read Chapter Eight, Authenticity, in *Emotionally Intelligent Leadership: A Guide for College Students* (Shankman & Allen, 2008). (Refer to Appendix A for an overview of the EIL model.) Prepare introductory comments based on your reading.

Room setup should have all participants facing each other in some manner (such as around a table or chairs in a circle).

Write a description of authenticity on the flipchart, based on the description in the Introduction section.

Download one copy of *My Life Is My Message* (see page viii). Each case study (four in all) should be on a separate sheet of paper; two of the case studies are longer than one page and may be printed double-sided.

Write the following questions for the *My Life Is My Message* section on a flipchart:

- What actions were in accordance with their values?
- What did they do that was truthful, genuine, real, or in accordance with who they really were?
- What message was this person's life sending?
- How did their background or personal history affect their message?

✦ Facilitator Tips

If the group is small (under ten) or participants are comfortable with each other, the first discussion can be done in one big group. If the group is newly formed, split participants into smaller groups of five or six.

There are several ways you can bring closure to the second activity. If participants aren't familiar with each other (for example, this session is the first time they've interacted), you may just want to end the activity with the last reflection. If participants are somewhat familiar with each other, you can have them share their responses in groups of two or three or, if you prefer, as one large group.

REFERENCE

Shankman, M. L., & Allen, S. J. (2008). *Emotionally intelligent leadership: A guide for college students*. San Francisco: Jossey-Bass.

✦ Introduction: Definitions

Ten minutes

Begin the discussion with a description of authenticity (FCH).

Read: "Authenticity means being the same on the outside as you are on the inside. Practice what you preach. Your walk talks; your talk talks; but your walk talks louder than your talk talks."

Ask participants whether they have heard any of these sayings. Ask them to share when or from whom they first heard them.

Share that all of these sayings describe what authenticity is.

- Being transparent—being the same on the outside as on the inside.
- Keeping promises.
- Being trustworthy—do you do what you say you will do—all the time? And then do you follow through?

Offer that authenticity is important but can be difficult to practice.

Ask participants if anyone has a formal definition of authenticity. Share the following definitions from the *Oxford English Dictionary*. Authenticity is:

- Being authoritative or duly authorized
- Being what it professes in origin or authorship, as being genuine
- Being real, actual
- Being entitled to acceptance or belief, accordance with fact, or as stating fact; reliable, trustworthy, of established credit

Consider the following questions:

- Which words in these definitions stand out to you? Why?
- Do you agree with these definitions? Why or why not? If not, then what does authenticity mean to you?

- In what ways would being authentic give someone "authority" or "acceptance" or "credit"?
- How would being authentic make someone "genuine" or "trustworthy"?
- Is "having character" the same as being authentic? Why or why not?
- What role do values play in being authentic?

✦ My Life Is My Message

Twenty minutes

Ask participants to create small groups of three or four. Assign each group one of the case studies and have each group choose a note taker. You can use the case studies provided or use your own (other suggestions include Elizabeth Cady Stanton, Frederick Douglass, William Wilberforce, Nelson Mandela, Bono of U2, and Aung San Suu Kyi). Ask the group to read the description of the person and identify the parts of the case study that illustrate authenticity.

Encourage the groups to respond to the following questions for discussion (FCH). (*Allow ten minutes.*)

- What actions were in accordance with their values?
- What did they do that was truthful, genuine, real, or in accordance with who they really were?
- What illustrates authenticity in this person's story?
- What message was this person's life sending?
- How did their background or personal history affect their message?

Reconvene the large group and ask one person from each small group to present a short summary of their discussion to the large group.

Ask participants to identify some of the common themes about authenticity in each person's life. Note these on the flipchart.

As an example, share the following story:

> Mahatma Gandhi is a man who was authentic. Legend has it that once, in a crowded train station, Gandhi was being pursued by a journalist who hoped to get an interview with the great public leader. Every time the journalist caught up to him, Gandhi would politely but repeatedly decline to answer the journalist's questions. As Gandhi's train was pulling away, the journalist cried to him, "Please! Give me your message for the people!" Gandhi immediately responded, "My life is my message!"

Ask participants to think about what the phrase "my life is my message" really means. How *do you* live out this statement? What does a person have to do to live that message?

← What's My Message?

Twenty-five minutes

Ask participants to return to their small groups to work through *What's My Message?* (Activity #1, SW).

Share with participants that now that they have seen how other people have led a life of authenticity, it's time to do a little self-examination.

Step 1

Ask them to consider the following questions:

- If my life is my message, then what message am I sending? The key question is not "what message do I *want* to send?" but rather "what message am I *actually* sending?

- Think about the activities and groups you're involved in. How do you interact with people in those groups? Do you treat everybody fairly? Do you take full responsibility for your actions? Do you follow through with what you commit to doing? Is there a difference in your personality or actions when you're around other people versus when you're alone?

- For example, some people might say "Do unto others as much as you can get away with," or "It's never too late to blame someone else for your life," or "Make resolutions and never follow through on them."

Ask participants to jot down some of their thoughts in response. (*Allow four minutes.*)

Step 2

Ask for participants' attention and offer that sometimes we send messages that we'd rather not. Ask the following questions:

- If this is true, what messages would you rather send?
- What kind of messages do you want people to take away from your interactions with them?
- What messages (positive and negative) do you think other people get from observing you in group activities?

For example, instead of some of the previously mentioned real messages that some people say to themselves, they might instead say "Always do your best and your best will always get better," or "The fastest way to future rewards is by following present joy."

Ask participants to jot down their thoughts. Repeat questions if needed. (*Allow four minutes.*)

Step 3

It's time to think about what changes participants can make to be sure the actual message they're sending is aligned with the intended message. Think about the following questions:

- What needs to be different about how you interact with others? (Think about family, close friends, coworkers, classmates and so forth.)
- How do you function under pressure? Do you give 100 percent effort to everything? When might you "let things slide"?

For example, if I want my life message to be "I always do my best, and my best will always get better," then changes I would make could be (1) to work to do my best, even when part of me wants to just get away with not doing so; (2) to focus on improving myself, even just a little bit, every time; or (3) to be optimistic.

Ask participants to write what they want to do to align their message. (*Allow four minutes.*)

Step 4

Ask participants to identify one action they can do in the next twenty-four hours that exhibits one of the changes they've just identified. Explain that this is an opportunity to make a commitment to authenticity. Looking at the example of wanting to stick with my life message of "always do my best," then today I'm not going to watch TV while I do my homework, or I'm not going to text or check Facebook in class. Ask participants: What are you committed to doing? (*Allow four minutes.*)

Allow feedback or follow-up conversation as time allows.

✦ Wrap Up

Five minutes

Begin with a quick check-in of how people feel about the session. Go around the circle and ask participants to share one word or phrase that highlights their thoughts and feelings about living in a more authentic manner.

After participants have shared their word or phrase, stress the idea that authenticity isn't just about what you value or what you say you value; it's about how your actions reflect your values. It's about turning your words into action. That's the only way you can be trustworthy or reliable. It's hard to do this all the time, but small efforts every day—like the ones you've just identified—lead to a life of greater authenticity.

Conclude by returning to the Gandhi quote.

✦ My Life Is My Message

Biography: Cesar Chavez

Cesar Estrada Chavez was born March 31, 1927, near Yuma, Arizona. Chavez was named after his grandfather, who escaped from slavery on a Mexican ranch and arrived in Arizona during the 1880s. Chavez's grandparents homesteaded more than one hundred acres in the Gila Valley and raised fourteen children. Chavez's father, Librado, started his family in 1924 when he married Juana Estrada. Cesar was the second of their six children. Librado worked on the family ranch and owned a store in the Gila Valley. The family lived in an apartment above the store.

Chavez began school at age seven, but he found it difficult because his family spoke only Spanish. Chavez preferred to learn from his uncles and grandparents, who would read to him in Spanish. In addition, Chavez learned many things from his mother. She believed violence and selfishness were wrong, and she taught these lessons to her children.

In the 1930s, Chavez's father lost his business because of the Great Depression, and the family moved back to the ranch. However, in 1937 a severe drought forced the family to give up the ranch. The next year, Chavez and his family packed their belongings and headed to California in search of work. In California, the Chavez family became part of the migrant community, traveling from farm to farm to pick fruits and vegetables during the harvest. They lived in numerous migrant camps and often were forced to sleep in their car. Chavez attended more than thirty elementary schools, often encountering cruel discrimination. Once Chavez completed the eighth grade, he quit school and worked full-time in the vineyards. His family was able to rent a small cottage in San Jose and make it their home. Then in 1944, Chavez joined the navy and served in World War II. After completing his duty two years later, Chavez returned to

California. He married Helen Fabela in 1948, and they moved into a one-room shack in Delano. Chavez again worked in the fields, but he began to fight for change. That same year, Chavez took part in his first strike in protest of low wages and poor working conditions. However, within several days the workers were forced back to the fields.

In 1952, Chavez met Fred Ross, who was part of a group called the Community Service Organization (CSO) formed by Saul Alinsky. Chavez became part of the organization and began urging Mexican-Americans to register and vote. Chavez traveled throughout California and made speeches in support of workers' rights. He became general director of CSO in 1958.

Four years later, however, Chavez left CSO to form his own organization, which he called the National Farm Workers Association (NFWA). The name was later changed to the United Farm Workers (UFW). In 1965, Chavez and the NFWA led a strike of California grape-pickers to demand higher wages. In addition to the strike, they encouraged all Americans to boycott table grapes as a show of support. The strike lasted five years and attracted national attention. When the U.S. Senate Subcommittee looked into the situation, Robert Kennedy gave Chavez his total support.

In 1968, Chavez began a fast to call attention to the migrant workers' cause. Although his dramatic act did little to solve the immediate problems, it increased public awareness of the problem. In the late 1960s, the Teamsters attempted to take power from the UFW. After many battles, an agreement was finally reached in 1977. It gave the UFW sole right to organize field workers.

In the early 1970s, the UFW organized strikes and boycotts to get higher wages from grape and lettuce growers. During the 1980s, Chavez led a boycott to protest the use of toxic pesticides on grapes. He again fasted to draw public attention. These strikes and boycotts generally ended with the signing of bargaining agreements.

Source: Sahlman, R. "Cesar Chavez." SPECTRUM Home & School. © KB Shaw. Adapted with permission.

Biography: Clara Barton

Clarissa Harlowe Barton was born December 25, 1821, in North Oxford, Massachusetts. Her father, Captain Stephen Barton, was a farmer, horse breeder, and respected member of the community. Her mother, Sarah, managed the household and taught Barton the importance of cleanliness.

Barton was the youngest of five children, and her two brothers and two sisters assumed much of the responsibility for her education. Her sister, Dorothy, taught her spelling, Stephen taught her arithmetic, Sally taught her geography, and David coached her in athletics. With their help, Barton received a vast and diverse education. By the time she started school at age four, Barton could already spell three-syllable words. She found school to be quite easy and studied such subjects as philosophy, chemistry, and Latin. Barton's only handicap was her extreme shyness.

At seventeen, Barton became a teacher in Massachusetts' District 9, located in Worcester County. She taught in several schools before establishing her own school in North Oxford. At the age of twenty-nine, after teaching for more than ten years, Barton yearned for a change. She entered the Liberal Institute in Clinton, New York, an advanced school for female teachers.

After a year in Clinton, Barton accepted a teaching position in New Jersey. She subsequently opened a free school in Bordentown, and the school's attendance grew to more than six hundred students. When the school board refused to offer Barton the high-paying position to head the school and hired a man instead, she found herself at a crossroads. Following a period of physical and emotional exhaustion, Barton moved to Washington, D.C., where she worked as a clerk in the U.S. Patent Office.

At the outbreak of the Civil War, Barton resigned from the Patent Office to work as a volunteer. She advertised for supplies and distributed bandages, socks, and other goods to help the wounded soldiers. In 1862, Barton was granted permission to deliver supplies directly to the front, which she did without fail for the next two years. In 1864, Barton was given the position of superintendent of Union nurses. After the war, she received permission from President Lincoln to begin a letter-writing campaign to search for missing soldiers.

During the years following the war, Barton lectured about her war experiences, continued her work at the Office of Correspondence, and worked with the suffragist movement. However, by 1869, Barton had worked herself into a physical breakdown. She followed her doctor's orders and traveled to Europe to rest and regain her health. During this trip Barton learned about the Treaty of Geneva, which provided relief for sick and wounded soldiers. Twelve nations had signed the treaty, but the United States had refused. Barton vowed to look into the matter. During this time Barton also learned about the Red Cross. She observed the organization in action while traveling with several volunteers to the front of the Franco-Prussian War.

When Barton returned to the United States in 1873, she began her crusade for the Treaty of Geneva and the Red Cross. After spending time at a spa in Dansville, New York, to improve her health, Barton moved to Washington, D.C., to lobby for her causes. Due to her efforts, the United States signed the Geneva Agreement in 1882. In addition, the American Red Cross organization was formed in 1881, and Barton served as its first president. Several years later, she wrote the American amendment to the Red Cross constitution, which provided for disaster relief during peace time as well as war.

Barton remained Red Cross president until 1904. During her tenure, she headed up relief work for disasters such as famines, floods, pestilence, and earthquakes in the United States and throughout the world. The last operation she personally directed was relief for victims of the Galveston, Texas, flood in 1900. In addition, she served as an emissary of the Red Cross and addressed several International Conferences.

In 1904, Barton was forced to resign her position as president. She experienced increasing criticism of her leadership style, and many felt it was time for the organization to be led by a larger, central administration. On May 12, Barton resigned. For the next eight years, she lived in her home at Glen Echo, Maryland, until her death on April 12, 1912.

The mission of her life can be summed up in her own words: "You must never so much as think whether you like it or not, whether it is bearable or not; you must never think of anything except the need, and how to meet it."

Source: Sahlman, R. "Clara Barton." SPECTRUM Home & School. © KB Shaw. Adapted with permission.

Biography: Amelia Earhart

"Courage is the price that life exacts for granting peace with yourself." These are the words of Amelia Earhart, one of the world's most celebrated aviators, a woman who broke records and charted new waters.

Amelia Earhart was the first child born to Edwin Stanton and Amy Otis Earhart on July 24, 1897, in Atchison, Kansas. Amelia and her sister, Muriel, who was born three years later, had a difficult childhood. Their father was an alcoholic and because he often lost jobs, the family traveled a great deal. The girls frequently missed school but still excelled academically. They enjoyed books and often recited poetry while doing their chores. Amelia and Muriel also loved sports, including basketball and tennis. Their parents encouraged them to try new things, and they did.

After graduating from high school, Amelia planned to attend college, but her plans were put on hold after she met four wounded World War I veterans on the street. After hearing of their plight, Amelia decided to study nursing. During the war, Amelia worked as a military nurse in Canada. At the war's end, she became a social worker at the Denison House in Boston and taught English to immigrant children.

Amelia enjoyed watching airplane stunt shows, which were quite popular during the 1920s. One day, after taking a ten-minute plane ride, Amelia knew she must learn to fly. By working several odd jobs and with the help of her mother, Amelia earned the $1,000 fee to take flying lessons. Ten hours of instruction and several crashes later, Amelia was ready to fly solo. She made her first solo flight in 1921. Except for a poor landing, the flight was uneventful. By the next year, Amelia had saved enough money to buy a plane of her own.

During the 1920s, Amelia lived with her mother and sister in Boston and continued teaching at Denison House. Flying was merely a hobby for her at that time. However, in 1928, Amelia received a call from Captain Hilton H. Railey asking her to join pilots Wilmer Stultz and Louis Gordon on a flight from America to England. Although she was only a passenger, Amelia became the first woman to cross the Atlantic on a plane called the Friendship on June 17–18, 1928. A publisher named George Putnam covered the story, and in 1931, the two married.

Amelia's 1928 flight brought her tremendous publicity, and she subsequently endeavored to justify this renown. On May 20–21, 1932, Amelia crossed the Atlantic on her own, establishing a new transatlantic crossing record of thirteen hours and thirty minutes. Amelia was celebrated throughout Europe and the United States and received a medal from President Herbert Hoover. Several years later, Amelia became the first woman to successfully complete the hazardous flight from Hawaii to California.

In June 1937, Amelia began what was to be her final flight. Amelia and navigator Fred Noonan set out in a twin-engine Lockheed Electra in an attempt to fly around the world. They departed from Miami, Florida, to South America, and then across the South Atlantic Ocean to Dakar, Africa. After crossing the Sahara desert, they flew to Thailand, Singapore, Java, and Australia. However, after departing Lae, New Guinea, for Howland Island, the U.S. Coast Guard lost contact with the plane. They received a final message on July 2 at 8:45 AM, and Amelia's tone was described as frantic.

The United States Navy searched extensively but never found a trace of the aviators or the plane. The mysterious disappearance of Earhart and her plane has raised considerable speculation throughout the years. Some believe that she and Noonan were captured and executed by the Japanese. Others speculate that President Roosevelt sent Earhart on a secret spy mission. However, none of the many theories about her disappearance have ever been confirmed. In 1939, Earhart's husband published a biography entitled *Soaring Wings*, in tribute to Amelia.

Source: Sahlman, R. "Amelia Earhart." SPECTRUM Home & School. © KB Shaw. Adapted with permission.

Biography: Harriet Tubman

Harriet Ross was born in Dorchester County, Maryland, in 1820. Her parents were from the Ashanti tribe of West Africa, and they worked as slaves on the Brodas plantation. In addition to producing lumber, Edward Brodas raised slaves to rent and sell. Life was difficult on the plantation, and Harriet was hired out as a laborer by the age of five.

Harriet did not like to work indoors, and she was routinely beaten by her masters. By her early teens, Harriet was no longer allowed to work indoors and was hired out as a field hand. She was a hard worker but considered defiant and rebellious. When she was fifteen years old, Harriet tried to help a runaway slave. The overseer hit her in the head with a lead weight, which put Harriet in a coma. It took months for her to recover, and for the rest of her life she suffered from blackouts.

In 1844, Harriet married a free black man named John Tubman. Harriet remained a slave, but she was able to stay in Tubman's cabin at night. Although she was married, Harriet lived in fear of being shipped to the deep South, a virtual death sentence for any slave. In 1849, her fears were realized when the owner of the Brodas plantation died and many of the slaves were scheduled to be sold. After hearing of her fate, Harriet planned to escape that very night. She knew her husband would expose her, so the only person she informed was her sister.

Harriet made the ninety-mile trip to the Mason-Dixon line with the help of contacts along the Underground Railroad. She had to hike through swamps and woodland. Harriet's trip was successful, and she settled in Philadelphia. She worked as a dishwasher and made plans to rescue her family. The next year, Harriet traveled back to Maryland and rescued her sister's family. She then returned to transport her brothers to the North. She went back for her husband, but he had remarried and did not want to follow her. In 1857, Harriet finally returned for her parents and settled them in Auburn, New York.

By this time, Harriet was becoming quite well known, and huge rewards were offered for her capture. Harriet was a master of disguise. A former master did not even recognize her when they ran into each other on the street. She was called "the Moses of her people" for leading them to freedom. In all, Harriet made 19 trips on the Underground Railroad and freed more than three hundred slaves.

With the arrival of the Civil War, Harriet became a spy for the Union army. She later worked in Washington, D.C., as a government nurse. Although Harriet won admiration from the military, she did not receive a government pension for more than thirty years. At the end of the war, Harriet returned to her parents in Auburn. She was extremely poor, and the profits of a book by Sarah Bradford entitled *Scenes in the Life of Harriet Tubman*, published in 1869, were a great financial help.

In 1870, Harriet married Nelson Davis, whom she had met at a South Carolina army base. They were happily married for eighteen years until his death. In 1896, Harriet purchased land to build a home for sick and needy blacks. However, she was unable to raise enough money to build the house and ultimately gave the land to the African Methodist Episcopal Zion Church. The church completed the home in 1908, and Harriet moved there several years later. She spent her last years in the home telling stories of her life to visitors. On March 10, 1913, Harriet died of pneumonia. She was ninety-three years old.

Harriet Tubman was not afraid to fight for the rights of African-Americans. Her story is one of dedication and inspiration. During her lifetime Harriet was honored by many people. In 1897, her bravery even inspired Queen Victoria to award her a silver medal.

Source: Sahlman, R. "Harriet Tubman." SPECTRUM Home & School. © KB Shaw. Adapted with permission.

What's My Message?

Step One: If my life is my message, then what message am I sending?

- How do you interact with strangers?

- Do you treat everybody fairly? Give an example.

- Do you take full responsibility for your actions? How do you do this? When don't you?

- How do you follow through on what you commit to doing?

- Is there a difference in your personality or actions when you're around other people versus when you're alone?

Step Two: What messages would you rather send?

- What kinds of messages do you want people to take away from your interactions with them?

(Continued)

- What messages (positive and negative) do you think other people get from observing you in group activities?

Step Three: Making changes!
- What changes do you need to make so that your actual message is more aligned with the message you want to send?

- What needs to be different about how you interact with others?

- How can you improve the alignment between your ideas and actions?

Step Four: Start with small steps
- What action(s) can you take in the next twenty-four hours that would exhibit one of these changes?

MODULE 13

Flexibility
Tracy Purinton

✦ Focus of Module

Flexibility entails being open and adaptive to changing situations. The best-laid plans don't always come to fruition, so emotionally intelligent leaders need to be responsive to change and open to feedback. By thinking creatively and using their problem-solving skills, emotionally intelligent leaders engage others in determining a new way to reach their goals. One way in which the emotionally intelligent leader demonstrates flexibility is by seeking out and using feedback from others. When others feel that their feedback is taken into consideration, they are more likely to support the final outcome or decision. Flexibility often yields better solutions. After all, each of us sees issues, problems, and challenges from a different vantage point. By working together with others and being flexible, we can achieve better solutions in terms of both outcome and process.

Primary Activities

Participants learn about the connection between flexibility and improvisational acting and then practice by participating in different experiential activities.

141

✦ Learning Objectives and Resources

- To learn and apply improvisation skills to expand the ability to think creatively and handle the unexpected
- To identify examples of when students have experienced an unexpected event and how they dealt with it
- To understand and experience that at times successful leadership depends on how well the leader reacts to unexpected circumstances
- To practice adaptive thinking as an interactive approach to influencing others

Total Time

Sixty to ninety minutes, depending on time available

Supplies

Expert Improv Actors worksheet (one per participant)

Key Rules of Improv worksheet (one per participant)

Your Improviser/Leader Profile worksheet (one per participant)

Flipchart, markers, easel

Pens, pencils (one per participant)

Audiovisual to support a PowerPoint or similar presentation, if preferred

Copy of *Emotionally Intelligent Leadership: A Guide for College Students*

✦ Facilitator Preparation Notes

Read Chapter Nine, Flexibility, in *Emotionally Intelligent Leadership: A Guide for College Students* (Shankman & Allen, 2008). (Refer to Appendix A for an overview of the EIL model.) Prepare introductory comments based on your reading.

Determine how much time you have available for this session. If a full ninety minutes is not available, consider including one of the following for a sixty-minute session; for a seventy-five-minute session, pick two of the following.

- *"Yes, and"* (fifteen minutes)
- *Conducted Story* (fifteen minutes)
- *Adapt Your Role* (fifteen minutes)

Prepare the following flipcharts or slides:

Today's World Requires
- Adaptability to changing situations
- Ability to work with different people
- Open-mindedness
- Juggling multiple demands

Learning Goals and Objectives
- To learn and apply improvisation skills
- To utilize improvisation skills for greater agility and flexibility
- To understand and experience leadership as *reacting*
- To grasp the structure and principles of adaptive thinking
- To effectively navigate the unexpected

Decide whether a small subgroup or the entire group will demonstrate the activity *Conducted Story*. If the entire group does the activity, then have everyone sit in a circle. One person starts a story and the group has to collectively tell a story that makes sense. As the facilitator, you can play the role of conductor, randomly pointing to participants to continue the story.

The instructions under *Conducted Story* assume a small group of six—adapt accordingly.

✦ Facilitator Tips

There may be participants who challenge the actor/leader analogy entirely, along the lines of, "I can understand how leaders might learn some things from actors, but how can we learn to be more authentic from people who lie professionally—or at least pretend to be someone else?" This may be an issue during the *Adapt Your Role* activity.

Ask the group to challenge that notion to see what other participants think. Also, offer the following:

- Just as actors play a variety of roles, we all play roles as people and as leaders. Each of you plays many different roles (student, member of a sports team, brother or sister, son or daughter, organization officer, sorority or fraternity member, and so on). Do you behave differently in each role? If so, do you feel like you are pretending or lying as you play different roles? Probably not, because beneath all those roles is the same person: you. The same can be said for actors.
- The second point is that the way actors do what they do actually requires them to connect with the emotion or feeling they are portraying as deeply as they can. Actors probably worry about the authenticity or "truth" of a portrayal almost more than anything else!

REFERENCE

Shankman, M. L., & Allen, S. J. (2008). *Emotionally intelligent leadership: A guide for college students*. San Francisco: Jossey-Bass.

✦ Introduction

Five minutes

Ask participants to introduce themselves. Introduce yourself, as appropriate.

Offer that creative and flexible thinking can make a big difference in how well you do your job and work with others.

Increasingly, the following are considered to be important leadership skills (FCH):

- The ability to work effectively in changing situations and in a variety of contexts
- The ability to work with different individuals and diverse groups
- A willingness to alter standard procedures (or even invent new ones!) when necessary
- The ability to juggle multiple demands and shifting priorities

These skills all require *flexibility*! We may think of ourselves as flexible and adaptable people, but let's think about how most of us react to change.

Ask the group, "What are some common reactions to unexpected change?" Record the responses (FCH). Feel free to add any of the following if they are not listed by participants:

- *Negative*: avoiding, blocking, resistance, impatience, confusion, controlling behavior
- *Positive*: optimism, confidence, seeing opportunities, adaptability

Note: Many people have a negative reaction to change, but change is a part of our reality. It is a constant in most (if not all) environments. Often we, as leaders, are introducing the change!

Suggest that flexibility helps us better manage personal and organizational change. Unexpected change happens to us all, and it is generally out of our control. The key is that we can control our reactions to it. We can improve our ability to accept change and adapt as needed.

✦ Outline and Setup

Five minutes

Share that participants will now practice ways to:

- Become more aware of their own thought and observational processes
- Think creatively in unpredictable situations
- Improve their mental agility or adaptability when something unexpected happens
- Listen more closely to get themselves and others "on the same page" (even if they don't know what that is!)
- Support the success of the team to keep moving in a positive direction

Highlight the learning goals and objectives on the flipchart by sharing the following ideas (FCH):

- In this session we are going to learn and apply improvisation skills to build on our ability to think creatively and handle the unexpected. We are introducing skills—*not* learning how to be funny.
- We will use improvisation skills for greater agility and flexibility in our leadership style and effectiveness.
- Our goal is to understand and experience leadership as reacting. As such, we need to know how to identify typical reactions or behaviors in unexpected situations.

- We want to grasp the structure and principles of adaptive thinking and learn an interactive approach to influencing our stakeholders, team members, and peers.

Offer that leadership is a dynamic process. Although everyone can be prepared for the ups and downs of leadership, rarely do leaders think about *how* to react to these ever-changing realities.

Improvisation can be a powerful tool for learning how to read unexpected situations and react to them with confidence.

Ask participants "How would you define improvisation?" After one or two participants volunteer answers, consider adding some or all of the following:

- Improvisation (or "improv") is the practice of acting and reacting (or of making and creating) in the moment.
- Improv is about responding to stimuli in your immediate environment and inner feelings.
- Improvisation can be applied to music, dramatic representations, art, cooking, and so on, but most often refers to improv comedy—it requires quick thinking and a tremendous amount of teamwork.
- Improv is unscripted, which requires quick reactions to situations that are in constant flux—just like life.

✦ Improv and Leadership

Ten minutes

Review *Expert Improv Actors* (Activity #1, SW). Ask participants to form groups of three to review the list and highlight the five most important points. (*Allow three to four minutes.*)

Solicit examples from small groups. After a few groups have shared their thoughts, ask: "What if we changed the term *improv actors* to *good leaders?*" Discuss the following:

- How does this list work? Ask for a few examples.
- What doesn't work?
- Can you think of additional characteristics that apply to one or both groups?

Note the overlaps and similarities between the two. Emphasize that improvisation offers a set of tools to improve numerous leadership skills, such as:

- Identifying opportunities
- Increasing flexibility and adaptability when working with others
- Taking responsibility and allowing others to do so as well
- Adding value to others on our team and increasing their creative responses
- Being prepared for the unexpected with greater confidence

◂ Rules of Improv

Fifteen minutes

Although improv is unscripted and seemingly haphazard, what allows it to work seamlessly is that all the actors improvise within a shifting, yet commonly understood framework. In fact, to understand the source of flexibility that is at the heart of improv, you have to understand a few key rules of improvisation.

Review *Key Rules of Improv* (Activity #2, SW) and highlight the following:

- Looking at the first and second rules, we all know how often we hear the phrase, "Yeah, but—" when a suggestion is made. "Yeah, but" is the same as saying "No"—a blocking word that limits creativity and participation.
- Instead, improv helps us shift to a "Yes, and . . ." mind-set. Try elaborating on ideas made by others with the words "Yes, and . . ." Saying "Yes" represents the acceptance of an idea; adding "and" takes the idea into the future. This makes the conversation more robust by encompassing everyone's contributions.

Shifting your whole perspective to *always* being ready to accept and build on what others say can be incredibly powerful! This can be a valuable skill in conflict management and brainstorming, in that it promotes creativity, active listening, and collaboration. It provokes others to add to an idea or solution, rather than dismissing it. "Yes, and . . ." shifts the focus to supporting the success of the team.

✦ "Yes, and . . ."

Fifteen minutes

Begin by sharing that the first fundamental skill of improvisation is accepting another's offer and then building on it.

Ask the group to form two lines facing each other, so that each person faces a partner. Ask each person to pick a topic that is relevant (if they are all from the same campus, it could be a campus issue, a student organization–focused topic, or other matter relevant to each party). Instruct participants to have a conversation in which each party has to respond by saying "yes, and" and build on each other's statements to cover the topics chosen, using "yes, and." (*Allow three to five minutes.*)

Consider the following questions:

- What was that like?
- What was hard about it?
- What was positive about it?
- Were you more creative? In what ways?
- Where or when is this kind of thinking helpful?

Summarize by suggesting that improv rules 1 and 2 are about finding a way to agree and move forward even when there's not obvious agreement (or in some cases, there is active disagreement).

✦ Listening with Logic

Five minutes

Remind participants that good improv requires listening intently. To do this, you need to be totally present. This requires that you hold back from playing out a story in your mind in anticipation of being called—because if you are not called, another person will respond in a different way and you'll be left behind.

Remind participants that the third key rule of improv is to be an active "high stakes" listener.

Listening to others is a great tool for leading in the moment. Place your attention on what the other person is saying, and stay open to possibility! When you stop trying so hard to think about how you're going to respond, you are actually much more open and available to think quickly and develop innovative ideas. The skill of building on and incorporating new ideas as they appear is incredibly valuable in organizations. This kind of thinking can cultivate key insights, inspiration, and high energy.

✦ Conducted Story

Fifteen minutes

Ask for six volunteers. Share that five will be the players and one will be the conductor. The goal of the conducted story is to have the players tell a story that moves seamlessly from one player to another. The goal of the conductor is to make the story flow as smoothly as possible, giving each person a turn.

Explain the following:

When the conductor moves from one player to another, the new player must continue on as though there was no pause. To start off, the conductor asks for a word from the audience (such as "dog food"), then points to one of the players. This person has to start a story that will be built on, sentence by sentence. The person stops talking as soon as the conductor stops pointing at him or her and points to another player (for example, "I was on my way to class this morning and ran into—"); that person picks up where the first person's sentence left off and keeps going. The key is listening, following along, and accepting what is happening in the story. The story continues, with each actor called upon by the conductor to invent the next step, until the actors bring the story to a conclusion involving the audience word (in this example, dog food) in some way.

After completion, lead a debriefing conversation with the following prompts:

- How well did you follow along without thinking ahead to what was next? What was it like?

- What are the advantages to this way of listening? The disadvantages?

- As a leader when might it be appropriate to listen this intently? When would it not be appropriate?

- Other than the obvious, how does this activity relate to leadership?

✦ Adapt Your Role

Fifteen minutes

Suggest that the best improv players invent new characters as often as possible. However, beginning improv players sometimes discover a comfortable character and keep inserting her or him into every sketch.
You can imagine how dull this gets.

Similarly, as people and as leaders, we all have reactions, habits, and behaviors that come up (for better or for worse) time and again when we work with others. But different situations require different responses, behaviors, and reactions, and they often require that you play a different *role* as a leader or active member of a team.

Being aware of your own "default character," common reactions, and preferred roles can be helpful as you think about the importance of flexibility and adaptability. The more aware you are, the more intentional you can be about what role you play as different situations arise.

Ask participants to complete *Your Improviser/Leader Profile* (Activity #3, SW). (*Allow five minutes.*)

Ask participants to form groups of three and share their responses with each other. (*Allow ten minutes.*)

In the remaining time, facilitate a discussion with the whole group. Use the following questions:

- Which roles are most common?

- How easy is it to imagine getting better (or more intentional) about switching roles?

- How do you know which role to use?

- How can we get better at our various roles?

- How do we improve our ability in shifting our roles, while remaining authentic?

✦ Wrap Up

Five minutes

Suggest to participants that many of the skills that actors develop can also improve our leadership, both as informal/formal leaders and as active members of groups and teams. The key rules of improv offer an adaptable model for working with others in a variety of contexts.

Return to the first set of ideas listed as important for effective leadership (FCH):

- Adaptability to work effectively in changing situations and in a variety of contexts
- The ability to work with different individuals and diverse groups
- Open-mindedness and a willingness to alter standard procedures (or even invent new ones!) when necessary
- An ability to juggle multiple demands and shifting priorities

Encourage participants to go out, be aware, be intentional, and practice!

Expert Improv Actors

Review the following list of characteristics of improvisational actors:

- Are present in the moment, curious, and engaged
- Listen intently
- Make specific suggestions and active choices
- Are action-oriented
- See the whole picture or scene as it is unfolding
- Meet the unexpected with a spirit of "Yes" rather than "No"
- Embrace change and seek to advance the development of the scene
- Present new ideas and leave the door open for others to do so
- Build on others' ideas and create connections and develop relationships
- Bring out the best in all other team members with the goal of making others look good (versus trying to stand out)
- Take risks
- View the unexpected as a valuable opportunity
- Are flexible, resilient, and able to play a variety of roles
- Have fun!

What if you changed the term *improvisational actors* to *good leaders*?

- Which statements in this list work? Mark with a "+"
- Which of the statements do not work? Mark with a "−"
- Which additional characteristics might apply to one or both groups?

Key Rules of Improv

Read through the following rules of improvisational acting:

1. The first rule—accept the offer—is never broken. All statements by improv actors are called "offers." Whatever an improv actor says—for example, "Hey, it's great to be back from the Amazon!"—the other actors must accept as reality. They can't say, "No, we're in an ice-cream store!" This is the rule that makes improv theater possible.

2. What makes improv work—what allows the group to create a satisfying, coherent story in the present moment—is the second rule, an extension of the first: the *Yes, and . . .* rule. This is the core rule of improvisational theater because it incorporates the rule of accepting the offer (*Yes!*) while requiring that an actor build on and extend what's been offered (*Yes, and . . .*).

3. The third rule is to be an active "high stakes" listener; this means to listen as if the scene's success relies on it. Be interested, not interesting!

4. The fourth rule is to adapt your role to the new reality. Don't be constrained by your own thinking about what will happen. Listen to what the other members of your team are saying, then adapt the role you are playing to fit as best you can. Be creative!

Which of these rules apply to leadership? In what ways?

(Continued)

Practice rule #2—write a scenario that describes a challenge you've experienced with leadership. Any time you find yourself writing "but" or any other contradicting comment, try inserting "yes, and" instead.

What happens when you apply rule #2?

What did you discover by writing your scenario using "yes, and"? How might this work for you in "real time"?

Your Improviser/Leader Profile

The following roles reflect typical approaches and roles that people take in leadership opportunities. Read through this list and answer the questions below.

Captain	Do it this way!
Initiator/Conceiver	Here's the future—follow me!
Supporter/Collaborator	I'll help you do it.
Accommodator	Let's make space or room for agreement.
Coach	You can do it!
Mediator	Let's bring all the different ideas together and see where we can go.
Observer	I'm going to see how things work before I jump in.
Joiner	I'll help! Tell me what I can do!
Challenger	I'm sure there is a better way to do this.

- Which role do you tend to play most often? Which is most comfortable? This is your default approach.

- Which role is most challenging for you?

- What are the strengths of your default approach?

- How does your default approach get in the way?

(Continued)

- Do any of these roles tend to push your buttons?

- Which of these roles are uncomfortable or do not feel natural?

- How might you go about practicing some of these behaviors or expanding your comfort zone?

- If you talk with others, what suggestions do they have for how to expand your improvisation comfort zone?

MODULE 14

Achievement 1: Ideal Versus Real

Sarah Spengler

✦ Focus of Module

Achievement is about being driven to improve according to personal standards. An important nuance of this capacity for emotionally intelligent leadership is the role of personal standards. Individuals often know achievement when they see and feel it. Instead of letting others define what achievement looks like, emotionally intelligent leaders pursue their passions and goals to a self-determined level of accomplishment. This drive produces results and may inspire others to become more focused in their efforts or to achieve at higher levels as well. No matter what the passion is, when we are committed to demonstrating emotionally intelligent leadership, we will pursue it to a high level of achievement.

Primary Activities

Participants reflect on their leadership abilities, then develop a personal action plan for development.

Learning Objectives and Resources

- To understand the concept of achievement in relation to emotionally intelligent leadership
- To gain new insights about leadership potential
- To develop an action plan for developing a specific leadership capacity

Total Time

Sixty minutes

Supplies

Impressions worksheet (one per participant)

Action Plan worksheet (one per participant)

Flipchart, markers, easel

Blank sheets of paper (two per participant)

Pens, pencils (one per participant)

Optional: Regular #6 or #10 envelopes (one per participant)

Copy of *Emotionally Intelligent Leadership: A Guide for College Students*

✦ Facilitator Preparation Notes

Read Chapter Ten, Achievement, in *Emotionally Intelligent Leadership: A Guide for College Students* (Shankman & Allen, 2008). (Refer to Appendix A for an overview of the EIL model.) Prepare introductory comments based on your reading.

Review the Intentional Change Theory as presented by Boyatzis and McKee in *Resonant Leadership* (2005) (optional).

Decide ahead of time whether the action plan that participants write will be taken with them or mailed at a later date.

If the mailing option is chosen, buy stamps for the envelopes and affix before distributing to participants. Be sure to have participants address the envelopes before they turn them in so that you can send them at a later date.

✦ Facilitator Tips

This session works best with a flexible seating arrangement so participants can move their chairs to better facilitate both small and large group discussion.

Before explaining each activity, share the following: "We are going to do another activity—I'll explain it first and then you can begin." This tends to minimize the participants' jumping into action before you are ready.

Because this design involves a combination of reflective writing and small group discussion, be prepared to move the participants quickly into the different configurations. Think ahead about how you want to pair participants up or put them into groups. Decide before you begin whether you will allow them to self-select or you will mix participants up intentionally.

When small groups report out, ask at the beginning that they report only highlights, in thirty seconds or less.

REFERENCES

Boyatzis, R., & McKee, A. (2005). *Resonant leadership*. Cambridge, MA: Harvard Business School Press.

Shankman, M. L., & Allen, S. J. (2008). *Emotionally intelligent leadership: A guide for college students*. San Francisco: Jossey-Bass.

✦ Introduction

Five minutes

Welcome participants and review the goals of this session:

- To better understand the concept of achievement
- To give you an opportunity to gain new insights about your own leadership potential
- To develop an action plan for developing a specific leadership capacity

Ask the group whether they have other goals for the session and respond to these as appropriate.

✦ Exploring the "Ideal"

Thirty minutes

Begin by explaining that participants will be looking at ideal leadership or personal qualities that they admire. In a sense, these are what we measure ourselves and our behavior against—sometimes unconsciously. When we become conscious of these qualities, we benefit in many ways.

Walk participants through *Impressions* (Activity #1, SW).

Instruct participants to write in the left column the names of four or five people, real or fictional, whom they admire. They should leave some space between the names. These people might have had a direct or indirect influence on them. They can be famous or not famous. (*Allow two to three minutes.*)

Next, ask participants to write in the right column some of the key characteristics that they admire. (*Allow two to three minutes.*)

Once finished, participants should look at the list of characteristics and circle the five that are the most important to them. (*Allow two to three minutes.*)

Ask participants to form small groups of four and share their lists with each other. They should keep a list of any characteristics that more than two of them had in common. (*Allow ten minutes.*)

Ask each group to share *briefly* (thirty seconds or less) which admirable characteristics they had in common. Record the characteristics on a flipchart (FCH).

After all groups have reported out, ask for a few examples of unique characteristics—those that only one person reported.

✦ Exploring What's "Real"—Who Are You as a Leader?

Thirty minutes

Next, state the following:

Now that you've thought about these ideal characteristics of others, you will get to take some time to think about yourselves specifically as leaders.

Ask participants to take a new blank sheet of paper and write down some of their best qualities as a leader. Ask:

What skills are you naturally pretty good at? What activities are more difficult for you to master?

After a few minutes, ask participants to look at their top four or five admired characteristics of others with their list of personal best qualities as a leader. (*Allow 3-4 minutes.*) Ask for volunteers to share what they see.

Now share the following comments:

- Where there is a gap between "ideal" and "real" is a place called your "learning edge."
- This edge reflects a place where you could spend some effort working to improve yourself.
- Consider picking one area to focus on developing your skills over the next six months.

Share with participants that they will be gathering back into the same small group of four to discuss this idea of the learning edge. Ask participants to gather with their earlier group and talk about their learning edges. Encourage participants to share their ideas on what kinds of experiences could help them test themselves and improve their skills in that area. (*Allow ten minutes.*)

☙ Developing a Learning/Leading Action Plan

Twenty minutes

Offer that the last conversation was meant to set the stage for the next activity. Based on the conversation in the small groups, ask participants to complete the *Action Plan* (Activity #2, SW). (*Allow five minutes.*)

Offer that these ideas will help them focus on what they want to do in the next few months. Ask participants to look again at their ideas and have them write more specifics about their action steps (such as dates, people's names, or book titles). Share that research tells us that intentions, when clearly stated and written or spoken, help us move toward our goals. (*Allow five minutes.*)

Variation: Have participants write an action plan as a "Memo to Self." Tell them to:

1. Write at the top of their list: "This is my action plan for growing my abilities/skills in _____."
2. Date it and sign at the bottom.
3. Fold up the list and put it in an envelope, address and seal it, and turn it in to the facilitator.
   - Share that you will mail it to them in a few months. Suggest that when they open the letter, they will have a chance to reflect on how much on their list they have accomplished.

Ask for volunteers to share an idea from their to-do lists. Continue for as long as time allows. (*Allow five minutes.*)

✦ Wrap Up

Five minutes

Share personal observations about the importance of following an action plan.

Offer the following quote from Eleanor Roosevelt: "You must do the things you think you cannot do."

Impressions

In the left column, list four or five people, real or fictional, whom you admire. Leave some space between the names. These people may have had a direct or an indirect influence on you. They may or may not be famous.

In the right column, list some of their key characteristics that you admire.

People	Characteristics

Circle two to three characteristics that you think you can develop over the next year.

Action Plan

Complete the following sentence stems. Refer back to Activity 1, if needed.

This is my action plan for developing my leadership potential in terms of _____.

List what you will do to develop this capacity.

I will:

A mentor to help me along the way:

Next week, I will:

Next month, I will:

By the end of the year, I will:

Signature:_____

Date:_____

MODULE 15

Achievement 2: Locus of Control
Sarah Spengler

✦ Focus of Module

Achievement is about being driven to improve according to personal standards. An important nuance of this capacity for emotionally intelligent leadership is the role of personal standards. Individuals often know achievement when they see and feel it. Instead of letting others define what achievement looks like, emotionally intelligent leaders pursue their passions and goals to a self-determined level of accomplishment. This drive produces results and may inspire others to become more focused in their efforts or to achieve at higher levels as well. No matter what the passion is, when we are committed to demonstrating emotionally intelligent leadership, we will pursue it to a high level of achievement.

Primary Activities

Through reflection and dialogue, participants explore the connections between locus of control, achievement, and leadership.

✦ Learning Objectives and Resources

- To understand what influences us in the decisions we make
- To learn about achievement in the context of emotionally intelligent leadership
- To develop a focus for pursuing additional learning and development after the session

Total time

Sixty minutes

Supplies

Internal and External Locus of Control worksheet (one per participant)

Blank sheets of paper (two per participant)

Flipchart, markers, easel

Music (soothing, calming instrumental), if desired

Flashcards, if desired

Copy of *Emotionally Intelligent Leadership: A Guide for College Students*

✦ Facilitator Preparation Notes

Read Chapter Ten, Achievement, in *Emotionally Intelligent Leadership: A Guide for College Students* (Shankman & Allen, 2008). (Refer to Appendix A for an overview of the EIL model.) Prepare introductory comments based on your reading.

Download *More to Explore* (see page viii).

Be familiar with the concept of locus of control prior to facilitating the session. For another session design that focuses solely on locus of control, see http://wilderdom.com/games/descriptions/LocusOfControlExercise.html.

Optional: If you choose to share with participants a list of influences, you can prepare a series of flash cards naming different possibilities. Include a variety of influences that they may find relevant—these could be parents, boyfriend or girlfriend, brothers and sisters, grandparents and other family, friends, grades or GPA, getting into grad school, getting a good job, the Dalai Lama, the Pope, the President, war in Iraq, terrorism, children in poverty, world hunger, global warming . . .

✦ Facilitator Tips

This session works best with a flexible seating arrangement that allows participants to move their chairs to form small groups or pairs quickly.

Because this design involves a combination of reflective writing and small group discussion, be prepared to move the participants quickly into the different configurations. Think ahead about how you want to partner participants or divide them into groups.

REFERENCE

Shankman, M. L., & Allen, S. J. (2008). *Emotionally intelligent leadership: A guide for college students*. San Francisco: Jossey-Bass.

✦ Introduction

Five minutes

Welcome participants and review the goals of this session:

- To understand what influences the decisions we make
- To learn about achievement and gain deeper personal insight
- To leave with ideas to explore further

Ask whether participants have any questions or additional goals for the session.

Ask participants to share what comes to mind when they hear the word *achievement*. Capture these words or phrases on a flipchart (FCH).

✦ Reflection

Thirty minutes

Ask participants to think for a minute about the following question:

> Do you influence, or are you influenced by, forces outside yourself? Or a little of both?

Share that in a few minutes they will draw personal diagrams of themselves and the influences around them. Let participants know that they will then have an opportunity to share this information with one other person in the room.

Demonstrating on the flipchart, ask participants to take a blank sheet of paper and draw a small circle at the center, in which they write their name or initials. Now ask participants to draw three or four concentric circles around the initial circle. Demonstrate again on the flipchart. Continue by suggesting:

The ones closer to the center are the layers that have the greatest influence on you: your behaviors and actions, your beliefs and values. Think about people, organizations, issues, and institutions that most strongly influence you. As you move out from the center, think about other people, organizations, issues, or situations that have some influence on you, but less so than those near the center. The circle farthest away represents things that have some influence on you, but in a more removed manner.

For example, where does global warming fit in your diagram? The wars in Iraq and Afghanistan? Your family and friends? The world economy? The earthquake in Haiti? Facebook? An organization you're involved in? Reality television? God?

Ask participants to fill in the circles and remember, the closer the circle is to the center, the stronger the influence.

Variation: Show flash cards here. Flip through the cards randomly and ask participants to figure out how strong that influence is in their lives and add them to their own diagrams in the appropriate circle. (*Allow seven to ten minutes. Play music if desired.*)

Ask participants to now select a partner and talk briefly about their diagram (sharing only what they are comfortable sharing). Discuss similarities and differences. (*Allow ten minutes.*)

Suggest that our lives are influenced by many different factors every day. From this exercise, we can see that we have different levels of what has a major influence on us and what has less influence. Ask the group to share some of those influences and describe the level of influence with the entire group. (*Allow ten minutes.*)

✦ Internal and External Locus of Control

Five minutes

Ask participants whether they have heard of *internal or external locus of control*. If anyone raises their hand, ask where that person learned about the terms. If no one raises their hand, ask two participants to each read a paragraph from *Internal and External Locus of Control* (Activity #3, SW). Be sure to emphasize that locus of control is at least partly learned from experience.

Add that when we better understand our locus of control and its influence on us, we learn how to make better decisions. We learn how to be more conscious of decisions ranging from what to wear and what to eat to whether to ask a question in class, volunteer on the weekend, or go to a party. Locus of control influences our behavior in various situations, like interpersonal conflicts, team projects, or even how we handle ourselves in our families.

✦ Reflection

Ten minutes

Ask participants to identify a situation where decision-making can be a challenge. (If participants are confused or cannot identify a situation, suggest challenges such as texting while driving, helping a friend cheat on an exam, or not being completely honest with a friend. Instruct participants to complete *Internal and External Locus of Control* (Activity #3, SW), beginning with the "I want" sentences in the *Internal* column. These statements should articulate their desired result from making this choice. (*Allow two to three minutes.*)

Now ask participants to complete the "They want" sentences in the *External* column—articulating what they think others want them to do or want from them in that situation.

Remember that neither "side" is better than the other—this is just one way of better understanding what forces may be affecting you in a given situation. (*Allow two to three minutes.*)

Ask participants to review what they've written and place an "X" at the point on the Internal-External continuum line that indicates what drives their behavior in that particular situation. Encourage participants to add other factors to the diagram to represent other forces that influence them.

✦ Wrap Up

Ten minutes

Refer back to the flipchart page about achievement created at the beginning of the session. Ask participants to think about how the concepts of internal and external locus of control relate to the EIL capacity of achievement. Ask participants to find a partner and discuss the following questions. (*Allow five to seven minutes.*)

- How does the concept of internal and external locus of control relate to leadership?
- What are at least two connections between you in relation to what you've thought about today?

Ask the group for a few examples of the connections they identified. Offer additional resources, if desired:

The concept of locus of control
  A web-based tutorial: Taking Control of Our Lives

The Far-Reaching Effects of Locus of Control
  www.units.muohio.edu/psybersite/control/index.shtml

A brief locus of control test
  http://discoveryhealth.queendom
    .com/lc_short_access.html

McClelland's motivation theory
> http://www.businessballs.com/davidmcclelland.htm

The concept of flow
> Csikszentmihalyi, M. (1990). *Flow: The psychology of optimal experience*. New York: Harper & Row.

Internal and External Locus of Control

Consider the following ideas:

External Locus of Control
External locus of control describes a person's belief that his or her behavior is guided by fate, luck, other people, or circumstances outside of that person's control.

Internal Locus of Control
Internal locus of control describes a person's belief that his or her behavior is guided by his or her own decisions and efforts.

Identify a challenge you currently (or often) face. Choose something where you are uncertain of the correct course of action. Describe that situation here (e.g., confronting a friend who has been engaging in unhealthy behavior).

Consider the definitions just offered.

Internal Locus of Control: **External Locus of Control:**

What do you want in this situation? What do others want you to do?
I want _____. They want _____.
I want _____. They want _____.
I want _____. They want _____.

As you read through your statements, from which direction do you see yourself being guided? Place an X on the following continuum to reflect where you are in relation to the type of control that is most strongly influencing your decisions. Identify the specific forces that you feel are most powerful in your decision making.

Internal _____**External**

MODULE 16

Optimism 1: The Power of Perception
Cathy Onion

✦ Focus of Module

Optimism is about being positive. Emotionally intelligent leaders demonstrate a healthy, positive outlook and display a positive regard for the future. Optimism is a powerful force that many overlook. When demonstrated effectively, optimism is contagious and spreads throughout a group or organization. In fact, optimism may be a learned skill—the more often we are able to see the positive, work to identify the best, and encourage others to be better, the more we can produce those results. With optimism, we focus on the best possible outcome, and as such, we align our thoughts in that way and work toward achieving that outcome. Research has found that being optimistic is an important element of emotional intelligence and leadership (Avolio & Luthans, 2006; Goleman, Boyatzis, & McKee, 2002).

Primary Activities

Through reflection and small group activities, participants explore the influences of their families and the power of perception to enhance their understanding of optimism.

179

⤝ Learning Objectives and Resources

- To understand how optimism can be a learned behavior
- To enhance personal perspectives on the power of perception
- To learn how to demonstrate optimistic thinking rather than pessimistic thinking

Total Time

Sixty minutes

Supplies

Assess Your Family worksheet (one per participant)

Illusions: What Do You See? worksheet (one per small group)

Flipchart, easel, markers

Audiovisual for PowerPoint or similar program, if desired

Copy of *Emotionally Intelligent Leadership: A Guide for College Students*

⤝ Facilitator Preparation Notes

Read Chapter Eleven, Optimism, in *Emotionally Intelligent Leadership: A Guide for College Students* (Shankman & Allen, 2008). (Refer to Appendix A for an overview of the EIL model.) Prepare introductory comments based on your reading.

The material covered in the *Illusions: What Do You See?* worksheet and the table "Explanatory Style of Optimists and Pessimists" can be presented in PowerPoint or a similar format if desired. The "Explanatory Style of Optimists and Pessimists" can also be made into a flipchart. Decide ahead of time which is preferred and plan accordingly.

Download the *Illusions: What Do You See?* worksheet (see page viii).

✦ Facilitator Tips

Decide on the basis of the group's dynamics whether the small group from *Illusions: What Do You See?* should gather again for *Two Sides to Every Story.*

REFERENCES

Avolio, B., & Luthans, F. (2006). *The high impact leader.* New York: McGraw-Hill.

Centre for Confidence and Well Being (n.d.). *What is optimism?* http://www.centreforconfidence.co.uk/pp/overview.php?p=c2lkPTQmdGlkPTAmaWQ9NTU=

Cutts, Emily (n.d.). *Learned optimism.* www.centreforconfidence.uk.co/pp/tools/LearnedOptimism.ppt

Goleman, D., Boyatzis, R., & McKee, A. (2002). *Primal leadership: Realizing the power of emotional intelligence.* Boston, MA: Harvard Business School Press.

Seligman, M. (2007). *The optimistic child: A proven program to safeguard children against depression and build lifelong resilience.* New York: Houghton Mifflin.

Shankman, M. L., & Allen, S. J. (2008). *Emotionally intelligent leadership: A guide for college students.* San Francisco: Jossey-Bass.

Sheperd, S. (2002). *Who's in charge: Attacking the stress myth.* Florida: Rainbow Books. Excerpt at http://www.rekindleyourheart.com/Site/Products_files/stressexcerpt.rtf.

☙ Introduce and Define

Five minutes

Ask participants how they would define optimism. Once several definitions have been offered, share the following definition from www.dictionary.com:

1. A disposition or tendency to look on the more favorable side of events or conditions and to expect the most favorable outcome
2. The belief that good ultimately predominates over evil in the world
3. The belief that goodness pervades reality

☙ Assess Your Family

Ten minutes

Using the preceding definitions, ask participants to use *Assess Your Family* (Activity #1, SW) and assess family members (parents, grandparents, siblings) and friends they see on a regular basis in terms of them being optimistic or pessimistic. (*Allow three to five minutes.*)

Continue by asking why they have those impressions. Consider the following questions:

- What kinds of attitudes do you often hear them express?
- What are common phrases they use?
- How do they explain good things that happen to them? Bad things that happen?
- How has their disposition affected you?

↞ Illusions

Ten minutes

Divide participants into small groups of no more than five. Provide each team with *Illusions*. Ask participants to identify what they see in each picture. Be sure to go through each picture, offering the perspective gained from *Illusions: What Do You See?*

Ask participants what these images might have to do with the subject of optimism. After a few responses, offer that our perceptions are individualistic. We may see the same image as someone else, but perceive it differently. Our perceptions are powerful forces that lead to thoughts, feelings, and behavior.

Conclude this segment with the following questions:

- What self-talk do you typically use when something doesn't go right or you can't figure something out?
- How much easier was it to spot the different images in the illusions when you were told what to look for? How does this relate to optimism? How does this relate to leadership?

↞ Views of the World

Fifteen minutes

Share with participants that Dr. Martin Seligman, director of the University of Pennsylvania's Positive Psychology Center, has conducted research on optimism. Seligman (2007) suggests, "The basis of optimism does not lie in positive phrases or images of victory, but in the way you think about causes" (p. 52). In addition, Seligman believes that pessimists and optimists explain the "why" of events in different ways, as shown in Table 16.1.

Table 16.1 **Explanatory Style of Optimists and Pessimists**

Success		Setbacks	
Optimists	**Pessimists**	**Optimists**	**Pessimists**
It was a result of hard work	Luck or a fluke or coincidence	A result of other factors	Their fault
Persistent—success can be maintained	Temporary—it won't last	Temporary	Permanent—will last a long time
Pervasive—success will positively impact other areas of my life	Specific	Specific—isolated to certain events	Pervasive— will undermine everything they do

Source: www.centreforconfidence.uk.co/pp/tools/LearnedOptimism.ppt.

Ask participants to think about their last setback or success and how they explained what had happened. Did they offer a pessimistic or optimistic explanation?

Ask participants the following questions:

- How can your viewpoint affect your level of optimism? Do you know someone who, from your perspective, is going through a terrible time yet seems to be handling it well (cancer, the loss of a loved one, and so on)?
- How might changing your perspective change your level of optimism?
- How is your outlook determined: externally or internally?
- What self-talk might you use to change your viewpoint or perspective?

✦ Two Sides to Every Story

Fifteen minutes

Share the following vignette with participants. Counselor and author Scott Sheperd has worked with many cancer patients. In an article about stress, Sheperd (2002) suggests the following:

> The phrase "Keep a positive attitude" has degenerated into "think good thoughts and only good things will happen."
>
> A "positive attitude" is now offered as a panacea to all the problems of the world. We have taken something that is profound and true—the idea that a positive attitude or belief system can play an important role in a fulfilled life, and we have trivialized it into a "magical incantation." Power, however, is about choices. (p. 2)

Divide participants into small groups (no more than six), and ask them to think of ten situations or events that some would see as positive and others as negative. Examples might include some of the following. (*Allow five minutes.*)

- Divorce
- Marriage
- Children
- Layoffs
- Illness
- Bankruptcy

Ask groups to report out and record ideas on a flipchart.

In the time remaining, ask participants any of the following questions:

- How can the same event be experienced as positive or negative?
- What makes a difference in the way you view the situation?
- When was the last time someone "made" you mad?
- Can someone actually "make" you mad or do you choose to be mad?

Offer that when you realize you have a choice, you can choose differently.

◆ Wrap Up

Five minutes

Remind participants that if they want things to change, they must be willing to work. Wrap up with this quote by author Scott Sheperd (2002):

> I don't believe our lives are problems that need to be solved, even if we are unhappy with them. We need less problem solving and a more creative way of looking at life. We need to focus less on specific situations and more on the big picture. Strangely, perhaps, this big-picture focus will help us with our specific situations.
>
> Most importantly, I believe we must look at what we are bringing to life, and not just what life is offering us. We must examine what our beliefs are and how they translate into our daily lives. Finally—we must be willing to work.
>
> Many people who come to seminars or read the books on managing stress or being successful want the fast fix. Fast fixes won't work. Revolution of any kind doesn't come easy. We cannot rely on the "Five ways to happiness" list. It is about having a belief system in place that enriches our lives. It is about using strategies that help us move through those events in our lives that we experience as tragic or painful. It is about seeing the beauty and strength that is around us in so many ways. We need to know what we can change and what we can't change. Then we have to have the courage to take action. This self-awareness takes work and, sometimes, can be very frightening. (pp. 4–5)

Illusions: What Do You See?

1. What two animals do you see?

2. How many legs does this elephant have?

3. What two pictures do you see?

4. What do you see?

Source: http://kids.niehs.nih.gov/illusion/illusions.htm#index

You may see . . .

1. A rabbit looking right or a duck looking left?
2. Four, five, or six legs?
3. A native American profile or an Eskimo looking into a cave?
4. A man playing a horn or a woman's face?

Assess Your Family

Think about your family members (parents, grandparents, siblings) and close friends. Decide which characteristic they generally display and write their names in the appropriate column.

Optimistic   Pessimistic

_____   _____
_____   _____
_____   _____
_____   _____
_____   _____
_____   _____

What statements do you often hear the optimists make? How do these statements impact those around them? You?

What statements do you often hear the pessimists make? How do these statements impact those around them? You?

MODULE 17

Optimism 2: Practice Optimism
Diana Wilson

✦ Focus of Module

Optimism is about being positive. Emotionally intelligent leaders demonstrate a healthy, positive outlook and display a positive regard for the future. Optimism is a powerful force that many overlook. When demonstrated effectively, optimism is contagious and spreads throughout a group or organization. In fact, optimism may be a learned skill—the more often we are able to see the positive, work to identify the best, and encourage others to be better, the more we can produce those results. With optimism, we focus on the best possible outcome, and as such, we align our thoughts in that way and work toward achieving that outcome. Research has found that being optimistic is an important element of emotional intelligence and leadership (Avolio & Luthans, 2006; Goleman, Boyatzis, & McKee, 2002).

Primary Activities

Participants will work with partners and in small groups to learn how to put optimism into practice.

❧ Learning Objectives and Resources

- To explore deeper meanings of optimism
- To foster optimism as a leadership capacity
- To practice optimism as it relates to participants' real experiences

Total Time

Sixty minutes

Supplies

Putting Optimism into Practice worksheet (one per participant)

Food for Thought (one per participant)

Flipchart, markers, easel

Index cards (one per participant)

Clear glass/cup with water filled halfway

Copy of *Emotionally Intelligent Leadership: A Guide for College Students*

❧ Facilitator Preparation

Read Chapter Eleven, Optimism, in *Emotionally Intelligent Leadership: A Guide for College Students* (Shankman & Allen, 2008). (Refer to Appendix A for an overview of the EIL model.) Prepare introductory comments based on your reading.

❧ Facilitator Tips

The participation required in this module's activities must be monitored to meet designated time limits. In addition, some participants may be reluctant to share their thoughts. Don't discount them or favor the talkative participants. If you give quieter participants a few moments of silence to gather their thoughts first, they will be more likely to share. Other participants may be eager to share too much. You may need to step in to redirect or move the discussion along.

REFERENCES

Avolio, B., & Luthans, F. (2006). *The high impact leader.* New York: McGraw-Hill.

Fox, M. J. (2009). Always looking up: The adventures of an incurable optimist. New York: Hyperion.

Goleman, D., Boyatzis, R., & McKee, A. (2002). *Primal leadership: Realizing the power of emotional intelligence.* Boston, MA: Harvard Business School Press.

Seligman, M. E. (1992). *Learned optimism: How to change your mind and your life.* New York: Harper.

Shankman, M. L., & Allen, S. J. (2008). *Emotionally intelligent leadership: A guide for college students.* San Francisco: Jossey-Bass.

✦ Introduction

Five minutes

Show participants a glass filled to half its capacity with water. Ask them to raise their hands if they would say "The glass is half full." Ask how many would say "The glass is half empty." Share that decades of research have proven that how you view the glass (figuratively, as analogous to a particular situation) has a meaningful impact on your future, how you understand other people, and the causes of events that occur every day. In fact, research shows that your view can affect your performance, your physical and emotional well-being, your academic or work achievement, and even the outcome of a project for which you are responsible (e.g., Seligman, 1992).

Share that the goal of this session is to encourage participants to think about the meaning of optimism and how they can foster this important capacity in themselves. Add additional observations about optimism as it relates to leadership based on your reading of the chapter in *Emotionally Intelligent Leadership: A Guide for College Students* (Shankman & Allen, 2008).

✦ Optimism Brainstorm

Five minutes

Divide participants into groups of three or four, with one participant designated as the note taker. Ask participants to discuss the following two questions. (*Allow two to three minutes.*)

- What is optimism?
- What is an optimist?

Have each group report on their brainstorm and record ideas (FCH).

Gauge whether the group is close to being on target, and offer the following definition if needed:

1. a doctrine that this world is the best possible world; 2: an inclination to put the most favorable construction upon actions and events or to anticipate the best possible outcome. (http://www.merriamwebster .com/dictionary/optimism)

✦ Learned Optimism

Fifteen minutes

Offer that there are times when we may need a little help being more optimistic, or maybe we need to help someone else learn to be more optimistic. Share the following quote:

Life is what happens to you while you're busy making other plans.
— John Lennon, "Beautiful Boy"

Ask participants to think of a time when a goal they had did not come to fruition (such as making the team, getting the job, being accepted into their dream school). If no one responds, ask participants if they have had anything similar happen to them. Ask for brief descriptions of the situation, then ask the participants how they reacted. Was it their own fault or did they interpret it as a temporary setback?

Share that we may not always have control over what happens in our lives, but we can choose how we respond. Optimists have positive feelings towards future situations, which causes them to respond differently to setbacks. There are many examples of people in the public eye that live life with this attitude. You have probably heard of Michael J. Fox, the actor who has been battling Parkinson's disease since 1991. His second memoir, *Always Looking Up: The Adventures of an Incurable Optimist* (2009), focuses on how his life and his family have been changed for the better as a result of his battling this debilitating disease.

Ask participants to silently finish this sentence, "When I think of the future, I feel . . . "

Ask participants to share the word or words they chose. After a few comments, offer that one primary difference between optimism and pessimism is how a person frames setbacks and obstacles:

- Those who frame situations pessimistically tend to see setbacks as difficult to move on from. They may go so far as to believe that the setback is their own fault.
- Optimists often view setbacks as temporary; they may see them as experiences to learn from. An optimistic frame may encourage a person to look at the situation and analyze the results in relation to external factors.

↞ Putting Optimism into Practice

Fifteen minutes

Instruct participants to find a partner to work with on *Putting Optimism into Practice* (Activity #2, SW). Explain that one partner reads a pessimistic statement while the other rephrases the statement into an optimistic one. Then alternate roles. As partners read through, they should be sure to record the optimistic statements below the pessimistic statements. *(Allow eight to ten minutes.)*

After the allotted time, ask each pair to read one of their new statements until the list is completed or until everyone has had a chance to share.

Conclude with the results of a (1992) study conducted by Dr. Martin E. Seligman, a renowned psychologist and clinical researcher. In just one example from his extensive research, he found that new sales personnel at Metropolitan Life who scored high on a test on optimism sold 37 percent more life insurance in their first two years than pessimists. (To learn more about

Seligman's research or to take any number of free questionnaires, including the Optimism Test, visit http://www.authentichappiness .sas.upenn.edu.)

✦ Optimistic Leadership

Ten minutes

Offer that optimism is a powerful, essential tool for every leadership toolbox. It is a key ingredient in leading and inspiring others to do their best work—and to even go beyond what they thought they could achieve.

Ask participants to think about organizations that they have joined and then consider the leader of that organization. Ask for a show of hands: how many would describe their organization as having a pervasive can-do attitude? Ask any of the following questions:

- Does the leader take risks and focus on the group rather than him- or herself? Give an example of how you know this.
- In what way(s) has the leader framed situations to help you feel you could accomplish anything if you worked hard and stayed positive?
- What happens to the mood of a group if someone says, "That idea will never work—we've tried it before" or "We can't do that; it won't be approved"?

Share that an optimistic leader will respond by staying focused on the vision and by turning challenges into opportunities.

Divide participants into small groups of three or four and distribute index cards. Ask participants to select a situation they have to face in the near future. Then ask them to imagine the worst case scenario. Next, have them jot down one action step they could take to stop the worst case scenario from happening. (*Allow two to three minutes.*)

Instruct participants to flip the card over. Ask them to write down the best case scenario and one action step they might take to make it happen. Encourage participants to get ideas from their group. This may inspire others to create new ideas and practice inspiring others. (*Allow two to three minutes.*)

Encourage participants to recognize that risk taking is part of leadership. Suggest that risk takers need to be optimistic; they need to believe that what they try will turn out well. Risk taking puts a leader's ability and effort on the line—and with an optimistic view, risk is seen more as an opportunity than a challenge. For optimists, the potential rewards for progress generally outweigh the risk of failure.

✦ Wrap Up

Five minutes

To conclude, share the following story:

While walking along a beach, a man saw in the distance what looked like a boy dancing. He was encouraged by the outward expression of someone dancing to the new day on the beach, and he approached the young man. As he got closer, he realized that the young man was actually running, leaning down, picking something up and then gently throwing it far out into the ocean.

As he came closer, he saw thousands of starfish the tide had thrown onto the beach. Unable to return to the ocean during low tide, the starfish were dying. He observed the young man picking up the starfish one by one and throwing them back.

After watching the seemingly futile effort, the observer said to the young man, "There must be thousands of starfish on this beach. It would be impossible for you to get to all of them. There are simply too many. You can't possibly save enough to make a difference."

The young man smiled as he continued to pick up another starfish and toss it back into the ocean.

"It made a difference to that one," he replied.

The older man shook his head at the impossible optimism of the young man, then turned away and walked home. That night, he sat for a long time thinking of the young man, and determined that the young man was really affecting the world and taking action to make a difference, something that the older man would have liked to do. That night he slept fitfully. In the morning, he awoke, went down to the beach, and again found the young man. Together they went along the shore, tossing starfish back into the ocean.—Author Unknown

Think about this example of optimism. There will be many times in life when you will be faced with adversity. How will you choose to feel about it? How will you choose to act? Encourage participants to keep *Food for Thought* (Module 17, Activity #3, SW) handy as a reminder for how to practice optimism.

Putting Optimism into Practice

Optimism is often understood as a reflection of how we view the world. Consider the following two different ways to view the same situation—taking an exam:

- I will never be prepared enough to do well on the exam. (Pessimistic statement.)
- I know I am smart and will do my best on the exam. (Optimistic statement.)

Rewrite the following statements to reflect an optimistic view.

1. It seems like I put myself in the same unhealthy situations over and over. I will never learn.
   Optimistic:

2. This game is too difficult to learn. I will never figure out how to play it well.
   Optimistic:

3. This event is going to fail. We are really unprepared and no one is doing their part.
   Optimistic:

4. I won't ever find someone to share my life with.
   Optimistic:

5. We have always done things this way. We can't change the process now.
   Optimistic:

6. I am too stressed out to get anything done.
   Optimistic:

7. Why should I put more effort into this class? The teacher doesn't like me.
   Optimistic:

8. I can't make it to the meeting. I'm too busy.
   Optimistic:

9. We have ruined so much of our environment. What is the point of being "green" now?
   Optimistic:

10. I don't see how this plan can possibly succeed.
    Optimistic:

Food for Thought

Reprinted with permission from *Funny Times*, PO Box 18530, Cleveland Heights, OH 44118.

The following thoughts reflect different perspectives on optimism. Which ones resonate with you?

> While we may not be able to control all that happens to us, we can control what happens inside us.
> —Benjamin Franklin

> An optimist sees an opportunity in every calamity; a pessimist sees a calamity in every opportunity.
> —Winston Churchill

> Optimism is the faith that leads to achievement. Nothing can be done without hope and confidence.
> —Helen Keller

> As we look ahead into the next century, leaders will be those who empower others.
> —Bill Gates

> Every person has the power to make others happy.
> Some do it simply by entering a room—
> others by leaving the room.
> Some individuals leave trails of gloom;
> others, trails of joy.
> Some leave trails of hate and bitterness

others, trails of love and harmony.
Some leave trails of cynicism and pessimism;
others, trails of faith and optimism.
Some leave trails of criticism and resignation;
others trails of gratitude and hope.
What kind of trails do you leave?
—William Arthur Ward

1. When might it be helpful to adopt one of these quotes on optimism? Describe that situation here.

2. Think about someone who you think would benefit from seeing one of these quotes on optimism. Take the time to share it with them and talk with them about how adopting this view or idea might be helpful. How did you benefit from this conversation?

To learn more about optimism, visit: http://www.authentichappiness. sas.upenn.edu.

MODULE 18

Initiative
Anthony Middlebrooks

✦ Focus of Module

Showing initiative, in the context of emotionally intelligent leadership, means wanting and seeking opportunities. Emotionally intelligent leaders understand and take initiative. Emotionally intelligent leaders have to both see the opportunity for change *and* make it happen. Demonstrating initiative means that individuals take action and help the work of the group move forward. Initiative requires self-understanding—knowing what you care about, what you are interested in doing, and believing that you can accomplish what you set out to do. Self-confidence and assertiveness are both essential components of initiative. Demonstrating initiative requires both stepping up and speaking out. To find new opportunities, you must know how to look for them and must truly want to make that change happen. Demonstrating initiative means that you take action. In his video *The Power of Vision* (1991), futurist Joel Barker suggests, "Vision without action is merely a dream. Action without vision just passes time. Vision with action changes the world."

Initiative combines thinking about possibilities, imagining a potential direction or action, and making it happen.

Primary Activities

Participants learn how to perform a new task or demonstrate a new talent, practice it, and then present their new talents to the larger group.

✦ Learning Objectives and Resources

- To practice initiative
- To explore the dynamics of transformational learning
- To identify the connections between teamwork and initiative

Total Time

Sixty minutes

Supplies

Transformational Team Learning: Instructions (one copy for the facilitator)

Transformational Team Learning: Small Group Leader Instructions (one per small group)

Copy of *Emotionally Intelligent Leadership: A Guide for College Students*

✦ Facilitator Preparation Notes

Read Chapter Twelve, Initiative, in *Emotionally Intelligent Leadership: A Guide for College Students* (Shankman & Allen,

2008). (Refer to Appendix A for an overview of the EIL model.) Prepare introductory comments based on your reading.

This activity works best if there are at least sixteen participants, divided into four groups of four or five. If possible, divide the group ahead of time and identify one person as the leader for each group. If you can't do this before the group gathers, do so at the beginning.

Download *Transformational Team Learning: Instructions* and *Small Group Leader Instructions* (see page viii). Include just *one* of the four listed facets of transformational leadership from *Transformational Team Learning: Small Group Leader Instructions* on each sheet: to do so, cut, paste, and print so that each small group leader gets a different facet on his or her instruction sheet.

This activity can be further enhanced by couching it within Senge's (1990) five disciplines, emphasizing shared vision, mental models, team learning, systems thinking, and personal mastery. The activity has implications for each of the other disciplines.

✦ Facilitator Tips

When setting up the activity, be efficient at the beginning to maximize the amount of time allotted.

Depending on the size of the small groups, the facilitator may assign one member of each group the role of "secret observer" to watch and take note of team dynamics over the course of the activity. This often adds an interesting perspective to the debrief.

The session can be extended by allowing more time for the activity and/or the debrief; this is highly recommended.

Explain that there are five versions of the worksheet: one for all participants, and four different worksheets for the small group leaders.

REFERENCES

Barker, J. (1991). *The power of vision* (VHS). United States: Starthrower Distribution.

Northouse, P. (2006). *Leadership: Theory and practice* (4th ed.). Thousand Oaks, CA: Sage.

Senge, P. (1990). *The fifth discipline: The art and practice of the learning organization.* New York: Doubleday.

Shankman, M. L., & Allen, S. J. (2008). *Emotionally intelligent leadership: A guide for college students.* San Francisco: Jossey-Bass.

✦ Introduction

Five minutes

Welcome participants and divide them into small groups. Share general observations about initiative and its relevance to emotionally intelligent leadership.

Explain that participants will now engage in an activity designed to give them practice and experience with the capacity of initiative. Assign a leader in each group or ask participants to choose a leader. Read aloud *Transformational Team Learning: Instructions*.

Each group has the following task:

1. Your team must learn to *do something new* that can be learned in less than fifteen minutes; for example, learning to juggle. All members must learn to do it. It must be an activity that no more than *one* member of the group has tried more than once.
2. Try to choose something to learn that's interesting, creative, valuable, and challenging; keep in mind that the other groups will be doing the same.
3. You must learn it from a credible source.
4. Be prepared to demonstrate your new skill to the large group.
5. You will be asked to describe how you felt during the learning process.

✦ Learn to Do Something

Fifteen minutes

Send participants out of the room to complete their challenge. Ask them to return prepared to share, demonstrate, and possibly teach others what they have learned.

As participants leave the room, give each small group leader one of the four different *Transformational Team Learning: Small*

Group Leader Instructions sheets. Explain that the leader should not let the other participants see those instructions.

Give participants a warning when half of their time is up. Assign one member of the group the role of timekeeper and give that person the time that they need to return to the large group.

← Presentations of Team Learning

Ten to fifteen minutes

Upon returning, ask each group to demonstrate what they learned. This can be quite fun and engaging. Feel free to ask some groups to teach the other participants the newly acquired skill or talent.

Congratulate each group on their success.

← Wrap Up

Twenty minutes

Solicit general impressions and insights from participants. Conclude with any or all of the following questions:

- How did the team learn? Describe your team's process. Give examples of who demonstrated initiative to facilitate the process.
- What facilitated the learning in your group? What inhibited or made it difficult?
- How did it feel to learn? Initially? Part way? Nearing competence?
- How did you relate to the leader? Others in the group?
- What does this activity teach you about demonstrating initiative?

Invite all the leaders from the small groups to the front of the room. Reiterate that each leader was asked to emphasize a different facet of a transformational leader. Ask leaders to comment on their roles, what they emphasized, and how this role enabled them to demonstrate initiative. After each leader speaks, read their specific assigned role.

Ask participants to discuss the extent to which they felt the leader and his or her behavior contributed to building the team and accomplishing the task.

Conclude with personal observations of the importance of demonstrating initiative effectively when it comes to emotionally intelligent leadership.

Transformational Team Learning: Instructions

Here is your group's task:

1. Your team must learn to *do something new* that can be accomplished in fifteen minutes; for example, learning to juggle, preparing a cappuccino, freehand drawing a perfect circle. All members must learn to do it. It must be an activity that no more than *one* member of the group has previously tried more than once.
2. Try to choose something to learn that's interesting, creative, valuable, and challenging; keep in mind that the other groups will be doing the same.
3. Members must learn it from a credible source.
4. Be prepared to demonstrate what members learned to do for the full group.
5. Observe yourself and others throughout the learning process. Describe how it felt to learn.

See page viii for download information.

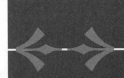

Transformational Team Learning: Small Group Leaders' Instructions

Leader: *Do not read this part out loud to your group.*

Here is *your* task as leader:

Transformational leadership has been defined as "the process whereby a person engages with others and creates a connection that raises the level of motivation and morality in both the leader and the follower" (Northouse, 2006, p. 176).

During this task you need to be a transformational leader who demonstrates initiative in your group. Specifically, you are to *emphasize and use* this facet of leadership:

[The facilitator will alter each leader's instructions to include just one of the following four facets.]

Idealized Influence or Charisma: "describes leaders who act as strong role models for followers; followers identify with these leaders and want very much to emulate them."

Inspirational Motivation: "leaders who communicate high expectations to followers, inspiring them through motivation to become committed to and a part of the vision . . . using symbols and emotional appeals to focus group members' efforts to achieve more than they would in their own self-interest."

Intellectual Stimulation: "leadership that stimulates followers to be creative and innovate, and to challenge their own beliefs and values as well as those of the leader . . . supports followers as they try new approaches . . . "

Individualized Consideration: "leaders who provide a supportive climate in which they listen carefully to the individual needs of the followers . . . act as coaches and advisers while trying to assist individuals in becoming fully actualized . . . "

See page viii for download information.

References

Northouse, P. (2006). *Leadership: Theory and practice* (4th ed.). Thousand Oaks, CA: Sage.

MODULE 19

Consciousness of Others
Marcy Levy Shankman and Scott J. Allen

✦ Focus of Module

Demonstrating consciousness of others means being aware of and attuned to those with whom you are working. Leadership is not a solo activity—it's based on relationships. Whether you think of a traditional leader-follower relationship or something more like a group of collaborators, the relationship among the people involved is essential. Consciousness of others includes the ability to empathize, inspire, influence, and coach. Teamwork, dealing with conflict and differences, and learning how to work effectively with others to bring about change are all essential capacities of emotionally intelligent leadership. Because the setting and situation for leadership changes so often, many variables affect leadership. Therefore it's essential that leaders learn how to work with others and incorporate them effectively in the leadership equation.

Primary Activities

Participants work together to accomplish the task of successfully jumping rope as a team.

✦ Learning Objectives and Resources

- To introduce the range of specific capacities that make up consciousness of others
- To learn how to work effectively together to accomplish a task
- To develop an analytical framework for applying consciousness of others to a group situation

Total Time

Forty-five minutes

Supplies

Working with Others worksheet (one per participant)

Pens, pencils (one per participant)

Jump rope that is about fifteen feet long—long enough for two people to jump in at the same time

Copy of *Emotionally Intelligent Leadership: A Guide for College Students*

✦ Facilitator Preparation Notes

Read Part Three, Consciousness of Others, in *Emotionally Intelligent Leadership: A Guide for College Students* (Shankman & Allen, 2008), and answer the reflection questions for yourself. (Refer to Appendix A for an overview of the EIL model.) Prepare introductory comments based on your reading.

Be sure you have a space large enough for participants to use a large jump rope.

Review the ten capacities of consciousness of others. Be familiar with them so that you can speak comfortably and quickly about each one.

✦ Facilitator Tips

This activity works best with at least fifteen participants.

For *EIL in Action* engage participants in conversation about their rationale for selecting the chosen capacities. Seek differences in volunteers so that participants can better understand the range of choices they have in contemplating different approaches to leadership.

Be sure participants have appropriate attire (for example tennis shoes versus high heels) for this activity. Remind participants that this activity is "challenge by choice."

REFERENCE

Shankman, M. L., & Allen, S. J. (2008). *Emotionally intelligent leadership: A guide for college students*. San Francisco: Jossey-Bass.

✦ Introduction

Ten minutes

Begin by sharing that consciousness of others is one facet of emotionally intelligent leadership that encompasses a wide range of capacities that we often associate with the "doing" part of leadership. Leadership doesn't happen in a vacuum, so we have to be just as aware of others as we are of ourselves and our context.

Refer participants to *Working with Others* (Activity #1, SW) and briefly review the range of capacities.

Ask participants to check one or two capacities that they think are most relevant to the demonstration of leadership. Solicit a few volunteers to share their thoughts—try to get different responses so that participants begin to see the range of perspectives on leadership.

✦ Activity

Twenty minutes

Share the following instructions with participants:

The goal of this exercise is to have *all* participants jump *through* the jump rope in succession. At least one person must jump through the rope each time it hits the ground. If the rope hits the ground without someone jumping through, or if it hits someone, the entire group must start over. Participants can jump only once each. There are no tricks here—you are simply jumping rope.

Upon completion of the task or after fifteen minutes (whichever comes first), use the following questions for initial discussion:

- How did you accomplish your goal?
- What were some of the difficulties?
- Did your group set a plan prior to attempting the task?
- What could have been improved?

✦ EIL in Action

Ten minutes

Instruct participants to form groups of three or four. Ask them to refer back to *Working with Others* (Activity #1, SW) and pick two or three capacities that would have helped the group accomplish this task more effectively or efficiently. Be sure to tell the groups that they will be asked to justify their selections. *(Allow five minutes.)*

Spend the remaining time soliciting ideas from the groups about the capacities they selected and why.

✦ Wrap Up

Five minutes

Ask participants to highlight a behavior of one team member that aligns with the facet of consciousness of others. For instance, who coached others well?

Have participants each share one observation they have about working with others. Encourage them to use language from the worksheet or from this session.

After this activity, encourage participants to consider the reflection questions at the end of *Working with Others* (Activity #1, SW). Offer that these questions are important to remember when they participate in group activities in the future.

Offer your own thoughts to conclude the session.

Working with Others

On the following list, check the three capacities you think are most important for effective leadership.

—— *Empathy*: Understanding others from their perspective
—— *Citizenship*: Recognizing and fulfilling your responsibility for others or the group
—— *Inspiration*: Motivating and moving others toward a shared vision
—— *Influence*: Demonstrating skills of persuasion
—— *Coaching*: Helping others enhance their skills and abilities
—— *Change agent*: Seeking out and working with others toward new directions
—— *Conflict management*: Identifying and resolving problems and issues with others
—— *Developing relationships*: Creating connections between, among, and with people
—— *Teamwork*: Working effectively with others in a group
—— *Capitalizing on difference*: Building on assets that come from differences with others

After a group activity, reflect on the following:

1. Why are the three capacities you chose the most relevant to you?

2. What happens when one of these capacities is overused? Why?

3. What happens if the other capacities (the ones you didn't check) are ignored? What is lost?

Reference

Shankman, M. L., & Allen, S. J. (2008). *Emotionally intelligent leadership: A guide for college students*. San Francisco: Jossey-Bass.

MODULE 20

Empathy
Ginny Carroll

✦ Focus of Module

Empathy is about understanding others from their perspective.
Emotionally intelligent leadership and, more specifically, the
capacity of empathy are about perceiving the emotions of others.
When leaders display empathy, they have the opportunity to
build healthier relationships, manage difficult situations, and
develop trust more effectively. Being empathetic requires an
individual to have a high level of self-awareness as well as awareness of others. The cliché "put yourself in someone else's shoes"
truly defines the capacity of empathy, because to identify
with the emotions of another person, you must first understand
your own emotions. Learning how to recognize and name your
emotions (some call this emotional literacy) is an essential stepping stone for demonstrating empathy.

Primary Activities

Participants practice their listening skills to understand and
enhance their perspective on what it means to demonstrate

empathy, and they learn how to connect empathy with emotionally intelligent leadership.

❖ Learning Objectives and Resources

- To increase participants' understanding of the concept of empathy
- To practice active listening skills
- To learn the difference between listening for feelings and listening for perspective

Total Time

Sixty minutes

Supplies

Flipchart, markers, easel

Copy of *Emotionally Intelligent Leadership: A Guide for College Students*

❖ Facilitator Preparation Notes

Read Chapter Thirteen, Empathy, in *Emotionally Intelligent Leadership: A Guide for College Students* (Shankman & Allen, 2008), and answer the reflection questions for yourself. (Refer to Appendix A for an overview of the EIL model.) Prepare introductory comments based on your reading.

Prepare two flipcharts. On one, write the following quotation:

Leadership is about empathy. It is about having the ability to relate and to connect with people for the purpose of inspiring and empowering their lives.—Oprah Winfrey

On the second, write the following:

Components of Empathy
- Inexactness
- Attention to the larger picture
- Context
- No exception for lawfulness

✦ Facilitator Tips

Be prepared to share personal observations of how the components of empathy connect with leadership.

REFERENCES

Baron-Cohen, S. (2003). *The essential difference: Men, women, and the extreme brain.* New York: Perseus Books.

Shankman, M. L., & Allen, S. J. (2008). *Emotionally intelligent leadership: A guide for college students.* San Francisco: Jossey-Bass.

✦ Introduction

Five minutes

Begin by offering the following observations:

Empathy is the ability to immerse oneself in another person's point of view and yet remain apart to be neutral. In our rapidly changing and diverse world, empathy is emerging as a critical leadership capability.

Empathy is the intersection of consciousness of context, consciousness of self, and consciousness of others.

Being empathetic requires you to have a high level of self-awareness as well as awareness of others. To be empathetic you must know what you are feeling in order to acknowledge and identify what others may be feeling.

Add personal comments as appropriate. Refer to the Oprah Winfrey quote (FCH). Ask for any comments or reactions.

✦ Components of Empathy

Ten minutes

In his 2003 book *The Essential Difference*, Cambridge University psychologist Simon Baron-Cohen asserts that empathy

Involves inexactness (one can only ever approximate when one ascertains another's mental state), attention to the larger picture (what one thinks he thinks or feels about other people, for example), context (a person's face, voice, action, and history are all essential information in determining that person's mental state), with no exception for lawfulness (what made her happy yesterday may not make her happy tomorrow). (p. 26)

Review Baron-Cohen's components of empathy (FCH) and ask for comments or opinions:

1. Inexactness
2. Attention to the larger picture

3. Context
4. No exception for lawfulness

Ask participants to connect these four points with leadership. Be prepared to offer personal observations if participants are not seeing the connections. For example, #2 is a factor in effective leadership—the ability to connect with a perspective that is beyond one person and that person's own goals.

Encourage participants to focus their attention during this session on their feelings as they relate to leadership and the context in which they lead.

✦ Listen to Understand

Forty minutes

Share that we can best demonstrate empathy by listening intently to others for two important messages being communicated—feelings and context.

Suggest that effective leadership requires us to recognize how context plays a role in the way people interpret and react to situations. Part of this requires us to realize that reactions will often include an array of emotions.

Empathy requires the ability to understand how others perceive situations based on *their* values and beliefs about the world. When we're empathetic, we take those ideas into consideration to the best of our ability. We can glean this information in numerous ways, including studying another person's demeanor. Their tone, body language, and the verbal language they use can tell us a lot. We can also learn from understanding how socioeconomic status or family of origin influences a person's experiences. These are just some ways to better understand how others perceive situations.

Ask participants to find a partner. After doing so, ask them to determine who will be the speaker and who will be the listener. Ask the speaker to tell the listener about a difficult situation they've experienced recently.

Share with the listeners that they are listening for feelings; to that end:

- Do not attempt to solve the problem. You are offering the speaker a mirror (reflection) to see the situation by asking questions that clarify feelings.
- Listen and speak only to the emotions being felt (feelings).

(*Allow five to ten minutes.*)

Next, ask the partners to switch roles.

Offer that another key approach is to listen for context and perspective. Context involves many variables. In this next conversation, the listener is to pay attention to and *ask questions* that will help to understand the history and context of the speaker's situation to better understand the speaker's perspective.

Spend five minutes as a large group talking about context and ask participants to discuss or brainstorm ways to get to context. Record their thoughts (FCH).

Ask participants to return to their partners in just a minute so that the speaker can tell the listener about a positive, happy situation experienced recently.

First share the following key points with the listeners:

- Do not attempt to solve the problem. You are only to ask questions that clarify context or what gave rise to the speaker's feelings. Seek to understand the speaker's perspective.
- Ask about why the speaker was involved in the situation and what made it important.

- Pay attention to body language. Study the speaker's demeanor.
- Remember, context includes a person's face, voice, action, and history.

Have partners spend five minutes with this next conversation. (*Allow five minutes.*)

When participants have finished, debrief by asking the following questions, as time allows:

- Which was more difficult for you to identify with—feelings or context?
- How did your partner respond when your reflection was accurate for both feeling and context?
- How often did you want to interrupt and add your own feelings to the conversation?
- What questions did you ask to identify feelings?
- What questions did you ask to clarify context?
- How does this activity apply to leadership?

✦ Wrap Up

Five minutes

Conclude with the idea that empathy is about putting yourself in someone else's shoes and relating to what that person is feeling. Empathy allows us to see the other side of an argument and to be more understanding.

Invite participants to purposefully watch and listen to get the best information they can about the people they work with.

Emotionally intelligent leadership is about paying attention and being intentional. The more we accurately identify our feelings with our context and the people with whom we're working, the more empathetic we will become.

Ask participants whether they have any final questions or comments. Conclude by sharing a personal observation about the importance of demonstrating empathy in the context of emotionally intelligent leadership.

Citizenship 1: Voices of Democracy
Jon Dooley

◆ Focus of Module

Citizenship, as a capacity of emotionally intelligent leadership, reflects our ability to recognize and fulfill our responsibility for others or the group. Emotionally intelligent leaders must be aware of what it means to be a part of something bigger than themselves. An essential component is to fulfill the ethical and moral obligations inherent in the values of the community. As a result, emotionally intelligent leaders know when to give of themselves for the benefit of others and the larger group. Demonstrating emotionally intelligent leadership requires us to recognize that being involved in a group is not a solo, self-oriented act. "To be a good citizen is to work for positive change on behalf of others and the community" (Higher Education Research Institute, 1996, p. 23). Citizenship also implies the broader concept of interdependence. When you demonstrate citizenship, you give of yourself and see yourself as responsible both for and to others. Interdependence, collaboration, and working effectively with others for the good of the organization or cause reflects the demands of leadership in the twenty-first century (Knapp, 2006).

Primary Activities

Participants listen to and reflect on a dialogue about the concept of citizenship, then work with others in small groups to identify problems and who is responsible for solving them.

⬳ Learning Objectives and Resources

- To enhance participants' understanding of citizenship
- To identify issues of concern that matter to participants
- To explore how leadership and citizenship happen at all levels of an organization or group

Total Time

Sixty minutes

Supplies

Formal Democracy Versus Living Democracy: An Argument (one per participant)

Flipchart, markers, easel

Copy of *Emotionally Intelligent Leadership: A Guide for College Students*

⬳ Facilitator Preparation Notes

Read Chapter Fourteen, Citizenship, in *Emotionally Intelligent Leadership: A Guide for College Students* (Shankman & Allen, 2008), and answer the reflection questions for yourself. (Refer to Appendix A for an overview of the EIL model.) Prepare introductory comments based on your reading.

Secure a space where participants can all stand and not be too close together.

Before the session, solicit two volunteers to read the dialogue in the worksheet; provide copies so they are prepared. If it isn't possible to prepare these individuals in advance, ask for two volunteers at the beginning of the session and prepare them appropriately.

Prepare flipcharts for the first two segments as follows:

1. Write "Citizenship" at the top, and then the following text:
   - Think back over the last year. Where have you heard or read any of these arguments?
   - Which voice in this dialogue best matches your own views?
2. Prepare a flipchart with three column headings:

Issue or problem	Those expected to solve the problem	Others to get involved

Be prepared to specify what community should be considered for the section on problem solving. This could be a small community, like an organization, or a larger community, like an entire campus or city.

✦ Facilitator Tips

Participants often equate the term *citizenship* with civic engagement or country identity. Be sure to point out that although this is certainly one form of citizenship that will be discussed during the session, citizenship is also found in other contexts—such as organizations, schools, and communities.

The first segment is focused on representations of citizenship from American democracy; the session can be adapted for groups with more diverse international populations as appropriate.

Be sure to read through the worksheet so you're familiar with content.

For *A Tap on Leadership*, give as little setup or explanation as possible and move seamlessly from the previous discussion to the instructions for the exercise. During a typical running of this activity, the participants may take several minutes to realize that they have the power to tap others and themselves; however, some groups may never realize they are allowed to do so. Once participants decide to tap themselves (unusual outcome) and/or others (expected outcome), the activity may end quickly. Be sensitive to the level of ability in the group and adapt the instructions accordingly if standing up and squatting down are not viable options. Consider having participants sit in chairs if physical concerns exist for anyone in terms of moving from a squatted position to standing.

REFERENCES

Eisenhower Leadership Program Grant (1995). *Citizens of change program: Application guidebook for the social change model of leadership development.* De Pere, WI: Citizen Leadership Development Center, St. Norbert College.

Higher Education Research Institute. (1996). *A social change model of leadership development: Guidebook version III.* Los Angeles: University of California Los Angeles Higher Education Research Institute.

Knapp, J. C. (Ed.). (2006). *For the common good: The ethics of leadership in the 21st century.* New York: Praeger.

Lappé, F. M., & Du Bois, P. M. (1994). *The quickening of America: Rebuilding our nation, remaking our lives.* San Francisco: Jossey-Bass.

Shankman, M. L., and Allen, S. J. (2008). *Emotionally intelligent leadership: A guide for college students.* San Francisco: Jossey-Bass.

✦ Introduction

Five minutes

Begin by asking participants what they first think of when they hear the word *citizenship*. Solicit ten to fifteen responses and write responses on the flipchart, until a pattern begins to emerge or similar responses are offered.

Share the perspective that we may equate citizenship with country or national identity—and this is certainly one form of citizenship that will be discussed during the session. We also should recognize that citizenship can be found in many other contexts—such as organizations, schools, and communities.

Offer that during this session, participants will be asked to consider an understanding of citizenship in a national context, explore its meaning in their own setting, and consider their personal stake in leadership and citizenship.

✦ Citizenship and Democracy

Twenty minutes

The facilitator should introduce the two volunteers who will be presenting a dialogue about the nature of citizenship, taken from the context of American democracy. As participants listen to the dialogue in *Formal Democracy versus Living Democracy: An Argument* (Activity #1, SW), ask them to consider two questions (FCH):

- Think back over the last year. Where have you heard or read any of these arguments?
- Which voice in this dialogue best matches your own views?

After the two volunteers have completed the dialogue, allow all participants to reread *Formal Democracy versus Living Democracy: An Argument. (Allow three minutes.)*

Divide participants into small groups of five or six to discuss their notes on the two questions posed. After a few minutes, share a third question for the groups to discuss: "What are some of the influences in your life—people, institutions, or experiences—that have shaped your views?" (*Allow ten minutes.*)

After the small group discussion, lead a large group discussion, asking participants for highlights or summaries of their conversation about the nature of citizenship. This discussion should set up the next segment and reinforce several key points from the definition of citizenship outlined in the model of emotionally intelligent leadership. Share any or all of the following, as needed:

- An important component of citizenship is taking responsibility for others or the group.
- Citizenship involves a commitment to the values, rules, goals, and mission of an organization or group (not just rights but also responsibilities).
- Citizenship sometimes requires personal sacrifice for the good of the group or even of one member.

Spend a few minutes eliciting responses to the dialogue and small group conversations before moving on to the next segment.

✦ Citizenship and Problem Solving

Twenty minutes

Ask participants to work with their small group to quickly identify ten of the most significant problems facing an organization, group, community, or society to which they all belong. (The facilitator should select one entity from among these four, depending on the composition and setting of the group.) (*Allow three minutes.*)

Once each small group has its list of ten, ask each group to quickly share their lists and record them (FCH). As a large group, develop a list of the top ten they would all agree on, using repeated responses to quickly identify the ten that were most frequently cited within the small groups.

Show the flipchart with the three-column table asking participants to name "Those expected to solve the problem" and "Others whose involvement is crucial if the problem is to be solved." For each of the top ten problems just identified, solicit participants' responses to record in the other two columns. Which individuals or organizations do the majority of participants think will take responsibility for solving each problem listed?

Once the columns are complete, ask participants to analyze the responses given and look for patterns, particularly in light of conversations from the first segment, *Citizenship and Democracy*. Here are some questions to consider:

- Do most people in our group, organization, community, or society expect problems to be solved by people in positions of authority or by average citizens?
- What is the responsibility of leaders to engage a broad range of citizens in problem solving?
- What is the responsibility of average citizens or members in problem solving?
- How can groups, organizations, communities, or society develop shared responsibility and shared accountability for problem solving?

At the close of the discussion, move quickly to the next segment.

❖ A Tap on Leadership

Ten minutes

Direct participants to an open area where they have room to spread out so they are unable to touch other participants and the facilitator can walk freely among the members of the group. Ask participants to close their eyes and sit (either on the ground or in chairs) in a hunched-over position with their eyes closed.

Begin the activity by repeating the following instructions verbatim:

> The directions for this activity are as follows: if you are tapped on the hand, you may stand up or straighten up; if you are tapped on the shoulder, you may stand up and open your eyes; if you are tapped on the head, you can do whatever you want.

Throughout the activity, the facilitator should repeat the instructions exactly as written, without inflection, being careful not to specify who has the power to tap participants. The facilitator should walk around the room slowly, tapping people at random, and asking various participants to repeat one or more of the instructions to help the group remember them. The facilitator should not tap every participant, thereby leaving several people in a seated position. The activity continues with constant repetition until all of the participants are released from their seated (or standing), eyes-closed position.

Once all participants have been released, assemble the group in a circle to debrief, and focus on the following questions:

- What did it feel like to be in the hunched-over, seated position?
- What did you hear? What did you see? What did you feel?
- Who had the power to release you in this activity? Repeat the instructions. Could you have tapped yourself on the head?
- For those who started tapping others: what made you decide to do that?
- How does this activity relate to citizenship and leadership?
- What are the characteristics of a good citizen?
- Who is responsible for creating change?

✦ Wrap Up

Five minutes

Reinforce key concepts about citizenship illustrated through the activities in this session:

- Citizenship is recognizing and fulfilling your responsibility for others or the group.
- Citizenship requires commitment.
- Citizens understand they are part of something bigger than themselves.
- Leadership and citizenship can and should happen at all levels in an organization or community.

Remind participants of the connections among citizenship, leadership, and social change. Close the session by asking participants to consider what they personally believe in so strongly as citizens that they as individuals are willing to empower themselves to take action and work for change.

Formal Democracy versus Living Democracy: An Argument

Please read the following passage:

Voice One: Democracy is one form of government, pure and simple. It depends on some key institutions: elected leadership, more than one party, and a balance of power. In the case of the United States, that means three branches of government.

Voice Two: But lots of countries have impressive institutions of democracy and still the majority of citizens live in misery. To work, democracy has to be more. It has to be a way of life—a way of life that involves the values and practices people engage in daily in all aspects of their public lives.

Voice One: Sure, it depends on some practices. The citizen has to vote, for example; the public official has to be honest. But the great thing about democracy is precisely that it doesn't require very much from citizens, leaving them free to pursue their private lives. That's what really matters to people.

Voice Two: Citizenship is a lot more than voting. And our public lives are much more than just our ties to government. Politicians are not the only people who live in a public world. Every one of us lives in a public world. But our public lives are rewarding—for ourselves and our society—to the extent that we have a real say in the workplace, at school, in the community, in relation to the media, and to human services, as well as in government.

Voice One: But democracy isn't about what goes on in the workplace or school. These institutions are *protected* by democratic government, but they certainly aren't the same thing as democracy. Furthermore, your ideas turn ordinary people into decision makers. Democracy works best when people elect *others* who are better qualified to keep the machinery of government running smoothly.

Voice Two: Citizens ought to determine the values upon which the decision makers act. It's these so-called experts—people who are supposed to be better qualified—who have gotten us into the mess we're in now! Experts don't have to be *on top* making the choices. Instead, they ought to be *on tap* to citizens who are choosing the directions our society ought to go in.

Voice One: But most people don't want to be involved. Public life is no picnic. It's nasty and getting nastier all the time. In a democracy, public life is a necessary evil. We minimize the nuisance by minimizing government—and by assigning public roles to others, to officials, in order to protect our private freedom.

Voice Two: But in reality there are millions of regular people discovering the *rewards* of public life at school, at work, and in the community. They are discovering that their voices *do* count. They're building strengths they didn't know they had—to communicate, to make decisions, to solve problems. Some are even discovering the *fun* of power!

Voice One: You've blurred some important distinctions. People you're talking about may be building their *character* through good works, but all that's required for *citizenship* is responsible voting—electing the best people to run our government.

Voice Two: Democracy requires a lot more of us than being intelligent voters. It requires that we learn to solve problems with others—that we learn to listen, to negotiate, and to evaluate. To think and speak effectively. To go beyond simple protest in order to wield power, becoming partners in problem solving. This isn't about so-called good work; it's about our vital interests. And it isn't about simply running our government; it's about running our *lives.*

Voice One: But what you're saying about the way it *ought* to be is irrelevant. Americans are apathetic.

Voice Two: No, Americans aren't apathetic. Study after study shows they're angry. Angry about being shut out of decision making. Angry that their democracy's been stolen from them.

Voice One: Our democracy hasn't been stolen. It's still in place. It's been in place for over two hundred years!

Voice Two: Democracy is never fully in place. It is always in flux, a work in progress. Democracy is dynamic. It evolves in response to the creative action of citizens. It's what we make of it.

(Continued)

Questions

- Think back over the last year. Where have you heard or read any of these arguments?

- Which voice in this dialogue best matches your own views? In what ways?

- What are some of the influences in your life—people, institutions, or experiences—that have shaped your views?

- What is the responsibility of leaders to engage a broad range of citizens or members in problem solving?

- What is the responsibility of average citizens or members in problem solving?

Reference

Lappé, F. M., & Du Bois, P. M. (1994). *The quickening of America: Rebuilding our nation, remaking our lives*. San Francisco: Jossey-Bass.

MODULE 22

Citizenship 2: Organizational Life
John Shertzer

✦ Focus of Module

Citizenship, as a capacity of emotionally intelligent leadership, reflects our ability to recognize and fulfill our responsibility for others or the group. Emotionally intelligent leaders must be aware of what it means to be a part of something bigger than themselves. An essential component is to fulfill the ethical and moral obligations inherent in the values of the community. As a result, emotionally intelligent leaders know when to give of themselves for the benefit of others and the larger group. Demonstrating emotionally intelligent leadership requires us to recognize that being involved in a group is not a solo, self-oriented act. "To be a good citizen is to work for positive change on behalf of others and the community" (Higher Education Research Institute, 1996, p. 23). Citizenship also implies the broader concept of interdependence. When you demonstrate citizenship, you give of yourself and see yourself as responsible both for and to others. Interdependence, collaboration, and working effectively with others for the good of the organization or cause reflects the demands of leadership in the twenty-first century (Knapp, 2006).

239

Primary Activities

Participants work in small groups to explore their concept of citizenship in an organizational context by defining and analyzing specific behaviors and conclude with a personal commitment to the practice of citizenship.

⤙ Learning Objectives and Resources

- To define citizenship behavior in the context of organizational life
- To explore why citizenship behaviors may not be demonstrated in organizations and how to increase the likelihood that they are
- To develop an action statement that reflects a personal commitment to demonstrate citizenship

Total Time

Sixty minutes

Supplies

Citizenship in Our Organizations worksheet (one per participant)

Falling Short of Expectations worksheet (one per participant)

Flipchart, markers, easel

Pens, pencils (one per participant)

Blank paper (one per small group)

Copy of *Emotionally Intelligent Leadership: A Guide for College Students*

⤙ Facilitator Preparation Notes

Read Chapter Fourteen, Citizenship, in *Emotionally Intelligent Leadership: A Guide for College Students* (Shankman & Allen, 2008), and answer the reflection questions for yourself. (Refer to

Appendix A for an overview of the EIL model.) Prepare introductory comments based on your reading.

Prepare flipchart with the following list:

- Practice exemplary citizenship.
- Help others practice citizenship by removing barriers.
- Hold ourselves and others accountable to citizenship.

Make sure enough space is available for the group to stand in a circle for the final activity.

Prepare a personal "I commit to ..." statement that can be shared at the start of *My Commitment to Citizenship* so that participants have an example to follow.

Prepare personal comments about commitment for the conclusion of the session.

Optional: Bring a laptop to the session so participant responses can be recorded. Then, send the compiled responses to participants at a later date as a reminder of the session.

✦ Facilitator Tips

The session is fairly fast-paced, so watch the time closely.

If you are working with participants who have the ability to follow up with each other, consider having a participant collect the notes from the small groups when they discuss strategies for helping members become more active citizens. If you have the ability to follow up, feel free to take on this responsibility.

REFERENCES

Higher Education Research Institute. (1996). *A social change model of leadership development: Guidebook version III*. Los Angeles: University of California Los Angeles Higher Education Research Institute.

Shankman, M. L., & Allen, S. J. (2008). *Emotionally intelligent leadership: A guide for college students*. San Francisco: Jossey-Bass.

↞ Introduction

Five minutes

Welcome the group and offer a chance for participants to quickly introduce themselves in thirty seconds or less; each should answer the following question: "What does citizenship mean to you?"

↞ Considering Citizenship

Eight minutes

Begin with the basic statement that today's session is about citizenship and the role it plays in leadership. Ask the group: What connection can you draw between citizenship and leadership? Record responses on a flipchart (FCH).

Summarize points made by the group and check with them to be sure that you've accurately summarized their perspectives.

Explain that, at its core, citizenship refers to the obligations and responsibilities we assume once we become part of a group. For example, as citizens of this country we agree to do certain things, such as pay taxes, serve on jury duty, and obey the law. Likewise, in the organizations and groups that you belong to, you have expectations to meet. Thus you may see yourself as a citizen of those groups.

Continue with the view that, as leaders, we need to concern ourselves with citizenship in three primary ways:

1. We need to be role models by practicing good citizenship in the commitments we make. We need to be the first to meet our obligations and exceed them.
2. We need to make it as easy as possible for others to meet their expectations.
3. We need to hold ourselves and others accountable to our obligations. Citizenship means little if there aren't consequences for falling short of our commitments.

Be sure to note that there are different degrees of citizenship. Someone can do the bare minimum and still be practicing citizenship. *Exemplary citizenship* means going far beyond basic expectations.

Summarize that emotionally intelligent leadership encourages us to (FCH):

- Practice exemplary citizenship
- Help others practice citizenship by removing barriers
- Hold ourselves and others accountable to citizenship

✦ Citizenship in Your Organization

Twelve minutes

Direct participants to *Citizenship in Our Organizations* (Activity #2, SW). Encourage participants to think about a student organization or group to which they belong and keep it in mind as they complete the worksheet. (*Allow five minutes.*)

Ask participants to form pairs and discuss what they wrote with their partner. If time allows, invite a few participants to share some of their exemplary citizenship practices with the rest of the group.

✦ Encouraging Citizenship

Twenty-five minutes
Review:

Because we've spent time defining what citizenship means and identifying areas where we fall short, we need to recognize that our members struggle with this as well.

Let's focus on how we, as people committed to demonstrating emotionally intelligent leadership, help others practice citizenship. Of course, the intention is not to fulfill others' obligations for them, or to lower the bar so they can more easily make it. Each person should maintain his or her personal responsibility as a citizen. However, we can identify obstacles that may be in others' way and remove those that we have control over. By doing so, we allow others to do their best.

Divide participants into smaller groups of four to six and ask them to complete *Falling Short of Expectations* (Activity #3, SW). Provide the following instructions. (*Allow ten minutes.*)

As a group, try to determine by consensus the top five reasons why group members fall short of their expectations. Think about those in your organization who are not carrying their weight. What do you see as the primary reasons for this? First identify five, and then try to rank them from one to five, with one being the most prevalent reason and five being the least.

Ask groups to report on their top five. Record on flipchart (FCH) and place a checkmark next to those that are repeated. Some groups may not have had time to rank them; that's OK.

Circle the top three to five reasons based on the small group reports (look for the ones with the most checkmarks). Assign one of the top responses to each of the small groups (for example, one group might be assigned "time commitment").

Explain that each group must now develop five practical ways that a leader can work to remove this obstacle so that group members can succeed. (*Allow eight minutes.*)

Invite groups to share their two solutions.

Option: Ask one participant to type the responses and commit to sending them to everyone else (recognize that person for his or her exemplary citizenship).

✦ My Commitment to Citizenship

Eight minutes

Ask participants to return to *Citizenship in Our Organizations* (Activity #2, SW). Each participant should choose one of the categories that they find most challenging. They should then turn that into an action statement that begins with "I commit to . . . " Offer a personal example. *(Allow three to four minutes.)*

Ask participants to stand in a circle. Each person in turn reads aloud their "I commit to . . . " statement.

✦ Wrap Up

Two minutes

Close with personal comments about commitment and the importance of following through on commitments made.

Citizenship in Our Organizations

Consider a group or organization in which you're involved. Write the name here: _____

In the table, fill in behaviors or actions that would constitute minimal, good, and exemplary citizenship for each of the categories. In the far right column, rate your own level of citizenship for each category.

Category	Constitutes minimal citizenship	Constitutes good citizenship	Constitutes exemplary citizenship	Self-rating
Attendance at meetings				
Participation in meetings				
Recruiting new members				
Participation in committees				
Seeking elected officer positions				
Attendance at organization's events				
Public relations/ promotions for organization				
Representing the organization externally				
Dues or financial commitments				
Fundraising activities				
Volunteering for tasks/duties				
Other				

Falling Short of Expectations

List reasons why group members have difficulty meeting expectations.

What can you do to influence the level of citizenship being demonstrated?

List what you consider to be the top five steps for influencing the level of citizenship in a group.

1. _____

2. _____

3. _____

4. _____

5. _____

MODULE 23

Inspiration 1: Vision and Motivation
Henry Parkinson

✦ Focus of Module

Inspiration requires that we motivate and move others toward a shared vision. Being perceived as an inspirational individual by others is an important capacity of emotionally intelligent leadership. Inspiration works through relationships. Effective leadership entails generating feelings of optimism and commitment to organizational goals through individual actions, words, and accomplishments. At times, inspiration is perceived as an ability held by one individual—the leader. In fact, inspiration is a social dynamic that is multidirectional. Although some may think that only charisma generates this feeling in others, inspiration can manifest in many different ways. For instance, some people are great at creating an environment that elicits inspirational acts from group members. Role modeling is another source of inspiration. Likewise, inspiration may come from how ideas are communicated through the leader's behavior. Finally, the quality of relationships both within and outside of the group generates inspiration for many. At the core of inspiration is a person's ability to unleash energy in others and provide direction for it.

Primary Activities

> Participants will create a vision that has personal meaning and will identify motivating factors that will lead to accomplishing their objective.

✦ Learning Objectives and Resources

- To develop a vision statement for a group or organization
- To learn how to represent a vision in multiple forms of expression
- To connect the work of achieving a vision with a person's motivation

Total Time

Forty-five, sixty, or ninety minutes

Supplies

Defining Vision worksheet (one per participant)

Party balloons (one per participant)

Pieces of scrap paper (one per participant)

Roll of masking tape

Flipchart, easel, markers

Copy of *Emotionally Intelligent Leadership: A Guide for College Students*

✦ Facilitator Preparation Notes

> Read Chapter Fifteen, Inspiration, in *Emotionally Intelligent Leadership: A Guide for College Students* (Shankman & Allen, 2008), and answer the reflection questions for yourself. (Refer to

Appendix A for an overview of the EIL model.) Prepare introductory comments based on your reading.

Determine how much time (forty-five, sixty, or ninety minutes) you want to spend on this module and plan accordingly.

- Option 1: forty-five minutes, which excludes *Organizational Logo: Parts I–III*. If participants are not part of the same group, only the forty-five-minute session is appropriate.
- Option 2: sixty minutes, which excludes *Organizational Logo: Part III*.
- Option 3: ninety minutes, which includes all listed activities.

Be sure scrap paper is the right size to be written on, rolled up, and tucked into a party balloon.

Create a filpchart with the following list:

Empower	Build Interest
Delegate	Plan
Be Inclusive	Set Clear Goals
Listen Well	Communicate Effectively
Praise in Public	Explain Why
Show Interest/Care	Be Positive
Allow Members to Try Their Ideas	Role Model
Be Self-Aware	Believe in Your Vision
Have Passion	Persevere

✦ Facilitator Tips

Ideally, this activity will take place in a large, open room.

The full ninety minutes is a good activity to do with an intact group. If you can gather the leadership of an organization, you can then explain that they are creating a vision that includes everyone's perspective, which means they now have ownership in this organization. The activity *Organizational Logo: Part III* offers an intact group a more in-depth experience with more tangible results.

Offer that this session initiates a process. Because a vision does not become a reality unless we are living it every day, participants need to understand the ongoing nature of this work.

To achieve a vision, a strategic plan should be implemented. This same activity can be used to develop a mission statement, goals, and action steps—all the elements of an effective strategic plan.

REFERENCE

Shankman, M. L., & Allen, S. J. (2008). *Emotionally intelligent leadership: A guide for college students.* San Francisco: Jossey-Bass.

✦ Introduction: Vision in a Balloon

Ten minutes

Begin by welcoming participants and sharing the perspective that inspiration often entails sharing a vision with others. Clarify that vision can mean many different things to people and organizations, but for the purposes of today's session, a vision represents a picture of the ideal future for an organization or group. Ask participants to think about a group or organization that they care deeply about. (For an intact group, ask them to focus on that group.)

Distribute balloons, scrap paper, and masking tape. Ask participants to write their ideal future for their organization or group on the piece of paper. Encourage them to describe this ideal future in ways that reflect what the group will be doing, how it will be known in the community, and who will be members and leaders. (*Allow five to six minutes.*)

Instruct participants to roll up the piece of paper and put it inside the balloon, then inflate and tie off the balloon. Ask participants to tape their balloon as high as they can on the wall or ceiling.

Ask for one or two volunteers to share what the balloons on the wall or ceiling represent (for example, visions are often beyond our easy reach but we know that they're there; visions need to be far-reaching, but attainable). Facilitators may suggest that it may take several people to get the balloons down, just as it takes a team of people to achieve a vision within an organization.

Conclude the exercise by having participants retrieve their balloons, pop them, and retrieve their written visions. (For the forty-five-minute option, skip to *Vision Statement.*)

✦ Organization Logo: Part I

Fifteen minutes

Divide participants into teams of four or five members. Ask them to share the visions that they wrote on their slips of paper and note common elements or themes. (*Allow five minutes.*)

Instruct the teams to create a logo that represents their ideal vision for their organization or group. The logos can include words, pictures, diagrams, and so on.

This should be a fun and creative exercise.

✦ Organizational Logo: Part II

Ten minutes

Ask participants to reconvene and present their logos to the larger group. (For the sixty-minute session, skip to *Vision Statement*.)

✦ Organizational Logo: Part III

Thirty minutes

Instruct participants to create a single logo that represents their collective vision. This new logo should include everyone's ideas.

After twenty-five minutes, provide a five-minute warning.

✦ Vision Statement

Twenty minutes

Explain that the next step is to develop a compelling statement that communicates participants' vision for their organization or group (and the ideas represented in the logo if the group completed those segments). This statement should be a point of pride and a clear expression of what the group or organization will become. Record the statement on *Defining Vision* (Activity #1, SW).

Note: If your group is not an intact group, consider pairing participants after ten minutes to have them talk through their vision, get feedback from their partners, and revise their statement. If you have an intact group and more time, you may want to divide the group back into their small teams and have them draft a vision statement. Then convene the larger group, share statements, and work on one vision statement using everyone's ideas.

✦ Wrap Up

Five minutes

Review a selection from the following motivating factors that help foster a shared vision (FCH):

Empower	Build Interest
Delegate	Plan
Be Inclusive	Set Clear Goals
Listen Well	Communicate Effectively
Praise in Public	Explain Why
Show Interest/Care	Be Positive
Allow Members to Try Their Ideas	Role Model
Be Self-Aware	Believe in Your Vision
Have Passion	Persevere

Use these examples as a transition to explain that developing a vision is a critical component of inspiring others. Vision development takes a while, so this is just the beginning. Encourage participants to revisit their vision statement from time to time. This will allow them to make appropriate changes and finalize what they want their vision to be. The most effective vision statements guide behavior and decision making for three to five years, so this statement should be both challenging and exciting.

Consider suggesting to participants that they think about where to display their vision statement (and the logo, if created)—ideally in a public place (such as an office, work space, or anywhere others can see it and be reminded of what their vision is).

Defining Vision

An effective vision should:

- Take you where you want to go
- Be far reaching, but attainable
- Change and adapt with the environment
- Be something you believe in and have passion for
- Give you direction for the future

Think about a group or organization that is important to you.

List it here: _____

Where do you see this group or organization in three to five years?

What do you want this group/organization to be known for five years from now?

What is your vision statement for this group/organization?

MODULE 24

Inspiration 2: Shared Values
Adam Peck

⚔ Focus of Module

Inspiration requires that we motivate and move others toward a shared vision. Being perceived as an inspirational individual by others is an important capacity of emotionally intelligent leadership. Inspiration works through relationships. Effective leadership entails generating feelings of optimism and commitment to organizational goals through individual actions, words, and accomplishments. At times, inspiration is perceived as an ability held by one individual—the leader. In fact, inspiration is a social dynamic that is multidirectional. Although some may think that only charisma generates this feeling in others, inspiration can manifest in many different ways. For instance, some people are great at creating an environment that elicits inspirational acts from group members. Role modeling is another source of inspiration. Likewise, inspiration may come from how ideas are communicated through the leader's behavior. Finally, the quality of relationships both within and outside of the group generates inspiration for many. At the core of inspiration is a person's ability to unleash energy in others and provide direction for it.

Primary Activities

Participants play a game that helps them define inspiration, watch video clips to deepen their understanding of inspiration, then explore the connection between inspiration and values.

← Learning Objectives and Resources

- To broaden participants' understanding of inspiration
- To analyze effective strategies for inspiring others
- To explore the connection between inspiration and values

Total Time

Sixty or ninety minutes

Supplies

Inspiration Bingo worksheet (one per participant)

Inspiration Bingo Answer Key (one copy)

Shared Values worksheet (one per participant)

Shared Values: Instructions (one copy per small group)

Pens, pencils (one per participant)

Small prizes (likely one per participant)

Audiovisual to support Powerpoint or similar program, if desired

Copies of *Braveheart* and *Animal House* in the appropriate video
    format (or Internet service for access to versions of these
    scenes on the Web)

Sticky notes (two notes per participant)

Tape

Flipchart, easel, markers

Copy of *Emotionally Intelligent Leadership: A Guide for College Students*

← Facilitator Preparation Notes

Read Chapter Fifteen, Inspiration, in *Emotionally Intelligent Leadership: A Guide for College Students* (Shankman & Allen, 2008), and answer the reflection questions for yourself. (Refer to Appendix A for an overview of the EIL model.) Prepare introductory comments based on your reading.

Determine how much time (sixty or ninety minutes) you want to spend on this module and plan accordingly. Follow the instructions as written.

Because most participants will complete the bingo card, be prepared to give a prize to each participant. Candy usually works well.

Set up AV and cue up *Braveheart* to play. Have *Animal House* cued to make a smooth transition to the second movie.

Make the following flipcharts and hang in a row on the wall for the shared values exercise. Once completed, fold up and tape so the writing is not visible.

1. In the top left-hand corner of one page, write "Values." At the bottom of the page, going from left to right, write the list of values provided. (If you are working with an advanced group or an intact group, you may want to substitute a values list previously created.)
2. At the top of a second page, write "Motivation," then "Intrinsic" and "Extrinsic" so that they form three column headers.
3. Label a third page "Analysis." Below that, list "First Value," "Second Value," "Third Value," and "Motivation."

Download *Inspiration Bingo* and *Answer Key* (see page viii) so that each small group has a copy.

✦ Facilitator Tips

For the bingo game, participants will use the bingo card to take notes on the presentation. Make sure to state each answer in a way that allows the participants to readily fill in the blanks. Consider pausing occasionally to track their progress.

Both movie clips are generally available on movie sharing sites such as YouTube. Search for "Braveheart speech" and "Animal House speech." Both movie clips contain mild profanity. If this is a problem for your group, simply cue the clips to start after the profanity.

Note: This exercise can be tailored to the tastes of the group by substituting movies other than the two suggested. If you want to choose your own clips, look for scenes that contrast between the speakers' abilities to inspire and influence others. One clip should demonstrate effectiveness; the other should give the group an opportunity to critique the speaker's approach. The more effective clip should feature a character who understands and appeals to the *values* of the people they hope to inspire. The less effective scene should show someone who fails to understand, or to appeal to, the group's values.

Using *Shared Values to Inspire Others* works best with ten or more participants. If you have a lower number of participants, you might want to cut down the list of values. A good rule of thumb is to have at least one value fewer than the number of participants. Review the *Instructions* to be sure that you're clear on what to do. If the group is larger than ten, divide into smaller groups of no more than ten and give each group a copy of *Shared Values: Instructions*.

Be aware that some members may resist selecting one value when so many values on the list are compelling. Remind participants that this exercise is in the context of leadership and that it is supposed to present a challenge to them.

Participants may demonstrate a bias toward intrinsic motivation. Participants may feel that being extrinsically motivated feels selfish or shallow. Be careful not to encourage this when you set up this exercise. Encourage participants to be completely honest; validate both choices as acceptable and good.

REFERENCES

Folger, R., Rosenfield, D., Grove, J., & Corkran, L. (1979). Effects of "voice" and peer opinions on responses to inequity. *Journal of Personality and Social Psychology, 37*(12), 2253–2261.

Shankman, M. L., & Allen, S. J. (2008). *Emotionally intelligent leadership: A guide for college students.* San Francisco: Jossey-Bass.

← Introduction

Five minutes

Be sure all participants have an *Inspiration Bingo* worksheet (Activity #2, SW). Encourage participants to use the card to take notes on the presentation.

Share that the focus today is on the topic of inspiration. Ask participants what other words come to mind when you say "inspiration." List these on the flipchart (FCH). Offer any of the following if participants don't suggest them:

Creativity	Excitement	Insight
Encouragement	Ideas	Motivation
Energy	Influence	Spirituality

Ask participants what these terms have in common. Although many of the terms may be inspired by others, they all reside within the individual. Another person cannot necessarily cause us to be *creative*, have *energy*, or be *encouraged* unless we choose to make that so (substitute other words the group brainstorms if appropriate).

Suggest that inspiration resides within the individual. One capacity of emotionally intelligent leadership is to inspire others to accomplish the group's goals.

Offer the following questions as guides for today's session:

- How is inspiration related to leadership?
- What causes you to be inspired?
- How can we use shared values to inspire others?

← William Wallace versus Bluto

Ten minutes

Play clips from *Braveheart* and *Animal House* (or other chosen clips) in sequence, without discussion in between.

Divide participants into small groups of no more than eight and offer the following questions for discussion. If desired, ask different groups to respond to different questions—allow five minutes for discussion and five for reporting out.

- To what shared values did William Wallace appeal?
  Notes: He appeals to their love of Scotland by calling them sons of Scotland; he appeals to their value of strength by noting that they have come in defiance of tyranny. He uses his reputation and humor to build credibility with the group. He helps them believe that their values are in jeopardy by saying, "What will you do without freedom; will you fight?" The group expresses that it values life more than freedom, but William Wallace reframes this by saying, "Aye, fight and you'll live—at least a while. And dying in your beds many years from now, would you be willing to trade all your days from this day to that, for one chance—just one chance to come back here and tell our enemies that they may take our lives, but they'll never take our freedom!" By doing so, he changes the values of the group and convinces them that freedom is more important than their lives.

- To what shared values did Bluto appeal?
  Notes: He plays on their spirit, guts, the opportunity to make lasting memories, and, to a certain extent, control (by saying, "This could be the greatest night of our lives, but you are going to let it be the worst").

- Which speech was more effective, William Wallace's rallying of the Scottish army or Bluto's rallying of his fraternity brothers? Why?
  Notes: At first no one follows Bluto, so he must not have hit on the values of the group. But he does come back and does a better job of appealing to the core values of the group. William Wallace uses his confidence, his

reputation, and his knowledge of the group to appeal to and even change the group's values. In the end, William Wallace likely has more credibility. Bluto was largely responsible for the mess the group was in, and not knowing who bombed Pearl Harbor probably didn't help his credibility. But he is charismatic, and that helps.

✦ How Does Inspiration Relate to Leadership?

Five minutes

Offer the following definition from Shankman and Allen (2008): inspiration is "that which motivates and moves others toward a shared vision."

Ask participants what stands out for them in this definition. After a few responses, offer the following: emotionally intelligent leaders depend on their knowledge of themselves and others to accomplish their goals and the goals of the group. Emotionally intelligent leaders know how to use shared values to motivate others.

Our values are our most important priorities. These may be family, hard work, or any of a number of other important aspects of our lives. The key point is that values influence.

An important factor of emotionally intelligent leadership is knowing how to use a group's shared values to motivate themselves and others.

✦ What Causes Us to Be Inspired?

Ten minutes

Suggest the following:

Many have said that both inspiration and leadership are in the eyes of the beholder. What may inspire some may not inspire others. We know that people will support and care most deeply about what they help to create. When you're tuned into emotionally intelligent leadership, you don't take risks when determining what values are most important to the group. You don't guess or ignore what is most important to the others in the group—you ask.

Once we know what a group values, we act on those values. We know that feeling valued and heard is important. For instance, research suggests that others will accept decisions they disagree with if they feel that they have been listened to before the decision is made (Folger, Rosenfield, Grove, & Corkran, 1979).

Inspiration is related to motivation. Although there is an element of what someone can do for you, motivation, like inspiration, is determined by each one of us. Consider that we can be motivated in two general ways:

- Extrinsic motivation exists when we are influenced by measures of success outside of ourselves.
- Intrinsic motivation exists when we are influenced by forces and feelings from within.

Ask participants to suggest different examples of each. Add the following, if needed:

- Extrinsic: titles, awards, the opinions of others whom they admire, or money
- Intrinsic: individual goals, feelings of personal accomplishment, a desire to do a good job or to help others

Offer that people may be motivated by either in different situations but generally have a preference for one over the other. Next, share the following:

As previously mentioned, for someone to be inspired, it must connect to their values. If I try to inspire someone with money who is more interested in significance, they will not only likely be less motivated, but it may even backfire and de-motivate them.

It is also important that the values that inspire others be shared by those involved. Otherwise, it may be unethical or may be seen by those they lead as pandering. It's important to remember that we can't be all things to all people.

Ask participants what they think needs to happen if the values of a leader do not match those of the people being led. After a couple of responses, offer that a leader may need to:

- Reevaluate his or her own core values
- Assess his or her fitness to lead the group
- Find someone within the organization to lead whose values match those of the group
- Persuade the group to change its core values

↙ Using Shared Values to Inspire Others

Twenty minutes

Remind participants that an important source of inspiration is our values. This next activity will illustrate how values can assist us in inspiring others. This exercise may also illustrate how difficult it can be to guess what a group may value most.

Draw participants' attention to the three flipchart pages hanging on the wall.

Use the values listed here and included on *Shared Values* (Activity #3, SW).

Challenge	Influence	Prosperity
Creativity	Order or Structure	Self-Reliance
Integrity	Power	Significance
Harmony	Progress	Spirituality

Ask participants to envision themselves in a leadership role. With this position or responsibility in mind, circle the one value on the list that is most important to them in this role. (*Allow one to two minutes.*)

Instruct participants to select the value that they believe will be most important to the group they are leading, using the list provided. (*Allow one to two minutes.*)

Ask each person which motivation style best describes their preference: intrinsic motivation or extrinsic motivation. Remind them that both choices are equally valid.

Ask each participant to place a sticky note above the value that is most important to them on the flipchart labeled Values. Ask whether intrinsic or extrinsic motivation is more inspiring to them. As these notes collect, the result should resemble a bar chart, which will easily reveal the values of the group in a graphical form.

Ask participants to form groups of six or eight. Use two or three of the following questions to facilitate discussion. If desired, reassemble the whole group for the last few questions.

- Note the values that seemed most important to this group based on the first flipchart. What did you think of these? Were you surprised? If so, why? If not, why not?
- Which values were of secondary importance to the group? What are the implications of these coming in second?
- Which values might conflict with each other? How might these influence motivation or inspiration?
  - Values in contrast with each other usually indicate disagreement within the group.
  - Values that conflict are not the best values to use to inspire the group, as they may be as likely to de-motivate as to motivate. Give examples if needed.

- Were there values that were less important to the group that surprised you?
- Did any of you assume that your top value would also be the top value of the group? If so, do you think this is a mistake that leaders often make?
- If you were leading this group, how could you appeal to these values to inspire this group?

Note: For the sixty-minute session, skip the following activity and proceed to wrap up.

✦ Problem Solving

Thirty minutes

Pose this situation to participants: You are all involved in an organization that is facing a budget shortfall, and you need to raise enough money to be sure you can continue to operate.

Ask small groups of four or five to develop a strategy to inspire the group to raise money, using the values that they've just identified. (*Allow ten minutes.*)

Have groups report out their recommendations. Note on the flipchart the values that are being used for motivation or inspiration (FCH).

Lead the group in an analysis of the suggested strategies, using the data collected on the flipcharts. Based on the values offered, decide as a group whether the driving motivation is intrinsic or extrinsic, then write this on the flipchart (FCH).

Encourage the group to brainstorm solutions and be sure their approach matches the values and motivational preferences of the group as reflected on the flipcharts.

✦ Wrap Up

Five minutes

Conclude with a short discussion asking participants to share observations about what they have learned about themselves and the topic of inspiration.

Use the following for final comments and/or a short discussion:

- Emotionally intelligent leadership requires us to demonstrate consciousness of self and others to lead effectively.
- Inspiration is a kind of motivation.
- Inspiration takes place inside the person leading and those led.
- Inspiration occurs when the person leading and those led have shared values.

Inspiration Bingo

Fill in as many blanks as possible.

IN	SP	IR	AT	ION
Intrinsically motivated people are motivated: A. Internally B. Externally	Inspiring leaders motivate others through s_____d values.	How is inspiration different from motivation?	Others are more likely to support even decisions they disagree with when they are c_____ed about the decision.	If the leader's values do not match those of the people that he or she leads, the leader should . . . (answer below)
Emotionally intelligent leaders use knowledge of s_____ and o_____ to inspire.	Leadership and inspiration are in the eyes of the b_____r.	Inspiration is defined as that which motivates and moves others toward a shared v_____.	People support and care about what they help to c_____.	A. Reevaluate . . .
For someone to be inspired, it must connect to their v_____.	Emotionally intelligent leaders know how to encourage those that they lead to motivate th_____s.	FREE SPACE	Values are the principles that guide our a_____.	B. Assess . . .
What is your top value? _____	Emotionally intelligent leaders a ____ rather than g _____ what followers and organizations value.	Extrinsically motivated people are motivated: A. Internally B. Externally	The best way to lead others is to make them feel h_____ and v_____.	C. Find . . .
Remember, you can't be all t _____ to all p_____.	Inspiration is an int_____able quality that can be hard to d_____.	Our values reflect our most important p_____.	We each c_____ to be inspired.	D. Persuade . . .

Shared Values

What values are most important to you when you serve in a formal or informal leadership role? What values do you think are most important to the group/organization? Complete the following.

Individual Values

From the following, select your *one* top value as it relates to leadership. Many of these values will be important to you, so give it careful thought.

Challenge	Influence	Prosperity
Creativity	Order or Structure	Self-Reliance
Integrity	Power	Significance
Harmony	Progress	Spirituality

Group Values

Now select the value you think will be most important to a group/organization of which you are a member. If you don't know the group/organization very well, take an educated guess.

Challenge	Influence	Prosperity
Creativity	Order or Structure	Self-Reliance
Integrity	Power	Significance
Harmony	Progress	Spirituality

(Continued)

Motivation

Which of the following two motivation preferences better describes you? Remember, both are equally valid. You might begin by asking yourself the following questions: When was the last time I was really motivated? What motivated me? Mark your general preference.

__*Extrinsic*: Extrinsically motivated people are motivated from outside themselves. They tend to be most motivated by recognition, awards, financial rewards, and the appreciation of others.

__*Intrinsic*: Intrinsically motivated people are motivated from within themselves. They tend to be most motivated by a sense of personal pride in accomplishment, achievement of individual goals, or a desire to help others.

Shared Values: Instructions

Exercise

Once you have identified your value, place a post-it note above the value that is most important to you on the flipchart page provided. When there is more than one post-it above a value, each should be placed above the previous one. The result should resemble a bar chart which will easily reveal the values of the group in a graphical form.

Analysis

Analyze the leadership challenge using the data collected. If you were the leaders of a group facing a budget shortfall, how would you use the data from this exercise to inspire the group? Remember, it's your job to raise the money.

Use the following guiding questions:

- Which values were most important to this group?
- Which values were of secondary or tertiary importance to the group?
- Did any values appear to be in contrast with each other? Were you surprised with the values that were most important to the group?
- Were there values that were not important to the group that surprised you? Did anyone assume that their top value would also be the top value of the group? If so, do you think this is a mistake that leaders often make, to assume that others feel the same way they do?
- If you were leading this group, how could you appeal to these values to inspire this group?

See page viii for download information.

MODULE 25

Influence
Gary Manka

← Focus of Module

The capacity of influence is fundamental to leadership; those who have this capacity demonstrate skills of persuasion. Emotionally intelligent leaders have the ability to persuade others with information, ideas, emotion, behavior, and a strong commitment to organizational values and purpose. They involve others to engage in a process of mutual exploration and action. Regardless of whether you hold a formal or informal position, you have the opportunity to influence. To influence others means that you believe in a desired end enough to share your ideas and create space for others. Having influence means that you effectively persuade others to join your cause, movement, solution, and so forth. This persuasion, as suggested by leadership scholar Bernard Bass (1997), means that you "display conviction; emphasize trust; take stands on different issues; present their most important values; emphasize the importance of purpose, commitment and ethical consequences of decision making" (p. 133).

Primary Activities

Participants explore different concepts of influence and
play a game that requires them to practice their skills
of persuasion.

← Learning Objectives and Resources

- To learn about different principles and stages of influence
- To practice skills of influence
- To develop a personal action plan for practicing skills of
  persuasion

Total Time

Sixty minutes

Supplies

Three Stages of Developing Leadership Influence worksheet
    (one per participant)

Spy Game Classifications (one per small group, cut up)

Six Principles of Influence worksheet (one per participant)

Developing Personal and Social Influence worksheet
    (one per participant)

Personal Persuasion Action Plan worksheet
    (one per participant)

Flipchart, easel, markers

Multiple decks of playing cards

- One deck of playing cards for facilitator to set up the
  card grid
- One deck of playing cards for each small group

Small containers for drawing spy classifications (one per small group)

Paper (one per participant)

Pens, pencils (one per participant)

Copy of *Emotionally Intelligent Leadership: A Guide for College Students*

✦ Facilitator Preparation Notes

Read Chapter Sixteen, Influence, in *Emotionally Intelligent Leadership: A Guide for College Students* (Shankman & Allen, 2008), and answer the reflection questions for yourself. (Refer to Appendix A for an overview of the EIL model.) Prepare introductory comments based on your reading.

Print an appropriate number of copies of the *Spy Game* classifications for each group. Cut out, fold, and place in small containers to be ready for the activity.

Be familiar with the curriculum and prepared to share personal examples, especially related to the *Six Principles of Influence*.

Prepare the following flipchart and display when participants enter the room:

> Effective leadership . . . is the influence of others in a productive, vision-driven direction and is done through the example, conviction, and character of the leader. —Brady and Woodward (2005)

Download *Spy Game* instructions, categories, and cards (see page viii).

Set up the *Spy Game* card grid pattern in a corner of the room before beginning the session and keep it hidden from participants.

Be cognizant of the time for the session; otherwise it is easy to exceed the anticipated sixty-minute length.

✦ Facilitator Tips

Pay close attention to the instruction sheet for the *Spy Game*. Be sure to set up the card grid in a discreet location. Be prepared for some initial frustration from the participants as they try to figure out what "intelligence" means and where to find it. If they do not discover the card grid after a couple of minutes, give them a hint as to its location.

During the *Spy Game*, intelligence gathering consists of participants viewing the card pattern and taking their observations back, as directed in the instructions. The gathering is strictly by memory; nothing else is allowed (no pen and paper, camera phones, and the like). Because of this people make mistakes in reporting back the pattern to the rest of their small group members. Although the directions mention the possibility of a spy, no one is actually assigned that role. Participants may jump to the conclusion that there is a spy because of misinformation from the intelligence gathering. This assumption is worth addressing during the debriefing of the activity.

Anticipate that the *Spy Game* activity will generate both excitement and minor mistrust among the participants.

REFERENCES

Bass, B. (1997). Does the transactional-transformational leadership paradigm transcend organizational and national boundaries? *American Psychology, 52*(2), 130–139.

Block, P. (1987). *The empowered manager: Positive political skills at work.* San Francisco: Jossey-Bass.

Brady, C., & Woodward, O. (2005). *Launching a leadership revolution: Mastering the five levels of influence.* New York: Business Plus.

Cialdini, R. B. (2007). *Influence: The psychology of persuasion.* New York: HarperCollins.

Collins, J. (2001). *Good to great: Why some companies make the leap . . . and others don't*. New York: HarperCollins.

Daft, R. L. (2005). *The leadership experience* (3rd ed.). Canada: South-Western.

Goleman, D. (1998, November-December). "What makes a leader?" *Harvard Business Review*.

Goleman, D. (1995). *Emotional intelligence*. New York: Bantam Books.

Shankman, M. L., & Allen, S. J. (2008). *Emotionally intelligent leadership: A guide for college students*. San Francisco: Jossey-Bass.

Watkins, M. (2007, October 3). "Infectious leadership." The Leading Edge. Boston: Harvard Business Publishing. http://blogs.hbr.org/watkins/2007/10/infectious_leadership.html

✦ Introduction

Five minutes

Begin by sharing the premise of this session:

Effective leadership is a form of influence that can't be bestowed or assigned, but must be earned. Influence is an integral part of effective leadership. For our purposes today, let's work with the definition of effective leadership as "the influence of others in a productive, vision-driven direction and is done through the example, conviction, and character of the leader" (Brady & Woodward, 2005, p. 7).

Offer that influence is a part of emotionally intelligent leadership because leaders are most effective once they've developed their own potential, expanded this potential with and through others, and grounded this understanding in the contexts in which we live and work. Review *Three Stages of Developing Leadership Influence* (Activity #1, SW).

Stage 1. Influence must first be groomed through personal growth. Before you can influence others you must understand and manage yourself (Goleman, 1998; Daft, 2005; Brady & Woodward, 2005).

Ask participants for examples of ways to develop or grow one's potential. Write responses on flipchart (FCH).

Stage 2. The ability to influence others is a direct result of personal growth. Personal growth must be expanded to occur outside of self through empathy, social awareness, and relationship management (Goleman, 1998; Daft, 2005; Cialdini, 2007; Brady & Woodward, 2005). Give examples, if needed.
Ask participants for examples.

Stage 3. The ability to influence self and others is also directly impacted by the organizational context we are in. More often than not, organizations can take on a life of their own and don't work as we had originally planned (Block, 1997; Watkins, 2007).

✦ Influence: The Double-Edged Sword

Ten minutes

Offer that influence occurs in many ways and comes from many sources. Often simple triggers are utilized in either negative or positive ways to influence our actions. We may change our behavior or alter how we make decisions because of a trigger. We tend to comply instinctively when triggers are experienced in our daily routines, even if we know better.

Review *Six Principles of Influence* (Activity #2, SW).

Reciprocation: "We should try to repay, in kind, what another person has provided us" (Cialdini, 2007, p. 7). This is an overpowering principle of persuasion when used and is based on the concept of *quid pro quo*. Uninvited gifts become obligations that enforce uninvited debt and triggers unfair exchanges.

Commitment and Consistency: "Once we have made a choice or taken a stand, we will encounter personal and interpersonal pressure to behave consistently with that commitment" (Cialdini, 2007 p. 57).

Provide an example of a time when those pressures caused you to respond in ways that justify your earlier decision.

Social Proof: "One means we use to determine what is correct is to find out what other people think is correct" (Cialdini, 2007, p. 116). Human nature tends to encourage us to view a behavior as more correct in a given situation to the degree that we see others performing it.

Ask participants for examples of social proof. This rule is more powerful when we are uncertain about a course of action and when we observe people just like us pursuing it (such as underage drinking).

Liking: "We most prefer to say yes to the requests of someone we know and like" (Cialdini, 2007, p. 167).

Share a personal observation of how common this phenomenon is: from young children to older adults, we all do it.

Authority: "We are trained from birth that obedience to proper authority is right and disobedience is wrong" (Cialdini, 2007, p. 216). The challenge with this form of influence is that we can easily fall into the trap of blind obedience in our decision making. Titles, uniforms, expensive clothes, and possessions all bolster a person's authority.

Ask participants what else reinforces a person's authority.

Scarcity: "Opportunities seem more valuable to us when their availability is limited . . . people seem to be more motivated by the thought of losing something than by the thought of gaining something of equal value" (Cialdini, 2007, p. 238).

Ask participants to raise their hands if they would agree with this statement. If time allows, ask for one or two volunteers to explain why they agree.

← The Organizational Context

Five minutes

Ask participants to consider these different forms of influence, and take a poll:

- Raise your hand if you think, in general, we influence the organizations we join.
- Raise your hand if you think organizations more often mold us.

Allow for one or two participants to support their position.

Offer that the question we need to ask ourselves is, do we influence the organization or does it influence us? It's our choice. We can be like robots in our own bureaucratic or hierarchical systems, in which case the influence is usually negative. On the other hand, if we learn to direct those systems instead, then the influence is often positive and fosters effective leadership. Peter Block (1987) defines this mentality as the ability to choose an entrepreneurial path over a bureaucratic path.

Jim Collins (2001) refers to this type of conscious thought as disciplined action whereby a balance of freedom and responsibility is achieved. Finally, consider what Michael Watkins (2007) suggests—that the behavior of leaders can be a positive or negative influence on the culture of leadership within the organization.

Read the following quote, if desired.

> For good or ill, the senior leadership of every organization is infectious. By this I mean that leaders' behaviors tend to be transmitted to their direct reports, who pass them on to the next level, and so on down through their organizations. Over time, they permeate the organization from top to bottom, influencing activity at all levels. Eventually they become embodied in the organizational culture, influencing the types of people who get promoted and hired into the organization, creating a self-reinforcing feedback loop—either positive or negative.—Michael Watkins, "Infectious Leadership"

✦ Developing Personal and Social Influence

Ten minutes

Introduce the work of Chris Brady and Orrin Woodward (2005) who have developed an influence scale that consists of five levels of leadership influence. Each level expands the influence of the previous level. Review *Developing Personal and Social Influence* (Activity #3, SW).

- Levels 1 and 2 focus on the personal growth of the leader.
- Level 3 is a transition level that consists of elements of both personal and social growth.

- Levels 4 and 5 focus on the leader's ability to influence others.

Explain that most leaders never ascend to the fifth level of influence because they can't keep their egos in check and are influenced by the wrong motives. Much like a standard transmission in an automobile, to perform at your best you have to gradually shift through a series of gears. Second gear builds on first gear, third gear on second, and so on. As such, you can't get to fifth gear directly from first gear. Even skipping one gear slows down the forward momentum. Developing levels of influence works in the same way.

← The Spy Game

Twenty-five minutes

Divide participants into small groups of equal numbers; each group should consist of five to ten members. Distribute a deck of playing cards to each group. Read the instructions verbatim (see *The Spy Game Instructions* worksheet). Distribute group member classifications when indicated on the instruction sheet. Tell participants that they are not to share these classifications with anyone.

Remind participants to follow the instructions carefully and wish them luck in their efforts to support the challenge at hand. (*Allow ten to fifteen minutes.*)

Conclude the activity when the time expires or until one group replicates the pattern from the card grid—whichever comes first.

In the remaining time, approximately ten minutes, discuss any of the following questions.

- How did you feel about your personal role in this activity?
- Who were the spies and what behaviors gave them away?
- How did you feel about the roles played by the other members in your group?
- What types of authority emerged or were present within your group?
- What other rules of influence were displayed by group members?
- What role did trust play in achieving your goal?

✦ Wrap Up

Five minutes

Share that influence comes from your ability to be in touch with yourself and others while understanding the context of environment. Leaders who do not operate on the premise of the common good are not really influencing, but rather manipulating and are primarily interested in personal gain.

Both influence and manipulation will take you places, but positive influences foster long-term achievement in society.

Ask participants to complete the *Personal Persuasion Action Plan* (Activity #4, SW).

Make personal observations to conclude the session.

Three Stages of Developing Leadership Influence

Stage 1. Influence must first be developed through personal growth. Before you can influence others, you must understand and manage yourself.

What aspects of your personality need further development?

Stage 2. The ability to influence others is a direct result of personal growth. Personal growth must be expanded to occur outside of self through social awareness and relationship management.

What do you need to do to become more aware of others, how they're feeling, and how you interact with them?

Stage 3. The ability to influence self and others is also directly affected by the organizational environment in which we work. More often than not, the organizations we create can take on a life of their own and don't work as we had originally planned them to work.

Think of an organization to which you belong. How would you describe the environment of this organization? What aspects of this organization are unpredictable?

References

Goleman, D. (1995). *Emotional intelligence*. New York: Bantam Books.

Watkins, M. (2007). "Infectious leadership." *The Leading Edge*. Boston: Harvard Business Publishing. http://blogs.hbr.org/watkins/2007/10/ infectious_leadership.html

Six Principles of Influence

Reciprocation: "We should try to repay, in kind, what another person has provided us" (p. 7).

Commitment and Consistency: "Once we have made a choice or taken a stand, we will encounter personal and interpersonal pressure to behave consistently with that commitment." (p. 57).

Social Proof: "One means we use to determine what is correct is to find out what other people think is correct. We view a behavior as more correct in a given situation to the degree that we see others performing it" (p. 116).

Liking: "We most prefer to say yes to the requests of someone we know and like" (p. 167).

Authority: "We are trained from birth that obedience to proper authority is right and disobedience is wrong" (p. 216).

Scarcity: "Opportunities seem more valuable to us when their availability is limited. In fact, people seem to be more motivated by the thought of losing something than by the thought of gaining something of equal value" (p. 238).

Place a check by the principles that are most obvious to you in your life.

Describe the ways in which you see these principles of influence in action. Think about people whom you consider influential. Which principles do they employ?

Reference

Cialdini, R. B. (2007). *Influence: The psychology of persuasion*. New York: HarperCollins Publishers, Inc.

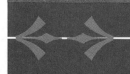

Developing Personal and Social Influence

The following model describes a way to develop your personal and social influence. After each level listed here, write your thoughts on how to complete each level—that is, what can you do to act on each level? Be specific.

Level 1: Learn—Everything from anyone.

Level 2: Perform—Persevere and work continuously hard.

Level 3: Lead—Extend personal abilities by expanding team.

Level 4: Develop Leaders—Find and develop other leaders while speaking truth and developing trust in every interaction.

Level 5: Develop Leaders Who Develop Leaders—Create a legacy that outlives the leader.

Reference

Brady, C., & Woodward, O. (2005). *Launching a leadership revolution: Mastering the five levels of influence.* New York: Business Plus.

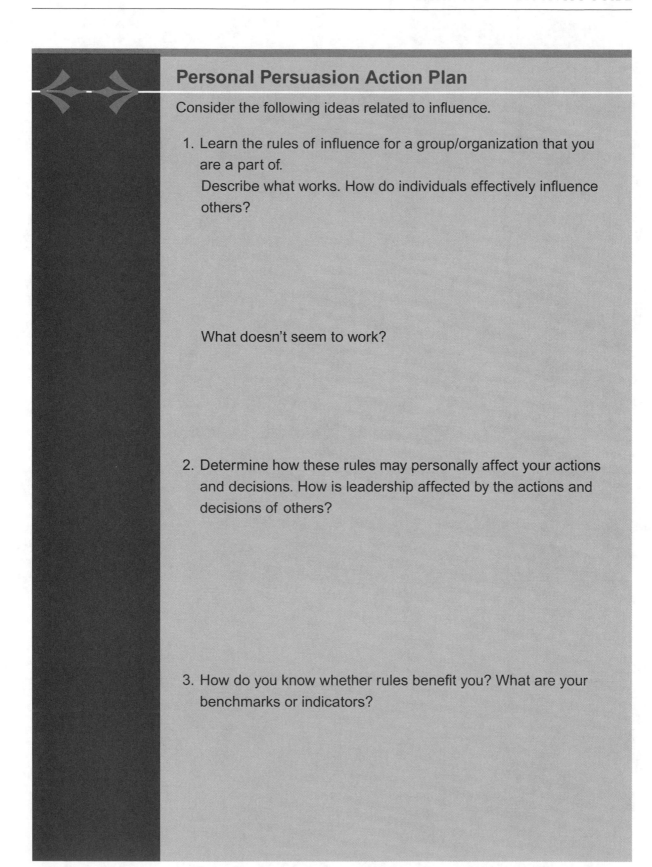

Personal Persuasion Action Plan

Consider the following ideas related to influence.

1. Learn the rules of influence for a group/organization that you are a part of.
   Describe what works. How do individuals effectively influence others?

   What doesn't seem to work?

2. Determine how these rules may personally affect your actions and decisions. How is leadership affected by the actions and decisions of others?

3. How do you know whether rules benefit you? What are your benchmarks or indicators?

4. Learn to recognize red flags or indicators when these rules are being used on you and how to say *"no"* when needed. What will you do or say when you recognize that the rules are not benefitting you?

Write your responses to the following:

I care about _____
(an issue, cause, organization, and so on). How do I feel about it? What do I think about it?

People I know with whom I want to share these thoughts are . . .

Here's a story I want to tell them about it . . .

Here's what I'd like them to think about it . . .

The Spy Game Instructions

At one time or another many of us have wanted to be like James Bond (007), Jason Bourne of the *Bourne Identity* series, or Sydney Bristow (from *Alias*). Imagine now that you are all government agents. This is your opportunity to gather secret intelligence and report that information back to headquarters. You must retrieve intelligence to resolve the current challenge before the opposing government agency does. The fate of your world is in your agency's hands.

Here are your instructions:

- This activity is called the Spy Game.
- You will be divided into equal, but competing groups.
- Each group will have to retrieve intelligence from another location in this room and re-create this intelligence back to your small group. Part of this challenge is discovering where the intelligence is located.
- Only one agent at a time from each group may go to the secret location to retrieve the intelligence information.
- Each agent is limited to one trip and may not return until every group member has had the chance to go at least once. There is no set order.
- You *may not* use any type of recording device when retrieving the intelligence information (such as paper, pens, camera phones). Only mental notes may be used.
- Everyone in each group is a government agent.
- There may be one agent in your group who is a spy.
- If you are a spy, you must try to stop or sabotage your group's progress without getting caught or drawing suspicion to yourself. Use the principles of influence when possible (Reciprocation, Commitment and Consistency, Social Proof, Liking, Authority, and Scarcity).
- Each group will have up to fifteen minutes to complete this assignment. We will conclude when one group successfully re-creates the intelligence information in their small group

and announces their success before another group does, or when the time expires, whichever comes first.

Your agent classification will now be assigned in writing. No one else is allowed to see your classification. Please memorize your assigned classification, then destroy the paper. You must be true to your classification.

Are there any questions before we begin? (Answer questions when appropriate and without divulging too much information other than what is in the instructions.)

You may begin now.

Fifteen minutes. Fourteen minutes and fifty-nine seconds . . . fifty-eight seconds . . . fifty-seven seconds . . .

See page viii for download information.

MODULE 26

Coaching

Darin Eich

✦ Focus of Module

Coaching entails helping others enhance their skills and abilities. Emotionally intelligent leaders know that they cannot do everything themselves. They need others to become a part of any endeavor. Coaching is about intentionally helping others demonstrate their talent and requires the emotionally intelligent leader to prioritize the time to foster the development of others in the group—not just themselves. Think about coaching as what you can do to help *train* and *prepare* another person. These words help connect coaching to emotionally intelligent leadership—doing what is necessary to help others for the challenges, tasks, or opportunities ahead. In a leadership context, coaching involves a willingness to learn from others. The relationship is reciprocal. One person does not know everything. Coaching others provides an easy vehicle for the learning to be shared and ideas to flow. At the heart of this capacity is the concept of developing others.

Primary Activities

Participants work in small groups to discuss experiences and ideas related to feedback, then practice giving and receiving feedback.

✦ Learning Objectives and Resources

- To develop communication and feedback skills
- To gain ideas from peers' feedback to improve leadership
- To apply the capacity of coaching as a way to enhance project effectiveness

Total Time

Forty-five minutes

Supplies

What Is Feedback? worksheet (one per participant)

Feedback Assessment worksheet (one per participant)

Feedback Activities (one copy)

Pens, pencils (one per participant)

Copy of *Emotionally Intelligent Leadership: A Guide for College Students*

✦ Facilitator Preparation Notes

Read Chapter Seventeen, Coaching, in *Emotionally Intelligent Leadership: A Guide for College Students* (Shankman & Allen, 2008), and answer the reflection questions for yourself. (Refer to Appendix A for an overview of the EIL model.) Prepare introductory comments based on your reading.

Prepare a personal story of feedback you have received that was helpful or a time when the feedback you received was either unhelpful or negative. Your story should be no more than two to three minutes long.

Prepare an observation about how the focus of the session contributes to better understanding of coaching and EIL.

⬦ Facilitator Tips

This activity can be personalized for an intact group that works together on a consistent basis. For the section on *Receiving Feedback*, have the participants think about a time when they worked together on a project and to talk about that experience, rather than selecting an issue they care passionately about.

The *Feedback Assessment* worksheet can be used repeatedly with different situations where participants need to receive feedback on an ongoing basis.

The *Feedback Activities* suggestions can be incorporated with intact groups so that feedback can be developed in their activities. These ideas can also be shared as part of the wrap up.

REFERENCE

Shankman, M. L., & Allen, S. J. (2008). *Emotionally intelligent leadership: A guide for college students.* San Francisco: Jossey-Bass.

← Introduction

Five minutes

Begin by sharing a personal story about feedback you have received that was helpful, unhelpful, or even negative. Share the value of that feedback. If it was unhelpful or negative, be specific about why you felt that way and what you learned from the experience.

Offer that this session is focused on:

- Developing communication and feedback skills
- Gaining ideas from peers' feedback to improve leadership
- Applying the capacity of coaching as a way to enhance project effectiveness

Share your observation as to how these ideas fit in with EIL and the capacity of coaching. Use this observation as a transition to the next section.

← Feedback Is Key

Fifteen minutes

Offer that we can improve our leadership or someone else's leadership by providing feedback. Feedback comes in many forms—the most valuable kind is that which recognizes strengths and provides ideas for improvement.

Ask participants to think of a time when they received helpful feedback and to raise their hand if what they heard was positive or about a strength. Now ask participants to raise their hand if what they heard was constructive or about an area of development. Ask how many of them knew what feedback was coming. Ask for one or two volunteers to share their thoughts about the experience.

Share that feedback can be validating or it can include new information. The benefit of receiving feedback is that it alerts you to how you're being perceived by others, and it can teach you about a blind spot you may not have been aware of.

Giving feedback is a skill that can be developed with practice. However, it takes awareness and creativity.

Ask participants to divide into groups of four. Using *What Is Feedback?* (Activity #1, SW), ask participants to think about how to give excellent feedback. Discuss, as a group, different types of feedback and the grade each would get. (*Allow five to seven minutes.*)

Solicit participant answers to the questions. Add the following, as needed:

- It takes awareness and sensitivity to identify the strengths and opportunities for growth in others.
- Creativity helps us suggest ideas for improvement based on strengths and opportunities.

Here is one system for grading feedback:

- A level feedback: Provides an idea for improvement based on an opportunity identified
- B level feedback: Provides an opportunity for improvement
- C level feedback: May not be truthful, is too generic, or generalizes unfairly
- D level feedback: Attacks the work
- F level feedback: Attacks the person, not the work

⬸ Receiving Feedback

Twenty minutes

Share that leadership requires us to become comfortable giving and receiving feedback. Solicit a few ideas about why this may be so.

Ask participants what they should do when they receive feedback. Suggest the following, if not offered:

- Don't immediately judge what someone shares—take the time to think about what might be learned from what's being shared.
- See what patterns exist.
- Listen with an open mind.
- Be appreciative, even if you don't agree with the feedback.

Ask participants to form pairs and spread out for conversations. Be sure they are far enough apart so pairs can talk without being overheard by others.

Instruct participants to think of an issue they have strong feelings about. Share that the goal of this next activity is to give participants a chance to convince their partner that their position is the appropriate one to take. Ask participants to decide which one will do the persuading; that person will have three minutes to persuade his or her partner to agree with him or her. After three minutes, ask the listener to give the speaker feedback on what the person did well and how the speaker might improve the argument. Remind participants of the suggestions offered in the previous conversation about giving feedback. (*Allow six to seven minutes.*)

Next, ask participants to switch roles and repeat. (*Allow six to seven minutes.*)

Use the following questions, in addition to your own, to facilitate a brief discussion:

- Who was comfortable giving feedback? Ask for one or two examples.
- Who was comfortable receiving feedback? Ask for one or two examples.

- In what ways does an open mind contribute to receiving feedback?
- What is difficult about receiving feedback?

Conclude this section with the thought that the more often we seek feedback, the more we can learn about ourselves. We begin to see patterns in the feedback we receive. As we learn these patterns, we become more clear about our strengths and our challenges. Feedback is a gift—the question is whether we're ready to accept it. The more we listen without judgment the more we have a better understanding of how others perceive us.

✦ Wrap Up

Five minutes

Conclude with the idea that emotionally intelligent leadership encourages us to learn how to give and receive feedback.

Leave participants with a brief overview of the *Feedback Assessment* (Activity #2, SW) as a tool for giving and receiving feedback.

What Is Feedback?

Feedback calls for both awareness and creativity. The person offering feedback needs to be aware of when to offer the feedback, who is receiving the feedback, and the point of giving the feedback. At the same time, feedback should be offered in a way that it can be heard and applied—this often requires creativity.

What if we were to grade the feedback given to a person on a scale from A Level (highest quality, most helpful feedback) to F Level (useless, demeaning feedback)? What does each kind of feedback look like? Describe these here:

A Level

B Level

C Level

D Level

F Level

Feedback Assessment

This form can be used to share feedback. Share this document with someone so that she or he can give you feedback. Or, try this approach with someone to whom you need to give feedback. This coaching is for

_____

    When was this feedback offered? What was the setting? The situation?

Consider successes, strengths, opportunities, and ideas.

1. What was done well? What small or large successes occurred?

2. What strengths of the individual did you notice that he or she can continue to use and build on?

3. What opportunities exist for development to the next level?

Other comments:

✦ Feedback Activities

Feedback Activity 1: Project, Presentation, or Leadership Style Feedback

Give feedback to others in your group. Write the feedback for them on the *Feedback Assessment* worksheet and then share it with them in person. Perhaps you are giving feedback to their project. Perhaps it is feedback on a person's leadership style. Try for A Level feedback: identify the person's strengths and opportunities and provide some ideas on how to use the opportunity for improvement and build on strengths. After each presentation or project, you can go one step beyond simply filling out the feedback sheet. You can share your feedback directly with the person.

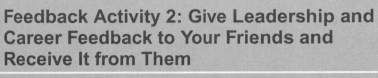

Feedback Activity 2: Give Leadership and Career Feedback to Your Friends and Receive It from Them

This is a 360-degree feedback activity. Many college students are thinking about their careers. We can assess our strengths, interests, and values and identify career areas that fit us. More important, though, is a comprehensive, 360-degree view. What do people we trust think about us? How would they assess our best-fit career areas, based on what they view our strengths, interests, or values to be? How would you give your friends feedback on this?

When you receive general and specific feedback from your friends, what themes emerge? Which kind of feedback was most helpful for you?

Feedback Activity 3: Assessing Feedback on the Web Through Public Comments

You will know the differences between A, B, C, D, and F level feedback when you experience them. A good place to see examples of bad feedback is any sequence of user comments online. Go to a website where people make a post that allows for feedback or comments. For instance, view a YouTube video of a performance or idea, an article, and so on. Grade the comments that people post. Did the comment attack the person? Was it hurtful? Was it too critical of the work without suggesting an opportunity for improvement? Was it too generic? Or did it encourage the person? Did it find positives about the work? Did it provide an idea for improvement? Quickly grade the feedback to determine what poor or excellent feedback looks like.

MODULE 27

Change Agent 1: For Organizations
Les Cook

⬥ Focus of Module

Being a change agent means you seek out and work with others toward new directions. As change agents, emotionally intelligent leaders look for opportunities for improvement or innovation—they think about possibilities and are future oriented. They see how change may benefit one person, an organization, or a whole community, and work to make this change happen. To be a change agent, you must possess certain skills, such as creative thinking and problem solving. In addition, you must have certain attitudes; for example, a comfort with risk taking and a desire to challenge the status quo. A change agent recognizes the importance of time. For change to be effective, you must consider the timing of a change effort and establish the appropriate level of urgency, knowing when to initiate a change and when to hold back.

Primary Activities

Participants work in pairs and small groups to analyze an organization and identify strategies to facilitate effective change.

✦ Learning Objectives and Resources

- To explore models of organizational change
- To learn how to analyze an organization
- To design strategies to create effective change within an organization

Total Time

Sixty minutes

Supplies

Quotes on Change (one copy)

Current State of Organization worksheet (one per participant)

Driving Forces for Change worksheet (one per participant)

Flipchart, markers, easel

Audiovisual for PowerPoint or similar program, if desired

Copy of *Emotionally Intelligent Leadership: A Guide for College Students*

✦ Facilitator Preparation Notes

Read Chapter Eighteen, Change Agent, in *Emotionally Intelligent Leadership: A Guide for College Students* (Shankman & Allen, 2008), and answer the reflection questions for yourself. (Refer to Appendix A for an overview of the EIL model.) Prepare introductory comments based on your reading.

Download *Quotes on Change* (see page viii) and cut apart the individual quotes. You have two choices for distributing these: (1) before participants arrive, tape each quote under a seat at random; or (2) at the beginning of the introduction, distribute the quotes (one per participant) until you run out.

Prepare an example for conducting a force field analysis to demonstrate the activity before the participants do it. Follow the same steps as those you will ask participants to follow:

- Describe the current structure of the organization.
- Describe the desired changes.
- List all the positive forces that drive change toward the desired state, then list all the constraining forces.
- Evaluate the strength of each force (1 = weak, 10 = strong).

Determine whether you want to conclude with a brief summary (two to three minutes) of either the five practices of exemplary leadership defined in *The Student Leadership Challenge* (Kouzes & Posner, 2008) or the eight-stage process outlined in *Leading Change* (Kotter, 1996). Prepare these summaries ahead of time. Consider putting on a flipchart or slide.

← Facilitator Tips

If participants ask what their focus should be, encourage them to think of an organization that they care about. It could be a volunteer organization, a special interest group, somewhere they work, or even their residence hall. This is an important point, as participants who do not hold a formal position of leadership can still become change agents for a group. This topic is especially relevant for emphasizing the informal leadership roles we all have the opportunity to play.

REFERENCES

Cramer, K., & Wasiak, H. (2006). *Change the way you see everything.* Philadelphia: Running Press.

Kotter, J. (1996). *Leading change.* Cambridge, MA: Harvard University Press.

Kouzes, J., & Posner, B. (2008). *The student leadership challenge.*
    San Francisco: Jossey-Bass.

Lewin, K. (1997). *Resolving social conflicts: Field theory in social science.*
    Washington, DC: American Psychological Association.

Peale, N. V. (2003). *The power of positive thinking.* New York: Fireside Books.
    (Original work published 1952)

Shankman, M. L., & Allen, S. J. (2008). *Emotionally intelligent leadership:
    A guide for college students.* San Francisco: Jossey-Bass.

Zander, R. S., & Zander, B. (2000). *The art of possibility: Transforming personal
    and professional life.* New York: Penguin Books.

✦ Introduction

Five minutes

Begin by sharing that inspiring others, demonstrating enthusiasm, cultivating ideas, and being willing to embrace change are essential characteristics of emotionally intelligent leadership.

This segment will explore the concept of change and how leaders can affect their organization by introducing, facilitating, and embracing change. Add additional thoughts as you see fit based on your reading of the chapter on change agents.

Offer that many different definitions of change suggest different ways for us to think about being a change agent.

Webster's defines change as "the ability to make different the form, nature, content, future course; to transform or convert; to substitute another or others for; to give and take reciprocally."

Suggest that while the dictionary offers one perspective on change, we can also think about change based on what others say. Direct participants to the different quotes (by directing them to either look under their chairs for the quotes or listen to the different participants as they read their quotes).

✦ Change Begins Within Yourself

Five minutes

Give the following summary of thoughts about change starting with the individual:

- In Dr. Norman Vincent Peale's *The Power of Positive Thinking* (2003; 1952), he describes the relevance of attitude, positive thinking, and belief in self as the engine to accomplish what we desire.
- In *The Art of Possibility: Transforming Personal and Professional Life* (2000), authors Rosamund Stone Zander

and Benjamin Zander assert the idea that life often resembles an obstacle course with various obstructions placed in our path. To be successful, individuals must spend more time living in possibility and looking to *what could be* rather than dwelling on the past and reminiscing about *what should have been* done.

- In *Change the Way You See Everything* (2006), authors Kathryn Cramer and Hank Wasiak define asset-based thinking as the concept of looking at the world as a glass that is half full rather than half empty. This idea connects with the EIL capacity of optimism. According to Kramer and Wasiak, asset-based thinking is a concrete and cognitive process designed to help individuals identify assets (possibilities, characteristics, talents, and strengths) that are available in themselves, other individuals, and the larger context.

Offer that each of these examples demonstrates the essential first step for participants to develop emotionally intelligent leadership and be change agents: to begin by believing in themselves and their ability to lead positive change within organizations or groups that they care about.

◆ What's Your Current State?

Fifteen minutes

Explain that the purpose of this session is to give participants an opportunity to begin to explore and create effective change within an organization or group. Reinforce that they don't have to hold a formal leadership role to make change happen.

To begin, ask participants to join with a partner to discuss the following questions. (*Allow seven or eight minutes.*)

- If they were to imagine the ideal for [insert name of organization they care about], what would it look like five years from now? Ten years?
- How can they be agents of change?

Ask participants to record their answers to the last two questions on *Current State of Organization* (Activity #1, SW). Ask for feedback from the group and record responses on a flipchart.

◈ Lewin's Force Field Analysis

Twenty-five minutes

The concept of force field analysis (Lewin, 1997) was an influential development in the field of social science and provides a framework for looking at the factors or *forces* that influence a situation. In the simplest terms, this framework promotes the idea that there are certain forces that help move individuals and organizations closer to a goal as well as forces that prevent us from reaching our desired goals.

Share that we will now have the opportunity to look at an issue from the perspective of opposing forces—those seeking to promote change (driving forces) and those attempting to maintain the status quo (restraining forces).

Ask participants to complete the *Driving Forces for Change* worksheet (Activity #2, SW). This activity offers the opportunity to conduct a force field analysis. If participants are having a difficult time selecting a focus for change, encourage them to think about the organization or group they just discussed with their partner. (*Allow ten minutes.*)

- Describe the current structure of the organization.
- Describe the desired changes.

- List all the positive forces that drive change toward a desired state and all the constraining forces.
- Discuss each force—which are fixed? Which can be changed?
- Evaluate the strength of each force (1 = weak; 10 = strong).

If participants struggle, share your example.

Ask participants to find a partner to talk through their analysis and discuss how to do the following. (*Allow ten minutes.*)

- Find ways to strengthen or add *driving* forces
- Find ways to weaken or remove *resisting or constraining* forces
- Recognize whether negative forces are too strong—in which case you may choose to abandon the project

Conclude with participants sharing an example of the following. (*Allow five minutes.*)

- What they identified as a helping force and how to strengthen it
- What they identified as a resisting or constraining force and how to weaken it

✦ Wrap Up

Ten minutes

Conclude with a brief summary of either the five practices of exemplary leadership defined in *The Student Leadership Challenge*

(Kouzes & Posner, 2008) or the eight-stage process outlined in *Leading Change* (Kotter, 1996). Here are further details on these options:

Researchers and leadership experts James Kouzes and Barry Posner have identified five practices of exemplary leadership:

- Challenge the process
- Inspire a shared vision
- Enable others to act
- Model the way
- Encourage the heart

Ask participants to examine how these practices might impact a leader's ability to create change.

John Kotter, in his book *Leading Change*, summarizes how change can occur within an organization; the eight stages are

- Creating a sense of urgency
- Establishing a guiding coalition
- Developing a vision or strategy
- Communicating the change vision
- Empowering participants for broad-based action
- Generating short-term wins
- Consolidating gains and producing more change
- Anchoring new approaches in the culture

Ask participants to offer their thoughts on which stages are most crucial for success.

Ask for final comments from participants, then offer your own.

☙ Quotes on Change

People are very open-minded about new things—as long as they're exactly like the old ones.—Charles F. Kettering, inventor

Change will not come if we wait for some other person or some other time. We are the ones we've been waiting for. We are the change that we seek.—Senator Barack Obama, during his presidential campaign

The mind has exactly the same power as the hands; not merely to grasp the world, but to change it.—Colin Wilson, philosopher

Never doubt that a small group of thoughtful, committed people can change the world. Indeed, it is the only thing that ever has.—Margaret Mead, anthropologist

There is nothing like returning to a place that remains unchanged to find the ways in which you yourself have altered.—Nelson Mandela, former president of South Africa

It is change, continuing change, inevitable change that is the dominant factor in society today. No sensible decision can be made any longer without taking into account not only the world as it is, but the world as it will be.—Isaac Asimov, author

See page viii for download information.

Current State of Organization

If you were to imagine the ideal for

_____

(insert name of group/organization), what would it look like five years from now? Ten years?

Re-read the definition of change agent and answer the following: How can you be an agent of change?

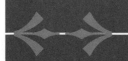

Driving Forces for Change

Every organization or group experiences multiple influences from both within and outside its boundaries. Some of these forces are encouraging change (driving forces); others are resisting change (restraining forces). Some of these forces can be initiated or halted; others will continue regardless of what anyone does. Some of these forces are positive, others are not.

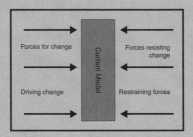

Provide the name of an organization or group you care about or are involved in:_____.

List all the positive forces (e.g., people, traditions, culture, external forces) that drive your organization toward evolving into a desired state; list all the constraining forces that are holding your organization back from evolving into a desired state.

Circle the forces that are critical to the future success of the organization or group.

Place a box around the forces that can be changed or influenced. Underline those that are out of your control.

Evaluate the strength of each force (1 = weak; 10 = strong) by placing a number next to it..

Change Agent 2: Be the Change
Gabrielle Lucke

✦ Focus of Module

Being a change agent means you seek out and work with others toward new directions. As change agents, emotionally intelligent leaders look for opportunities for improvement or innovation—they think about possibilities and are future oriented. They see how change may benefit one person, an organization, or a whole community, and work to make this change happen. To be a change agent, you must possess certain skills, such as creative thinking and problem solving. In addition, you must have certain attitudes—for example, a comfort with risk taking and a desire to challenge the status quo. A change agent recognizes the importance of time. For change to be effective, you must consider the timing of a change effort and establish the appropriate level of urgency, knowing when to initiate a change and when to hold back.

Primary Activities

Participants work in small groups and on their own to define the primary characteristics and skills required of change agents.

✦ Learning Objectives and Resources

- To practice creative problem-solving skills
- To explore the dynamics of working together in a newly formed group
- To identify challenges and characteristics of change agents

Total Time

Forty-five minutes

Supplies

Flipchart, markers, easel

Copy of *Emotionally Intelligent Leadership: A Guide for College Students*

✦ Facilitator Preparation Notes

Read Chapter Eighteen, Change Agent, in *Emotionally Intelligent Leadership: A Guide for College Students* (Shankman & Allen, 2008), and answer the reflection questions for yourself. (Refer to Appendix A for an overview of the EIL model.) Prepare introductory comments based on your reading.

✦ Facilitator Tips

Be prepared to assert that not everyone takes on the role of change agent or is comfortable doing so. It is important to share with the group that although there are well-known change agents throughout world history, we need to remember there are also significant change agents in our day-to-day lives. Have some examples of everyday and contemporary change agents in mind to share with the group.

For the first activity, decide how small the groups should be—groups of six, seven, or eight. By counting off, you can separate participants who may be clustered together and familiar with each other.

REFERENCE

Shankman, M. L., & Allen, S. J. (2008). *Emotionally intelligent leadership: A guide for college students*. San Francisco: Jossey-Bass.

✦ Introduction

Five minutes

Begin with a quick review of Appendix A: EIL Overview.

Ask participants to focus on the definition of change agent and ask for a few responses to the following question: Why does the capacity of change agent fall under the facet *consciousness of others*?

Acknowledge participants' responses and add that this is a role needed in any leadership process. Change allows people and systems to move toward what is desired or what comes next for a group, organization, or community.

✦ Moving a Group Forward

Twenty minutes

Ask participants to count off into small groups as you've determined in your preparation. Ask each group to identify three similarities all members of their group share. Explain that *obvious* common aspects are not allowed; for example, if all are in college, being a college student doesn't count. (*Allow five minutes.*)

Ask each of the small groups to report out to the large group what they have in common. Use the following questions for discussion:

- If we are talking about being a change agent, why would we do this activity?
- What skills and techniques did your group use to move through the process?

Acknowledge responses, then offer the following if not identified by the participants:

- Group members asked questions, listened, observed, assessed, and integrated the information that was presented to identify the core items that members of each group had in common.

- A change agent's role in the leadership process requires that these skills be in place to enable working with others in new directions.
- In a five-minute period, each small group participated in creative problem solving to discover what they had in common. On a larger scale, change agents have to identify stakeholders who can help them make change happen. The first step in that process is often finding common ground for that group of stakeholders.
- A change agent needs the motivation and energy to not only convene a group but also unite and build consensus with diverse stakeholders.

✦ Characteristics and Challenges for Change Agents

Fifteen minutes

Ask participants to brainstorm the characteristics of a change agent. Record the responses (FCH). Add the following, if not suggested by participants:

- Strong communication skills
- Strong facilitation skills
- Ability to listen and observe
- Ability to integrate multiple approaches
- Ability to establish trust and confidence
- Ability to manage people and resources
- Ability to lead people
- Ability to easily detect, sense, and manage controversy
- Desire and skill to overcome resistance

Ask the group why change agents need to manage controversy and overcome resistance.

Ask participants to brainstorm challenges for a change agent. Record responses (FCH). If the following are not identified, the facilitator should bring up:

- Being resistant to change
- Being satisfied with the status quo
- Being invested in the status quo

Remind participants that being a change agent is not often a popular role because people may be resistant to change. Sometimes just the thought of change will cause people to rebel or react negatively.

✦ Wrap Up

Five minutes

Conclude the session by suggesting that change agents who promote interactions and initiatives that serve the greater good can move individuals, organizations, and communities into new ways of being. Ask participants for comments or questions.

Ask participants to take a moment to think about someone who has been a change agent in their lives. Ask how this person has made a difference in their life. Solicit a few examples.

Close with this question: Where and when will you be a change agent?

MODULE 29

Conflict Management 1: It's About Relationships

Mary Peterson

✦ Focus of Module

Conflict management is about identifying and resolving problems and issues with others. Emotionally intelligent leaders understand that conflict is part of any leadership experience. When managed effectively, conflict can foster great innovation. At times conflict is overt and may involve anger, raised voices, or high levels of frustration. Other times conflict is below the surface and shows itself only through cliques, side conversations, and apathy. Emotionally intelligent leaders are aware of these dynamics and work to manage them.

Primary Activities

Participants complete two assessments, one personal and one organizational, and work in small groups to better understand how to manage conflict.

✦ Learning Objectives and Resources

- To explore connections between honesty and conflict
- To identify the quality of personal and organizational interactions as they relate to conflict management
- To develop strategies to create an environment where conflict is managed constructively

Total Time

Sixty minutes

Supplies

Honesty article (one per participant)

Honesty Continuum worksheet (one per participant)

Personal Interactions Assessment worksheet (one per participant)

Organizational Interactions Assessment worksheet (one per participant)

Flipchart, markers, easel

Audiovisual to support PowerPoint or similar program, if desired

Copy of *Emotionally Intelligent Leadership: A Guide for College Students*

✦ Facilitator Preparation Notes

Read Chapter Nineteen, Conflict Management, in *Emotionally Intelligent Leadership: A Guide for College Students* (Shankman & Allen, 2008), and answer the reflection questions for yourself. (Refer to Appendix A for an overview of the EIL model.) Prepare introductory comments based on your reading.

Read the *Honesty* article.

Complete the *Honesty Continuum* and assessment worksheets prior to facilitating the module.

Prepare a flipchart or slide with the following:

Discussion Questions
- What is one action you can take to increase the quality of interactions in your organization?
- How have you seen organizations stifle differing opinions? What was the effect?
- What are some ways that organizations can create a supportive atmosphere where constructive conflict can occur? What might be the results?

Facilitator Tips

By completing the *Honesty Continuum* and assessment worksheets, you will be better equipped to facilitate the discussion because you will have had time to reflect on your experience.

In this module, participants are expected to deal with the challenging subjects of honesty and truth. This may affect individuals' willingness to share, so it is important to be considerate of what participants may be feeling.

REFERENCE

Shankman, M. L., & Allen, S. J. (2008). *Emotionally intelligent leadership: A guide for college students*. San Francisco: Jossey-Bass.

✦ Introduction

Five minutes

Ask participants to raise their hand if they like conflict. If applicable, ask one or two to explain why.

For those participants who do not like conflict, ask one or two to explain why.

Share that, in general, most people dislike conflict. People enjoy harmony in relationships. Conflict takes us out of our comfort zones and forces us to experience feelings that make us uncomfortable or unhappy. Ask participants why conflict management is an important capacity of leadership. After a couple of responses, review the capacity of conflict management in Appendix A: EIL Overview.

Outline the learning objectives highlighted at the beginning of this module.

✦ Honesty Article

Ten minutes

Ask participants to read the *Honesty* article (Module 29, SW). (*Allow five minutes.*)

Lead a discussion with participants about key points from the article.

✦ Honesty Continuum

Ten minutes

Share with the participants that they now have an opportunity to assess their levels of honesty by completing the *Honesty Continuum* (Activity #1, SW). (*Allow five minutes.*)

Once all participants finish, ask them to share with the person next to them one observation they made about themselves after completing the *Honesty Continuum*.

Ask participants to explain what connection they see between honesty and its role in or impact on conflict management. After a few volunteers offer their thoughts, add the following as needed:

- When people are honest in a considerate and understanding manner, it can aid in making conflict a positive experience.
- Trust and respect are built through honest communication. The potential for change is then more likely to be realized. Without honesty, negative feelings toward the person emerge and communication is stifled.

✦ Personal and Organizational Interactions Assessment

Thirty minutes

Share with the participants the following:

For conflict to be managed in a productive manner, we need to reflect upon our interactions. Understanding conflict at personal and organizational levels will help tremendously.

When individuals are in a leadership position, they often believe they should eliminate conflict at all costs. This is not healthy, nor will an organization grow and move forward.

We usually don't think about creating an environment where we can disagree or understand one another's point of view. The following assessment will help you better understand where you and your organization stand.

Ask each participant to complete the *Personal Interactions Assessment* (Activity #2, SW). Ask participants to think about their place in an organization or group (as either a leader or member) when completing the assessment. Remind them to explain why they choose the ranking they do. (*Allow five to seven minutes.*)

Share with the participants that they will now have the opportunity to examine interactions within an organization they are actively involved in.

Ask each participant to complete the *Organizational Interactions Assessment* (Activity #3, SW). Again mention that they'll need to explain why they choose the ranking they do. (*Allow five to seven minutes.*)

Next, divide the participants into groups of four to six, depending on the size of the large group. If there are participants from the same organization, assign them to the same group.

Ask the small groups to discuss the following questions (FCH):

- What is one action you can take to increase the quality of interactions in your organization?
- How have you seen organizations stifle different opinions? What was the effect?
- What are some ways that organizations can create a supportive atmosphere so constructive conflict can happen? What might the results be? (*Allow the remaining time for this discussion.*)

✦ Wrap Up

Five minutes

Ask participants to share final thoughts they have. Encourage a few comments about the small group conversations and a few observations based on the assessments.

Conclude by suggesting that conflict management starts when people are honest and willing to create an environment where healthy conflict is encouraged.

Honesty

Almost any difficulty will move in the face of honesty.
When I am honest I never feel stupid.
And when I am honest I am automatically humble.
—Hugh Prather, *I Touch the Earth, the Earth Touches Me*

Webster's New Collegiate Dictionary defines *honest* as

1 (a) free from fraud or deception; legitimate, truthful (b) genuine, real (c) humble; 2 (a) reputable, respectful (b) good, worthy; 3—credible, praiseworthy; 4 (a) marked by integrity (b) frank, sincere (c) innocent, simple.

The *American Heritage College Dictionary* defines dialogue as 1—a conversation between two or more people; 5—an exchange of ideas or opinions.

Why use two different dictionary sources? To ensure an honest exchange of ideas, of course. So, according to *The Modern Mary Peterson Dictionary*, the definition of an honest dialogue would be the combination of the two sources: *a legitimate, frank conversation with yourself or two or more people, in which ideas and opinions are shared to create good and worthy ideas of integrity.*

You may now be asking why a definition of honest dialogue would include a conversation with yourself as one of its possibilities. To have honest dialogue with others, you need to be free from fraud and deception of self (*Webster's* 1a). It begins with you.

The definition seems so straightforward and simple, but it is difficult for humans to achieve. In fact, we have even created levels of honesty. Most people would say they value honesty in themselves and in others with whom they interact. You may recall, in the movie *A Few Good Men,* when Jack Nicholson's character responds to the Tom Cruise character, who has demanded, "I want the truth." With an angry and strong intonation, Nicholson's character replies, "You want the truth? You can't handle the truth!" In some sense, that exchange says it all. We fight against the very thing we cry out for. We humans sure are complicated.

(Continued)

Some people will tell you they are being as honest as they can. The key is "as they can." This takes us back to having an honest dialogue with ourselves before doing it with others. Some believe being honest means being rebellious or difficult. For example, at a planning meeting facilitated by a colleague, a participant spoke up, saying he did not like a particular activity they were being asked to do. He said he didn't understand why they were being asked to draw a picture of their vision for the organization. He apologized for being honest. Jeffrey replied, "Honesty is not rebellion."

Honesty isn't rebellion. The truth was, this man really *did* understand why we were doing the vision exercise. He was not being honest with himself about the fact that it was hard for him to think outside the box and be creative and visionary. In his mind that statement would have been admitting a weakness. However, after being given some support and encouragement, he did an excellent job with his vision picture.

If we could only get over being independent and become more *interdependent*. Feeling secure in asking for help, rather than struggling on our own or dismissing the activity or challenge, is a step toward honesty with you.

Honesty Continuum

List at least three examples of times when you responded with the level of honesty suggested.

Then think about the eventual outcomes of your level of honesty; what actually happened?

When was I . . .

Completely Honest?   *Outcome(s)*

1.

2.

3.

Somewhat Honest?   *Outcome(s)*

1.

2.

3.

(Continued)

Somewhat Dishonest?   *Outcome(s)*

1.

2.

3.

Completely Dishonest?   *Outcome(s)*

1.

2.

3.

Personal Interactions Assessment

To what extent do you agree or disagree with the following statements? Use the scale and place your ranking next to the number for each statement. Next, explain why you chose that ranking. In your responses, be consistent about the aspect of yourself that you are assessing (for example, as a formal leader or as a member of an organization or group).

Agree	*Somewhat Agree*	*Somewhat Disagree*	*Disagree*
4	3	2	1

___1. I am totally honest in all I have to say.
    Why?

___2. I prefer taking the time to understand others' points of view rather than to convince people of my own views.
    Why?

(Continued)

___ 3. I frequently ask people questions about their views.
Why?

___ 4. I think a lot about the differences in thinking that lead to conflict among people.
Why?

___ 5. I often change my ideas as a result of conversing with others.
Why?

Organizational Interactions Assessment

To what extent do you agree or disagree with the following statements? Using the following scale, place your ranking next to each statement number and explain why you chose that ranking.

Agree	*Somewhat Agree*	*Somewhat Disagree*	*Disagree*
4	3	2	1

___1. My organization encourages people to take the time to communicate openly, even about difficult issues.
Why?

___2. My organization provides training and development for the skills needed to engage in constructive conflict.
Why?

___3. People respect different viewpoints and individual differences.
Why?

___4. Dissent and questioning are encouraged.
Why?

MODULE 30

Conflict Management 2: Learning Confrontation Skills

Michael Hayes

✦ Focus of Module

Conflict management is about identifying and resolving
problems and issues with others. Emotionally intelligent
leaders understand that conflict is part of any leadership experience.
When managed effectively, conflict can foster great innovation.
At times conflict is overt and may involve anger, raised voices,
or high levels of frustration. Other times conflict is below the
surface and shows itself only through cliques, side conversations,
and apathy. Emotionally intelligent leaders are aware of these
dynamics and work to manage them.

Primary Activities

Participants discuss key elements of conflict, conduct an
organizational audit, and role play a constructive confrontation
with a partner.

✦ Learning Objectives and Resources

- To explore the roots of conflict
- To learn strategies for managing conflict
- To practice key communication skills for managing conflict

Total Time

Sixty minutes

Supplies

Basic Organizational Audit worksheet (one per participant)

Scenarios worksheet (one per participant)

Flipchart, markers, easel

Audiovisual to support PowerPoint or similar program, if desired

Copy of *Emotionally Intelligent Leadership: A Guide for College Students*

✦ Facilitator Preparation Notes

Read Chapter Nineteen, Conflict Management, in *Emotionally Intelligent Leadership: A Guide for College Students* (Shankman & Allen, 2008), and answer the reflection questions for yourself. (Refer to Appendix A for an overview of the EIL model.) Prepare introductory comments based on your reading.

Prepare the following flipcharts or slides:

Roots of Conflict
- Power struggles
- Differences in values or priorities
- Apathy
- Time
- Leadership style

Strategies
1. Communicate honestly
2. Listen to all perspectives
3. Summarize all perspectives
4. Find common ground
5. Make a decision

Healthy Confrontation
1. Initiate contact
2. Establish rapport
3. Identify the issue
4. Agree on the problem
5. Obtain commitment
6. Offer support
7. Praise success

← Facilitator Tips

Review the talking points of the module so that you are comfortable with the information that you will be sharing.
Manage your time carefully with the lecturettes.
If you share too many examples or tell stories to illustrate the key points, you will run out of time. Similarly, if you ask for participants to comment, be sure to ask them for brief responses.

REFERENCES

National Panhellenic Conference (2006). *Something to talk about: Confrontation skills*. Indianapolis, IN: NPC.

Scott, S. (2004). *Fierce conversations: Achieving success at work and in life, one conversation at a time.* New York: Berkley Books.

Shankman, M. L., & Allen, S. J. (2008). *Emotionally intelligent leadership: A guide for college students.* San Francisco: Jossey-Bass.

✦ Introduction: What Does Conflict Mean to You?

Ten minutes

Begin with a quick review of Appendix A: EIL Overview. Ask participants to focus on the capacity of conflict management. Share the perspective that when we look at personal relationships, organizational life, and working with others on causes that we are passionate about, conflict is inevitable. Emotionally intelligent leadership recognizes this and offers ways to think about how to manage and address conflict. With EIL, we can work through conflict productively. When this happens, our organizations and members continue to grow.

Ask participants to share what comes to mind when they think of conflict. Solicit a few responses from the group and record them (FCH).

Ask the following questions to encourage a deeper understanding of conflict:

- How many are positive? How many are negative?
- Why do we often associate conflict as a negative experience?
- How and when might conflict be seen as positive?

✦ Roots of Conflict

Fifteen minutes

Share that we can better understand conflict by looking at what Shankman and Allen (2008) identify as the roots of conflict (FCH):

- Power struggles
- Differences in values or priorities
- Apathy
- Time
- Leadership style

Offer the following thoughts:

Let's visit each of these quickly. What might the conflict around power look like? What might be happening? It usually exists as individuals or different factions of an organization vie for control.

The second root of conflict centers on values and priorities. When there is a difference in the values of the individuals and/or within different factions of a given group, conflict will occur. It could be something esoteric concerning commitment to the mission of the group or something as tactical as how the organization is fulfilling its mission. It might manifest itself in how people buy in and work for the betterment of the organization or cause.

The third root, apathy, might occur when some deal with the ensuing conflict by withdrawing or becoming resentful about how things are being done. How else might apathy be a source of conflict?

When the authors mention time, why might this potentially cause conflict? How people choose to spend their time is a reflection of their values and priorities. If this is the case, then you can see how someone who is dedicated to an organization and someone who isn't can be in conflict over how they spend their time.

And the last root, leadership style: in what ways might one's leadership style cause conflict?

After one or two comments, highlight the importance of honest self-understanding, especially in terms of knowing our own strengths and limitations. This includes being brutally honest with ourselves in terms of how we respond to conflict. Share that some of us face conflict head on, whereas others are conflict averse. In either scenario, we can manage ourselves and have the ability to work through the conflict.

← Finding the Truth

Fifteen minutes

Offer that our ability to be honest about how we manage conflict is paramount. This means being honest with ourselves and the individuals with whom we work about why conflict exists. Ask participants whether this is easy to do. Why or why not? Solicit two or three comments.

Highlight that Susan Scott, in her book *Fierce Conversations* (2004), discusses the notion of "ground truth" versus "official truth." Ground truth is what is occurring in the fabric of the organization, and everyone inside the organization knows it. "Official truth" is what the organization wants people, especially on the outside, to think is happening. It is easy to see how both internal and interpersonal conflict might arise in these circumstances. Remind participants of the five roots of conflict mentioned previously. Ask participants how they would reduce the disparity between these two different types of truths, thus lessening the opportunity for conflict.

Share with participants that they will now conduct a *Basic Organizational Audit* (Activity #4, SW).

Walk participants through the following questions, allowing time for them to write their thoughts:

- Where are you succeeding? Where are you failing?
- Is conflict a by-product of what's happening in your organization/group? If so, in what ways?
- What needs to change for your organization to work through conflict more effectively?

Suggest that possible next steps include:

- A difficult discussion with a member who may have not met his or her obligations
- An apology from the leader to the group about the leader's own breach of commitment
- Revisiting procedures and protocol—or . . . ?

Whatever steps are taken, honesty is key. Remember the two truths and how important it is to understand them.

✦ So, What's Next?

Ten minutes

Share with participants that understanding how to work through conflict enables emotionally intelligent leaders to work through conflict. Shankman and Allen (2008) discuss five strategies for working through conflict in a positive manner (FCH):

1. Communicate honestly
   - Be open and encourage all parties engaged to be honest.
2. Listen to all perspectives:
   - Be sure to encourage all parties to voice perspectives.
   - Facilitate the conversation.
3. Summarize all perspectives:
   - Cut through the rhetoric.
   - Succinctly summarize to ensure that all concerned have been understood.
4. Find common ground.
5. Make a decision:
   - First seek consensus.
   - Be prepared to make a decision if consensus can't be reached.

Offer that one critical step in effective conflict management is confronting individuals. We often associate negative feelings with the notion of confrontation. Ask for a few thoughts as to why confrontation elicits negative feelings. Then offer the following:

Confrontation is a necessary component of leading people and organizations. Let's work through a model that can help make confrontation a little easier to manage.

First, it's important to understand the context and remember that confrontation is about the evaluation and potential redirection of behavior. In plain English, this means you separate the person from the behavior.

Second, be willing to listen to the reasons surrounding the behavior. When you understand the rationale behind the behavior, the conversation will be more honest and reflective of the parties involved.

Share with participants what healthy confrontation looks like. Review the following seven components adapted from the National Panhellenic Conference's *Something to Talk About* program (FCH):

1. Initiate contact.
   - Make contact with the person to be confronted.
   - Consider time and place (be sure it is an appropriate setting, such as a private space).
2. Establish rapport: create a sense of mutual trust and respect.
3. Identify the issue or problem.
   - Talk together to clarify that the behavior in question is an issue.
   - Do not ask "why" questions; instead, ask "what" questions.
   - If no agreement is reached, return to step 2.
4. Agree on the problem.
   - Be sure that a specific problem is defined as the focus for changing.
   - If the confronted person does not agree, she or he will lack the necessary motivation to address it.
5. Obtain a commitment.
   - Agree on a commitment about addressing the problematic behavior.
   - Be sure the commitment is acceptable to both parties and attainable.
6. Offer support on keeping the commitment: set a time or date to check back in with the person on how the commitment has been kept, and if it hasn't been by that date, head back to step 5.
7. Praise success. Remember, confront in private, praise success in public, as appropriate.

With these steps, we can address areas for potential conflict before they escalate.

Share these additional tips, as appropriate:

- Have conversations in person—not by texting, email or Facebook.
- Use "I" statements about observable behavior, rather than "you" statements that sound accusatory.
- Nonverbal messages need to be consistent with verbal messages.
- Avoid generalizations.
- Be sincere.
- Be prepared, especially if the person doesn't believe there's a problem.
- Don't minimize your point—say what is necessary; otherwise you reduce the effectiveness of your message.

If time allows, answer questions from participants.

← Wrap Up

Ten minutes

Ask participants to partner with someone in the room and have them pick a *Scenario* (Activity #5, SW) to work through. Remind participants to use the model just discussed to practice their confrontation skills. (*Allow three to four minutes.*)

Ask for a few volunteers to comment on what it was like to initiate the confrontation. Then ask for a few volunteers to discuss how it felt to be confronted. (*Allow three to four minutes.*)

Conclude with the observation that this opportunity to practice confrontation is a critical skill in conflict resolution. Confrontation is a skill that everyone can add to their leadership toolbox. It will be one that enables us to continue to do extraordinary things within our organizations, in our relationships, and in our lives.

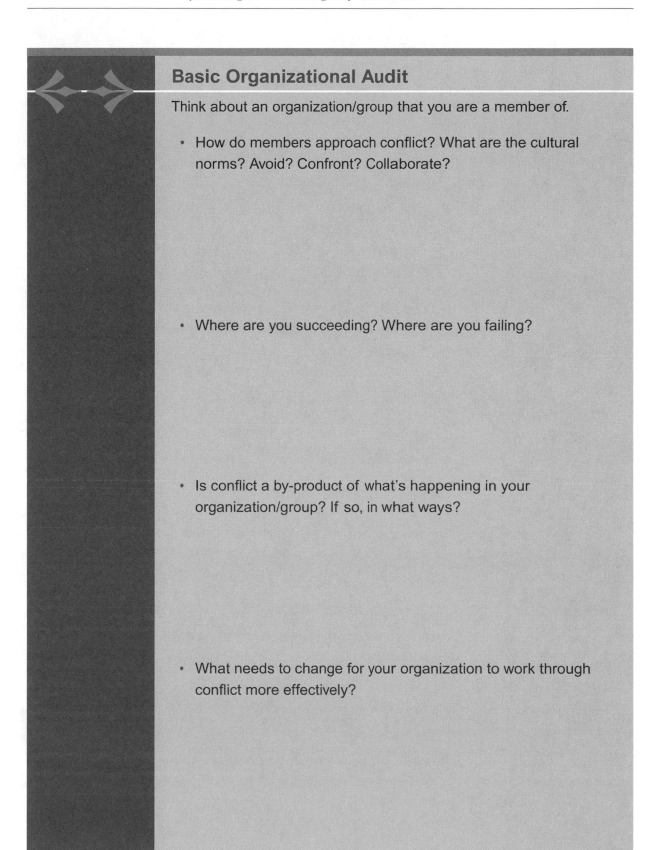

Basic Organizational Audit

Think about an organization/group that you are a member of.

- How do members approach conflict? What are the cultural norms? Avoid? Confront? Collaborate?

- Where are you succeeding? Where are you failing?

- Is conflict a by-product of what's happening in your organization/group? If so, in what ways?

- What needs to change for your organization to work through conflict more effectively?

Scenarios

Confrontation Model

1. Initiate contact.
2. Establish rapport.
3. Identify the issue or problem.
4. Agree on the problem.
5. Obtain a commitment.
6. Offer support on keeping the commitment.
7. Praise success!

Using this confrontation model, consider the following three scenarios. What would you do? Answer the questions that follow each of the scenarios.

Scenario One: A committee chair has failed to perform his or her duties on an important committee.

- What do you need to do to communicate honestly?

- How will you be sure to listen to all perspectives?

- What skills will you need to use to summarize all perspectives?

- What will you do to find common ground?

- How do you envision a decision getting made? Who's involved? How?

Scenario Two: A senior member has stopped attending meetings, and the member's historical perspective of your organization is missed.

- What do you need to do to communicate honestly?

- How will you be sure to listen to all perspectives?

- What skills will you need to use to summarize all perspectives?

- What will you do to find common ground?

- How do you envision a decision getting made? Who's involved? How?

Scenario Three: A friend has cheated on a recent exam or taken credit for work performed by someone else.

- What do you need to do to communicate honestly?

(Continued)

- How will you be sure to listen to all perspectives?

- What skills will you need to use to summarize all perspectives?

- What will you do to find common ground?

- How do you envision a decision getting made? Who's involved? How?

Source: Adapted from Shankman and Allen (2008).

MODULE 31

Developing Relationships 1: Networking
Paige Haber

✦ Focus of Module

Developing relationships is about creating connections between, among, and with people. It is a skill as well as a mindset. This capacity requires emotionally intelligent leaders to build relationships and create a sense of trust and mutual interest. Simply put, individuals, groups, and organizations are stronger, smarter, and more effective when they are rooted in and facilitate positive relationships. Some people assume you have to be outgoing or social to be effective at developing relationships; however, networking experts have discovered that the people who are best at developing relationships are not necessarily gregarious. They possess a combination of skills and the understanding that they need to listen well, know themselves, and know how to develop rapport with others. People who understand the valuable role that others play in making their own lives rich and fulfilling are often the best at developing relationships, regardless of personality type.

Primary Activities

Participants will practice networking skills and develop a networking action plan.

✦ Learning Objectives and Resources

- To learn about the benefits of and strategies for networking
- To practice basic networking skills
- To identify important people with whom to connect

Total Time

Sixty minutes

Supplies

Personal Networking Web worksheet (one per participant)

Personal Networking Action Planning worksheet (one per participant)

Flipchart, markers, easel

Soft music (optional)

Audiovisual to support PowerPoint or similar program, if desired

Copy of *Emotionally Intelligent Leadership: A Guide for College Students*

✦ Facilitator Preparation Notes

Read Chapter Twenty, Developing Relationships, in *Emotionally Intelligent Leadership: A Guide for College Students* (Shankman & Allen, 2008). (Refer to Appendix A for an overview of the EIL model.) Prepare introductory comments based on your reading. Prepare a flipchart or slide as follows:

Benefits of Networking
- Increases access to information and opportunities
- Enhances understanding of others
- Maximizes effect on others
- Helps develop meaningful relationships
- Improves communication and interpersonal skills
- Builds credibility

Prepare a personal example of the *Personal Networking Web*. This web should be drawn on a piece of flipchart paper or put in a slide presentation program so participants can see it. Be sure to include a variety of different individuals, organizations, groups, family members, teammates, and family friends that you know personally or through someone. These different stakeholders should surround your name and be connected to you or other components of your web through solid lines. Use dashed lines for less direct connections.

✦ Facilitator Tips

Preparing short personal examples (two to three minutes) will be helpful so that you can provide examples throughout the module on:

- Finding common ground with someone and how this developed into a meaningful relationship
- A positive networking experience

The activity *Things in Common* should take fifteen minutes, which will allow you five minutes for follow-up discussion.

REFERENCE

Shankman, M. L., & Allen, S. J. (2008). *Emotionally intelligent leadership: A guide for college students*. San Francisco: Jossey-Bass.

✦ Introduction

Three minutes

Welcome the group and share that the focus of this session is developing relationships. Building and developing relationships is a key component of emotionally intelligent leadership, as you need others to be working with you toward your shared goal. Offer a quick review of Appendix A: EIL Overview.

Suggest that developing relationships is also an important capacity in our personal and professional lives.

✦ Things in Common

Twenty minutes

Ask participants to stand up, walk around, and partner with someone they don't know well. Everyone should have a partner; allow one group of three if necessary.

Ask each pair to introduce themselves to one another by name and find something unique they have in common. Emphasize that this must be something out of the ordinary and should be as detailed as possible (for example, we were both Girl Scouts and won the most number of cookies sold three years in a row). (*Allow two to three minutes.*)

Ask a few of the pairs to share with the group what they had in common.

Ask each pair to partner up with another pair. (If there is an odd number of pairs, allow three pairs to join together.) Each pair should introduce themselves to the next pair by name and share what they had in common. Now, as a new group, encourage them to find common ground. (*Allow five minutes.*)

Once groups have found common ground, ask a few groups to share what they have in common.

Continue this process of joining subunits until there is one large group or the activity has gone on for fifteen minutes.

Facilitate a large group discussion using any of the following questions:

- What new information did you learn about in this activity?
- How did your feelings toward others in the group shift as you went through the activity?
- Based on your conversations, what further questions do you have for others in the room?

Emphasize that building rapport through commonalities will help form a feeling of connection. This feeling of connection allows for free-flowing conversation. Initial connections with people also provide a foundation from which a more significant relationship can be developed.

At this point, feel free to offer a personal short example about finding common ground with someone and how this developed into a meaningful relationship, as appropriate.

← Networking Basics

Ten minutes

Ask participants to share what comes to mind when they hear the word *networking*.

Offer that networking means finding or making connections with others. Sometimes, however, the idea of networking may sound manipulative. This comes from the notion that networking is about "using" people to get what you want. Although this does happen, networking is really about finding connections with others and viewing the relationship as mutually beneficial. It is not about manipulating others. People don't need to be outgoing or extroverted to be good at networking.

There are many benefits of networking (FCH). Share the different benefits and engage the group in conversation about what each means and how they have seen these benefits in their own lives. Networking:

- Increases your access to information and opportunities (the people you know are in contact with many other people as well)
- Enhances your understanding of others
- Maximizes your effect on others
- Helps you develop meaningful relationships
- Improves your communication and interpersonal skills
- Builds credibility

As we can see, there is definitely some truth in the old saying "It's not what you know, it's who you know." Share a personal example of a positive networking experience when at least one of the listed benefits was experienced.

Ask the group, "Where and how can you find opportunities to network in your lives?" Record the answers for all to see (FCH).

Be sure the following sources are shared:

- Professors and teachers (past, current, and future)
- Classmates
- Coaches, bosses (current and past), mentors
- Family members and family friends
- Roommates and friends (and their parents)
- Campus or professional associations/organizations

Emphasize the importance of getting involved in different opportunities. Not only is the experience important, but making a personal connection with many people is also helpful.

✦ Personal Networking Web

Fifteen minutes

Share that in this next activity participants will be asked to create a personal networking web, to identify the different networks and relationships in their lives, and to identify opportunities for growth.

Share your own personal web (FCH) and answer any questions. Ask participants to put their name in the center of *Personal Networking Web* (Activity #1, SW) and begin drawing their web.

Encourage participants not to think too much. If a person's name or the name of an organization emerges, put it down. It is likely that there is a potential opportunity. When and if there are connections between the different stakeholders, feel free to draw connecting lines between them. (*Allow eight to ten minutes.*)

✦ Personal Networking Web Sharing

Five minutes

Ask participants to connect with another person to share their webs with one another (after they have found a common ground). Encourage participants to add to their web if they think of others to add as a result of sharing with and listening to their partner.

After the pairs have shared their webs, emphasize that everyone in this room is connected to everyone else's web because we are all part of this same experience. There are an infinite number of possible connections and opportunities out there, and sharing these with people helps the world continue to be more and more interconnected. Option: relate this personal web to social networking sites such as Facebook, Ning, or LinkedIn.

Share the following quote as a way to summarize this segment.

The way of the world is meeting people through other people.—Robert Kerrigan

← Personal Networking Action Planning

Five minutes

Ask participants to complete *Personal Networking Action Planning* (Activity #2, SW). This exercise gets participants thinking about how they can use their networks and how they can continue to build their personal network. (*Allow three to four minutes. Play music in the background, if desired.*)

← Wrap Up

Two minutes

Share that developing relationships is a capacity that we can always continue to enhance and develop. There are many opportunities in our lives to connect with people and develop relationships that will be helpful for us, for others, and for our purpose, cause, or vision. Encourage participants to think about how they can build relationships so that they purposefully grow, develop, and maintain connectivity.

Personal Networking Web

Think about the people and organizations that provide you with opportunities to grow (e.g., friends, family, employers, mentors, coaches, supervisors, pastor, rabbi, alumni, current and former classmates). Identify the different networks and relationships in your life that can or will make a difference in who you become or what you do. Don't think too much about this. If a person's name or the name of an organization comes up, go with it. Write it down and draw a line to your circle. If there are connections between the different individuals or groups that you think of, feel free to draw connecting lines between them.

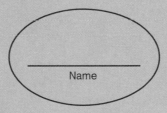

Think about the following questions and jot down your thoughts:

What will you do to develop these relationships?

How can you benefit from these relationships?

What do you contribute to continually cultivate these relationships?

Personal Networking Action Planning

Looking at Activity 1, what patterns do you see in your personal networking web? How would you describe any gaps that you see?

What opportunities do you see in your personal network web that you can use, personally or professionally, in the next three months?

What potential connections with your network can you facilitate for a friend or classmate?

What connections or relationships may require some additional attention or reconnection to maintain this relationship in the future?

How do you see your personal networking web changing in the next three years?

What steps can you take at this point in your life to expand your personal networking web?

MODULE 32

Developing Relationships 2: Finding Each Other

David Zamansky

✦ Focus of Module

Developing relationships is about creating connections between, among, and with people. It is a skill as well as a mindset. This capacity requires emotionally intelligent leaders to build relationships and create a sense of trust and mutual interest. Simply put, individuals, groups, and organizations are stronger, smarter, and more effective when they are rooted in and facilitate positive relationships. Some people assume you have to be outgoing or social to be effective at developing relationships; however, networking experts have discovered that the people who are best at developing relationships are not necessarily gregarious. They possess a combination of skills and the understanding that they need to listen well, know themselves, and know how to develop rapport with others. People who understand the valuable role that others play in making their own lives rich and fulfilling are often the best at developing relationships, regardless of personality type.

Primary Activities

Participants engage in a series of activities to develop relationships among one another.

✦ Learning Objectives and Resources

- To discover commonalities among participants that may not be immediately apparent
- To practice communication skills
- To explore the dynamics of perspective and perception

Total Time

Sixty minutes

Supplies

Drawing Shapes (half as many as participants: one per pair)

Blank paper (two per participant)

Pens, pencils (one per participant)

Random object (something common and neutral, like a purse or a chair)

Rope (a section long enough to stretch across the room to divide the group in half)

Copy of *Emotionally Intelligent Leadership: A Guide for College Students*

✦ Facilitator Preparation Notes

Read Chapter Twenty, Developing Relationships, in *Emotionally Intelligent Leadership: A Guide for College Students* (Shankman & Allen, 2008). (Refer to Appendix A for an overview of the EIL model.) Prepare introductory comments based on your reading.

Be prepared to have a theme for the *Human Camera* exercise. Consider inspiration, energy, focus, and the like. You can give each pair a different theme or some pairs the same theme.

Download *Drawing Shapes* (see page viii) and make a copy for each pair of participants in the *Back-to-Back Communication* exercise.

Have your chosen random object ready for the *Perspectives* exercise.

Have the rope ready to stretch across the center of the room.

✦ Facilitator Tips

If the group is larger than twenty, divide participants into more than one group for the first exercise, *Threads of Commonality*. The goal of this activity is to help people notice that we all share commonalities (liking your favorite sports team, going to the same concert you went to two years ago, having the same extracurricular activity).

Anticipate that participants will be talking about trust and identifying differing perspectives on the same exercise. Discussions should be focused on stepping into the shoes of someone different from you to develop deeper relationships. Knowledge of one's feelings combined with the knowledge of how others are feeling in different situations creates trust, respect, and connections.

For the *Back-to-Back Communication* exercise, arrange participants in parallel lines with listeners on one side and participants with drawings on the other. Try to space those side by side so that they are not too close to each other to minimize the likelihood of looking at each other's drawings.

For the *Cross the Line* exercise, instruct the listeners from the *Back to Back* exercise to be on one side and their partners with the drawing on the other side.

REFERENCE

Shankman, M. L., & Allen, S. J. (2008). *Emotionally intelligent leadership: A guide for college students*. San Francisco: Jossey-Bass.

✦ Introduction: Threads of Commonality

Five minutes

Ask the participants to form a circle.

Once in a circle, inform them that we all have commonalities with each other no matter how different we are; these threads of commonality help us develop relationships.

Ask one participant to introduce him- or herself and talk about him- or herself until another participant can politely interrupt because he or she has found something in common with what the original participant was saying. Then that participant will introduce him- or herself until someone else finds something in common. Proceed until everyone has had a turn.

Suggest that we all now know each other a little more and all of us share something in common. Give examples to highlight, if desired.

✦ Human Camera

Fifteen minutes

Ask participants to partner with someone they do not know. Let pairs know that one half of the pair will have their eyes closed with a hand on the partner's shoulder. The partners with sight will lead their "blind" partners around the room and stop at five different places based on an overall theme that the facilitator announces. When the partners stop, they will say "Click." At the "click" sound, the "blind" partners will quickly open and close their eyes to get a brief look at what their "seeing" partners are trying to show them.

Inform the group that the partners with sight can take their partners to any part of the room and show them whatever they wish. This should be a creative journey or story that is being told with five "pictures."

Give each pair a theme. (*Allow five to six minutes.*)

Once everyone has finished, gather the group in a circle to reflect on the experience. Consider the following questions:

- How did it feel to be led around by a person with sight?
- For the person who could see, how did you create your story?
- What kind of a story was your partner trying to show you?
- What level of trust was involved in this experience?

← Back-to-Back Communication

Twenty minutes

Have participants find a new partner whom they don't know. Instruct the pairs to sit back to back.

Explain that in this exercise, one person will have a blank piece of paper and a pen or pencil, while the other partner will have a drawing with various shapes on it (see *Drawing Shapes*). The partner with the blank piece of paper is not allowed to talk during the exercise while the other partner gives instructions on how to create a drawing.

After ten minutes, consider the following questions:

- In this exercise, which was harder: giving the directions or following the instructions?
- What is important to remember when giving instructions to others?
- Which is more important for developing relationships—speaking or listening? Give your reasons why.

- In what ways is listening important to developing relationships?
- How hard is it to truly listen?

Conclude with the idea that listening closely to others and trying to better understand where others are coming from are important when developing relationships.

✦ Perspective Exercise

Ten minutes

Arrange participants in a circle, put an object in the middle, give everyone a pencil and paper, and tell them to write about what they see and how they feel about it. (*Allow two to three minutes.*)

Have various volunteers, or everyone if possible, share what they wrote.

Do a quick debrief about how this exercise demonstrates how we often have different perspectives about the same "thing." Encourage participants to comment on how important it is to recognize differences in how we approach the world and each other. Ask participants to describe examples of what was shared according to how they might be described:

- Detailed or general
- Pragmatic or romantic
- Functional or descriptive

Conclude by asking, "What does this exercise have to do with developing relationships?". After a few responses, offer that in general, the potential to have different perspectives on relationships is natural and should be expected. The key is remembering that differences do exist and we need to be open to hearing about them.

⊰ Cross the Line

Five minutes

Stretch the rope across the center of the room, with half the group on either side. Quickly go to each group separately and tell them they have two minutes to strategize how they will get as many members from the other group as possible to cross over the rope to their side of the rope (without using any kind of physical touch) in two minutes or less. After two minutes they should begin.

⊰ Wrap Up

One to two minutes

Conclude by highlighting the times in our lives when we draw lines between ourselves and others. Share that it is only when we "cross the line" and see the situation through someone else's eyes that positive relationships are created.

Drawing Shapes

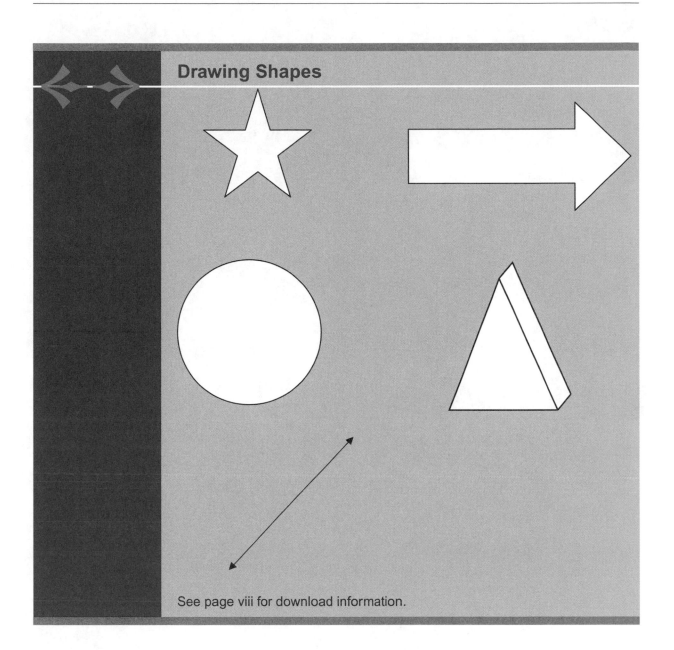

See page viii for download information.

MODULE 33

Teamwork

Karyn Nishimura Sneath

✦ Focus of Module

Teamwork is about working effectively with others in a group. Emotionally intelligent leaders know how to work with others to bring out the best in each team member. By facilitating good communication, creating shared purpose, clarifying roles, and facilitating results, emotionally intelligent leaders foster group cohesion and truly develop a sense of togetherness that leads to desired results. Teamwork is about knowing when to assert and when to hold back. Many leadership experts propose that sometimes the most influential act of leadership is to take a step back and follow. When you know how to work well with others, you create an environment where working together is expected.

Primary Activities

Participants create a collage representing what is important to them as they work in a team, then discuss key characteristics with the group.

✦ Learning Objectives and Resources

- To articulate personal perspectives on teamwork
- To explore different definitions of teamwork
- To identify a personal commitment to enhance collaboration skills

Total Time

Sixty minutes

Supplies

Flipchart, easel, markers

Transparent tape

8 1/2 by 11 paper (one per participant)

Magazines

Optional: glue or glue sticks

Optional: scissors

Copy of *Emotionally Intelligent Leadership: A Guide for College Students*

✦ Facilitator Preparation Notes

Read Chapter Twenty-one, Teamwork, in *Emotionally Intelligent Leadership: A Guide for College Students* (Shankman & Allen, 2008). (Refer to Appendix A for an overview of the EIL model.) Prepare introductory comments based on your reading.

Be prepared to share a personal story of a team that worked well together and one that did not (one to three minutes each). The goal of sharing this story is to offer lessons you have learned when you did not share or verbalize your assumptions about teamwork.

In advance, gather enough magazines to provide at least one for each participant. Be sure to bring a good mix of magazines to choose from (not just women's fashion magazines or a year's worth of *Sports Illustrated*). You can go to the local library and ask for past monthly magazines that will be recycled or destroyed.

Depending on your current supplies, bring a few pairs of scissors. Some people will want them—others will be happy to simply tear pictures and phrases out of the magazines.

◈ Facilitator Tips

During the art activity, some participants may have some anxiety about their artistic abilities. Remind them that they are not being judged or graded on their creation. This is just a visual representation of teamwork.

If you yourself feel uncomfortable with such a project, create an example in advance of the session to get a feel for the nervousness a participant may feel.

The individual sharing time can really get away from you—be sure you know how many participants you have in advance so that you can think through the amount of time you have or are willing to devote to each activity. If the group is larger than twenty, divide into smaller groups of six to eight people and allow two minutes of sharing per person.

REFERENCE

Shankman, M. L., & Allen, S. J. (2008). *Emotionally intelligent leadership: A guide for college students.* San Francisco: Jossey-Bass.

✦ Introduction

Fifteen minutes

Begin with a quick review of Appendix A: EIL Overview. Ask participants to focus on the definition of teamwork. Ask for participants to raise their hands if they have been involved in a team that worked really well together. Ask which of the following they experienced:

- People contributed.
- Team members felt valued.
- The team accomplished a lot—together.

Offer that it is likely that many of us have also been involved in teams that didn't work as well. Ask for a show of hands. Suggest that sometimes teams break down because people have different agendas, goals, and even assumptions about success.

Share a personal story about a time when a team you were involved in didn't work well because team members had *different assumptions* about how to work together as a unit.

Offer that by sharing this story, you hope that participants will be reminded that we can learn from our mistakes. An important first step is to think intentionally about our assumptions about teamwork. We all carry perceptions about teamwork from parents, teachers, coaches, and other mentors, as well as visions and parables that have guided our thoughts about working as a cohesive unit.

Instruct participants that they will now have some time to put some of those perceptions on paper.

✦ Art Activity: Creation Time

Ten minutes

Give each participant a sheet of blank paper, some markers, tape or glue, and at least one magazine. Ask them to create a visual representation of specific phrases or images that convey their assumptions about teamwork. They can trade magazines, use just one magazine, or use their own artistic skills and creativity.

Encourage participants to stay focused on the task: representing what is important to them individually as they work in a team (by sharing resources).

Share with participants that they will have a chance to share their individual creation with others, so drawings can be realistic or abstract. Let those with any anxiety about their artistic abilities know that they can simply tear out images from the magazines to express their ideas if desired.

✦ Individual Sharing

Twenty minutes

Invite each participant to share the themes in his or her artwork. They do not have to share every detail, but they should tell others what is most important to them regarding teamwork.

Note: If the group is larger than twenty, divide into smaller discussion groups of six to eight people and allow two to three minutes per person.

✦ Debrief

Ten minutes

After all have had a chance to share their artwork, facilitate a large group conversation. Consider the following questions:

- What commonalities did you hear as we shared our assumptions about teamwork? Write up responses on a flipchart (FCH). Label the flipchart "Commonalities."

- What are our differences?
- What are some lessons to keep in mind as we work to strengthen our team and our team relationships?
- What are our commitments to each other as we focus on collaboration and team contributions? Write up responses on another page of the flipchart (FCH). Label this flipchart "Commitments."

← Wrap Up

Five minutes

Review the commonalities and commitments written from the previous conversation on the two flipchart pages (FCH). Try to summarize and even combine the commonalities for a more concise list.

Review the commitments generated from the last question. Suggest that this is an important list to keep in mind in the future.

Close with the following quotation:

Teamwork is the ability to work together toward a common vision. The ability to direct individual accomplishments toward organizational objectives. It is the fuel that allows common people to attain uncommon results.—Andrew Carnegie (1835–1919), American businessman and philanthropist

MODULE 34

Capitalizing on Difference 1: Exploring Privilege
Tara Edberg

⬸ Focus of Module

Capitalizing on difference is about building on assets that stem from differences between people. Capitalizing on difference suggests that differences are seen as assets, not barriers. Difference may mean race, socioeconomic status, religion, sexual orientation, or gender as well as ability, personality, or philosophy. When capitalized on, these differences create a larger perspective—a more inclusive view. Emotionally intelligent leaders use these differences as an opportunity to help others grow, develop, and ultimately build on them. Whatever they may be, you have the capacity to learn about these differences. When you capitalize on these assets, you understand the power that can be drawn from a wider perspective, set of ideas, talents, or world views. To capitalize on difference, you must possess a desire to learn, have an open mind, and be willing to change your mind. Doing this can be challenging—and also rewarding for you, the people with whom you interact, and the cause or organization that you serve.

Primary Activities

> Participants explore their understanding of difference through watching a video clip, personal reflection, and writing about areas of privilege in their own lives.

☚ Learning Objectives and Resources

- To explore the concepts of social identity and privilege
- To learn how multiple perspectives influence your perceptions
- To experience how different personalities and perceptions influence a group task

Total Time

Sixty minutes

Supplies

Diversity Wheel worksheet (one per participant)

Privilege Statements worksheet (one per participant)

Glory Road (movie)

Audiovisual equipment to show the *Glory Road* clip

Flipchart, markers, easel

Copy of *Emotionally Intelligent Leadership: A Guide for College Students*

☚ Facilitator Preparation Notes

> Read Chapter Twenty-two, Capitalizing on Difference, in *Emotionally Intelligent Leadership: A Guide for College Students*

(Shankman & Allen, 2008). (Refer to Appendix A for an overview of the EIL model.) Prepare introductory comments based on your reading.

Have *Glory Road* cued to the scene where Coach Haskins announces he is going to play only the black players.

Familiarize yourself with the *Diversity Wheel* and *Privilege Statements* activities and the activity that the participants will do. Prepare a two-minute personal example of your own social identity that you can share with participants (for example, "I work with a fraternity, and sometimes when I walk into their house I am the only woman there. At that point my gender becomes my salient identity").

Write your own privilege statements. You can add these to the worksheet if you'd like.

← Facilitator Tips

Watch *Glory Road* in its entirety, if you have not seen it previously.

If you have never written privilege statements, you may want to read "White Privilege: Unpacking the Invisible Knapsack" by Peggy McIntosh (1989), or additional information on privilege, before facilitating this module.

You should anticipate some resistance to the word *privilege* and the concept in general. Some participants will deny that they have privilege. This module may challenge some participants to think about concepts they may have not examined.

Asking participants to move past accepting difference to celebrating it can be a challenge. Be prepared for resistance, confusion, and/or disagreement.

REFERENCES

McIntosh, P. M. (1989, July-August). White privilege: Unpacking the invisible knapsack. *Peace and Freedom*, 10–12.

Shankman, M. L., & Allen, S. J. (2008). *Emotionally intelligent leadership: A guide for college students*. San Francisco: Jossey-Bass.

✦ Introduction

Five minutes

Begin by showing the scene from *Glory Road* where Coach Haskins announces he is going to play only the black players. After watching the scene, ask participants to comment on what they saw. Consider the following questions:

- What sort of differences did the team recognize within itself?
- How were these differences an asset to the Texas Western team?
- In what ways was the team strengthened by these differences? How was the team challenged?

Transition to the next activity by suggesting that before we can use difference as an asset, we must first understand what differences are. Explain how this capacity fits within the model of emotionally intelligent leadership. Provide a quick review of Appendix A: EIL Overview. Suggest that capitalizing on difference also means that we must have a solid understanding of ourselves before we can lead others.

✦ The Diversity Wheel

Fifteen minutes

Explain the concept of social identity and refer to examples on the *Diversity Wheel* (Activity #1, SW).

Offer that our identities can change. When we think about ourselves, we see multiple dimensions that make up who we are. At any point, these identities may be more salient to us. The idea of saliency is that there are times in our lives (or even in our day) when certain aspects of our identity will be more important to us. This may be based on our environment, our interactions, or an activity we're engaged in. When we look at the Diversity Wheel, it is imperative to realize we are all at different points. Some of us are more connected to our race than to our gender. Others are more aware of their class than their religion.

Share a personal example.

These aspects give us an opportunity to understand ourselves, especially how we react to others.

Ask participants to now use the *Diversity Wheel* model and circle which aspects make up their social identity. They should feel free to circle aspects from either or both wheels. (*Allow four minutes.*)

Have participants locate a partner and discuss whether there are any pieces missing from the *Diversity Wheel* model and which aspects they feel influence them most. (*Allow five minutes.*)

⬥ Privilege Statements

Fifteen minutes

Share that with difference comes privilege. Ask participants for their understanding or definition of the word *privilege*. After a couple of volunteers speak, share the following:

> I have come to see privilege as an invisible package of unearned assets that I can count on cashing in each day, but about which I was "meant" to remain oblivious. Privilege is like an invisible weightless knapsack of special provisions, maps, passports, codebooks, visas, clothes, tools, and blank checks. (McIntosh, 1989, p.1)

With this perspective, ask participants to consider whether privilege comes with each aspect of identity. (*Allow one or two minutes.*)

Review *Privilege Statements* (Activity #2, SW). Ask participants to circle the ten privilege statements that apply to them. (*Allow five to seven minutes.*)

Ask participants to share a statement of their choice.

With the time remaining, use the following questions for discussion:

- What are the social influences that affect your identity?
- Had you thought about this topic before? If so, what caused you to think about it? If not, how will you think about this in the future?
- How does knowing this information about people you are leading or who are members of your organization help you in your leadership?
- How does this knowledge of yourself influence you as a leader?

✦ "Change the Tire" Activity

Fifteen minutes

Divide participants into small groups of four or five. Share with the group that you are now going to shift to a different perspective.

Set the scene. (*Allow five minutes.*)

> You are all riding in one car through the desert. You realize that the right rear tire has just gone flat. Your objective is to work as a team to identify a list of tasks you will need to complete to change the tire and get back on the road. You do not have a cell phone or any other means of communicating for help. You are one hundred miles from the closest service station. The car has an automatic transmission and a normal-sized spare tire.

Give the teams five minutes to complete their lists. Tell participants to number the tasks so that the total is evident. If possible, send teams to separate areas to develop their lists.

When the teams return, ask for the total number of items from each list and chart these totals on the flipchart. There will normally be a significant variance in the totals. Ask the team with the lowest total to review its list starting with step #1.

Ask the group which steps were left out. Normally some significant steps are left out. For instance:

- Pull the car off the highway.
- Stop the car and put it in park.
- Open the door or the trunk.

(The key here is to have fun while pointing out what's missing.)

Once you have identified some of the steps that were missed by the first team, be sure to tell them that they aren't being picked on; every group that shares its list will be analyzed by the whole group. Then go to the next team, starting with Step #1, and go through part of their list, pointing out some of the missing steps. Continue with the next team, giving each team an opportunity to review parts of their list. Be sure to keep it lighthearted and fun.

Ask the participants what they learned from this activity. If not already voiced by volunteers, supplement their responses with some of the following thoughts:

- People perceive the same process differently.
- People who are given the same goal will often approach it from different perspectives.
- Steps that are critical to the success of a process can be left out or placed out of sequence.
- If people perceive that a process has fewer steps, they will have different expectations.

✦ Wrap Up

Five minutes

Begin by asking participants how they connect this last activity with the first two. Feel free to share your own thoughts.

Conclude with the following discussion questions as time allows:

- What part of today did you find easy? What was challenging?
- What are the benefits of having people with different strengths on your team?
- Why is it important to celebrate differences?
- When was a time that you capitalized on difference? What happened as a result?
- Based on today's activities, what action steps can you take to enhance your own leadership?

The Diversity Wheel

Diversity refers to the multifaceted ways in which human beings can be both similar and different. The Diversity Wheel model illustrates the primary and secondary dimensions of diversity that exert an effect on each of us at home, at work, and in society. Although each dimension adds a layer of complexity to individual identity, it is the dynamic interaction among all the dimensions that influences self-image, values, opportunities, and expectations. Together, the primary and secondary dimensions of diversity give definition and meaning to our lives by contributing to a synergistic, integrated whole—the diverse person. *Circle the dimensions that relate to you.*

Primary Dimensions

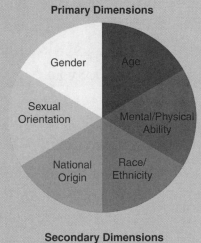

Secondary Dimensions

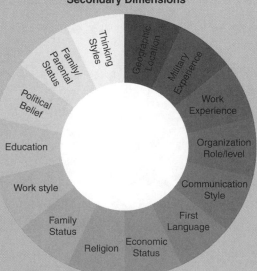

Source: Tara Edberg, referenced from *Implementing Diversity* © 1996. Irwin Professional Publishing.

Privilege Statements

Consider the following:

> I have come to see privilege as an invisible package of unearned assets that I can count on cashing in each day, but about which I was " meant " to remain oblivious. Privilege is like an invisible weightless knapsack of special provisions, maps, passports, codebooks, visas, clothes, tools, and blank checks. (McIntosh, 1999, p. 1)

With this definition in mind, circle up to ten statements that you believe are true for you.

1. I make a dollar to every seventy-eight cents a woman makes.
2. I feel safe walking down the street at night without a fear that I will be sexually assaulted or raped.
3. I can speak about my political beliefs without being considered overly religious.
4. When I go shopping, I can do so without being followed or harassed.
5. When I am out in public, I do not have to worry that people may think I am a terrorist.
6. The academic calendar revolves around my religious calendar/holidays.
7. When I watch TV, I see people of my race widely represented in a positive manner.
8. I believe no one thinks I am unhealthy, unfit, or unemployable because of my body type.
9. I can be reasonably sure that when I wear a symbol of my religion, people do not fear me.
10. I can criticize my government without being seen as an outsider.
11. I can be talkative or moody without it being attributed to my gender.
12. I can slap another man's rear end after a football game and say "Good Game" without it being attributed to my sexuality.
13. I can turn on the TV and see family units similar to mine depicted positively on TV.
14. I have traveled to other countries and toured several states in the United States.

(Continued)

15. When I testify in a court of law, I am sworn in on my religion's holy book.

16. I can enter every building on campus without worrying about the route I take.

17. I am sure that no one thinks I am unintelligent because of my accent.

18. I can buy new clothes, go out to dinner, or see a dentist, doctor, or lawyer when I need to.

Source: Adapted from McIntosh, P. M. (1989, July-August). White privilege: Unpacking the invisible knapsack. *Peace and Freedom,* 10–12.

Now consider the following questions:

• What are the social influences that affect your identity?

• Had you thought about this before? If so, what causes you to think about these things? If not, how will you think about this in the future?

• How does this knowledge of yourself influence your leadership?

• Do you know this information about people with whom you work? If so, how? If not, how might you learn it?

MODULE 35

Capitalizing on Difference 2:
Our Identities

Susana Muñoz

✦ Focus of Module

Capitalizing on difference is about building on assets that stem from differences between people. Capitalizing on difference suggests that differences are seen as assets, not barriers. Difference may mean race, socioeconomic status, religion, sexual orientation, or gender as well as ability, personality, or philosophy. When capitalized on, these differences create a larger perspective—a more inclusive view. Emotionally intelligent leaders use these differences as an opportunity to help others grow, develop, and ultimately build on them. Whatever they may be, you have the capacity to learn about these differences. When you capitalize on these assets, you understand the power that can be drawn from a wider perspective, set of ideas, talents, or world views. To capitalize on difference, you must possess a desire to learn, have an open mind, and be willing to change your mind. Doing this can be challenging—and also rewarding for you, the people with whom you interact, and the cause or organization that you serve.

Primary Activities

Participants create a braid of colored yarn reflective of their identity and work in small groups to develop an action plan.

✦ Learning Objectives and Resources

- To reflect on the multiple identities with which participants identify
- To explore the concept of what an inclusive campus looks like

Total Time

Sixty minutes

Supplies

Braids of Multiple Identities worksheet (one per participant)

Action Planning worksheet (one per participant)

Flipchart, markers, and easel

Yarn (eight different colors, cut into ten-inch pieces; enough for three pieces per participant)

Bowl

Strips of small paper (one per participant)

Pens, pencils (one per participant)

Audiovisual to support PowerPoint or similar program, if desired

Copy of *Emotionally Intelligent Leadership: A Guide for College Students*

✦ Facilitator Preparation Notes

Read Chapter Twenty-two, Capitalizing on Difference, in *Emotionally Intelligent Leadership: A Guide for College Students*

(Shankman & Allen, 2008). (Refer to Appendix A for an overview of the EIL model.) Prepare introductory comments based on your reading.

You will need to prepare your own personal stories about which identities are most apparent in your daily life. Be comfortable with speaking about how these identities impact your values and actions.

Prepare the following flipcharts or slides:

- Ground rules of communication

  Speak your truth with care.

  Be open to challenges as well as gestures of support.

  Be open to learning.

- To create a more inclusive campus, what can we

  Start doing?

  Stop doing?

  Continue doing?

← Facilitator Tips

Conversations about differences can be emotionally charged. Each of us brings our own perspective and life experiences into our own identity development. It is important that facilitator(s) set ground rules of communication that promote validation of individual viewpoints.

The term *braids of multiple identities* comes from the theory of critical race feminism, specifically from a Chicana scholar named Francisca Gonzalez. Here's an example of a personal statement:

> When I think about my multiple identities, I think about the weaving of different identities to form new ones, I think about the strength it carries as we unmask our personal nuances to gain clarity of ourselves. Most importantly, I think about how messy my "braids" may seem to

others but to me it's my form of resistance. My braids of multiple identities is my story, and within my story we each have different meanings, feelings, values, histories, and experiences, which depending on the social context are often validated or stifled.

REFERENCES

Gonzalez, F. E. (1999). Formations of "Mexicana"ness: Trenzas de identidades multiples [Growing up Mexicana: Braids of multiple identities]. In L. Parker, D. Deyhle, & S. Villenas (Eds.), *Race is . . . race isn't: Critical race theory and qualitative studies in education* (pp. 156–172). Boulder, CO: Perseus.

Shankman, M. L., & Allen, S. J. (2008). *Emotionally intelligent leadership: A guide for college students.* San Francisco: Jossey-Bass.

✦ Introduction

Five minutes

Begin with a quick review of Appendix A: EIL Overview. Ask participants to focus on the definition of *capitalizing on difference*. Make a short comment about the importance of the topic to college campuses and student development.

Review the ground rules of communication (FCH):

- Speak your truth with care. *(Verbal and nonverbal)*
- Be open to challenges as well as gestures of support.
- Be open to learning. *(About yourself, about others, about our communities)*

Solicit additional suggestions from participants and record them.

✦ Braids of Multiple Identities

Thirty minutes

Offer that today, we are going to reflect on our own *Braids of Multiple Identities* (Activity #3, SW). Assign participants to groups of four.

Give the following instructions:

You will create your own braids using three colors of yarn. One color can reflect an identity and you will "name" your identity to match any color of your choice. Give more time to choosing your three key identities and the colors that represent them; don't worry if you're unable to finish braiding your yarn. If someone in your group doesn't know how to braid, be sure to take the time to show them. Once everyone in your group has chosen their identities and yarn colors, I will ask you to discuss your identities in response to the following questions:

What are your multiple identities? (Give an example of one for yourself.)

What do (or might) your multiple identities mean as a student leader?

Explain when or how your multiple identities are validated or invalidated on your college campus.

Walk around the groups and listen intently to the conversations. Provide clarification if asked, or if you notice the conversation is not exactly on target. Give participants "five minute" and "one minute" warnings.

Reconvene the group and ask for volunteers to share their thoughts and the activity. Ask for comments about the activity. Add additional questions as desired.

✦ Taking Action

Twenty minutes

Suggest that now that we've discussed our multiple identities, it's time to turn our attention to how we can turn this conversation into *Action Planning* (Activity #4, SW) for our organizations or institutions.

Have participants return to their small group and think about how to be more inclusive of the multiple identities of others by responding to the following questions (FCH):

To create a more inclusive campus/organization, what can we

- Start doing?
- Stop doing?
- Continue doing?

(Allow ten minutes.)

Reserve ten minutes for each group to report out their ideas.

✦ Wrap Up

Five minutes

Ask participants what message they want to give to their fellow participants about how individuals can work to create a community/organization that capitalizes on difference.

Distribute small pieces of paper and ask participants to form a large circle. Instruct participants to write a short message of encouragement, advice, or wisdom and place it in a bowl. When everyone is finished, pass the bowl around the circle, allowing each participant to select a message from the bowl and read it out loud.

Offer final thoughts as appropriate.

Braids of Multiple Identities

Individuals are composed of different identities. Consider the diagram:

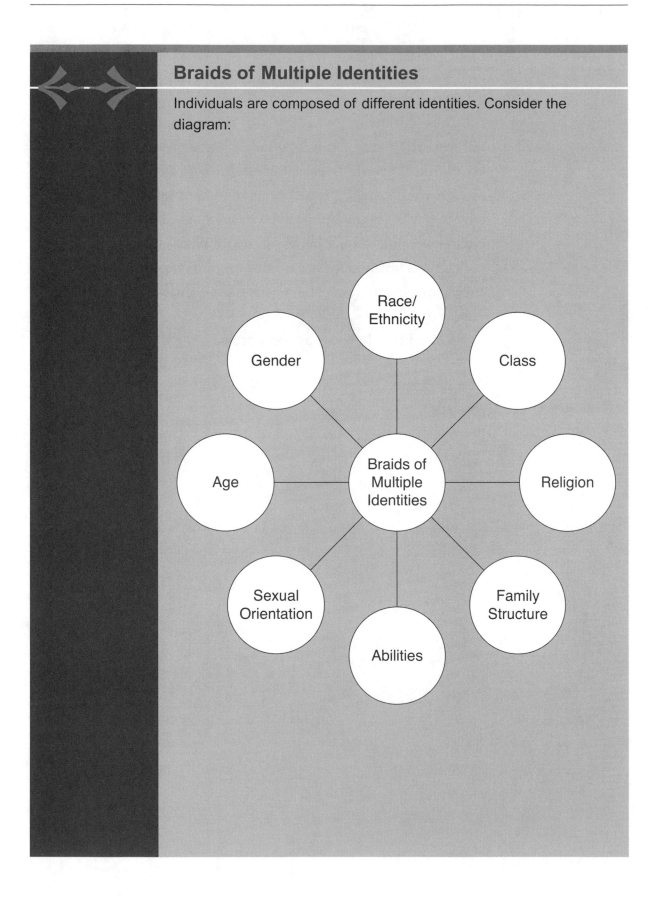

These are just some examples of different identities that individuals possess. From the identities shown, choose three that reflect the most influential aspects of who you are, or write your own. The point is to identify the most influential aspects of who you are.

1.

2.

3.

What do your multiple identities mean for you as a leader?

When or how are your multiple identities validated or invalidated?

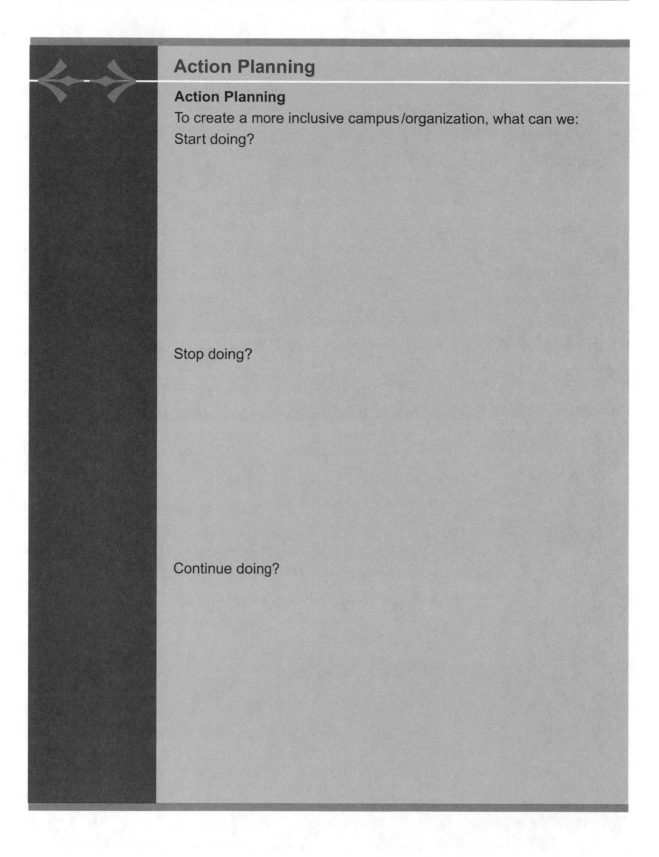

Action Planning

Action Planning

To create a more inclusive campus/organization, what can we:
Start doing?

Stop doing?

Continue doing?

APPENDIX A: EIL OVERVIEW

Leadership is available to all of us. In fact, you do not need a formal title or position to lead others (think of Gandhi and Martin Luther King, Jr.). Sometimes you make a conscious decision to pursue a leadership role; other times the opportunity simply presents itself and you "step up." Either way, we agree with Joseph Rost (1993), who suggests that leadership is "an influence relationship among leaders and followers who intend real changes that reflect their mutual purposes" (p. 102). In other words, leaders and followers often collaborate toward a common end point. Each of us, often in a moment's notice, move from leader to follower depending on the context. So we suggest that leaders and followers can behave in an emotionally intelligent manner—it's not just about emotionally intelligent leadership, it's about emotionally intelligent followership as well.

Emotionally intelligent leadership asserts that an individual must be conscious of three fundamental facets that contribute to the leadership dynamic: consciousness of context, of self, and of others. These three facets overlap yet are independent of each other. Each facet consists of specific capacities that can be developed. A person's ability to monitor all three facets intentionally will enhance the person's ability to lead effectively.

Consciousness of Context

- *Environmental awareness:* Thinking intentionally about the environment of a leadership situation. The larger system, or environment, directly influences an individual's ability to lead. Aspects of the environment affect the psychological and interpersonal dynamics of any human interaction.

Emotionally intelligent leaders are in tune with a variety of factors such as community traditions and customs, the political environment, and major institutions (e.g., religion, government).

• *Group savvy*: Interpreting the situation and/or networks of an organization. Every group has written/unwritten rules, ways of operating, customs and rituals, power dynamics, internal politics, inherent values, and so forth. Emotionally intelligent leaders know how to diagnose and interpret these dynamics. Demonstrating group savvy enables one to have a direct influence on the work of the group.

Consciousness of Self

• *Emotional self-perception*: Identifying your emotions and reactions and their impact on you. Emotional self-perception means that individuals are acutely aware of their feelings (in real time). In addition, emotional self-perception means understanding how these feelings lead to behaviors. Having emotional self-perception also means that emotionally intelligent leaders have a choice as to how they respond. This capacity enables one to differentiate between the emotions felt and the actions taken. In most situations, both healthy and unhealthy responses are available.

• *Honest self-understanding*: Being aware of your own strengths and limitations. Honest self-understanding means that an individual celebrates and honors their strengths and talents while acknowledging and addressing limitations. Honest self-understanding means accepting the good and bad about one's personality, abilities, and ideas. When emotionally intelligent leaders demonstrate honest self-understanding, they embody a foundational capacity of effective leadership—the ability to see a more holistic self and understand how this impacts their leadership.

- *Healthy self-esteem:* Having a balanced sense of self. Emotionally intelligent leaders possess a high level of self-worth, are confident in their abilities, and are willing to stand up for what they believe in. They are also balanced by a sense of humility and the ability to create space for the opinions, perspectives, and thoughts of others.

- *Emotional self-control:* Consciously moderating your emotions and reactions. Although feeling emotions and being aware of them is part of this statement, so too is regulating them. Emotional self-control is about both awareness (being conscious of feelings) and action (managing emotions and knowing when and how to show them). Recognizing feelings, understanding how and when to demonstrate those feelings appropriately, and taking responsibility for one's emotions (versus being victims of them) are critical components of this capacity.

- *Authenticity:* Being transparent and trustworthy. Authenticity is a complex concept that emphasizes the importance of being trustworthy, transparent, and living in a way in which words match actions and vice versa. This is no small order. Being authentic means, in part, that emotionally intelligent leaders follow through on commitments and present themselves and their motives in an open and honest manner.

- *Flexibility:* Being open and adaptive to changing situations. The best laid plans don't always come to fruition, so emotionally intelligent leaders need to be responsive to change and open to feedback. By thinking creatively and using their problem-solving skills, emotionally intelligent leaders engage others in determining a new way to reach their goals.

- *Achievement:* Being driven to improve according to personal standards. An important nuance of this capacity is the role of personal standards. Individuals often know achievement when they see and feel it. Instead of letting others define what achievement looks like, emotionally intelligent leaders pursue their passions and goals to a self-determined level of accomplishment.

This drive produces results and may inspire others to become more focused in their efforts or at to work increased levels as well.

- *Optimism:* Being positive. Emotionally intelligent leaders demonstrate a healthy, positive outlook and display a positive regard for the future. Optimism is a powerful force that many overlook. When demonstrated effectively, optimism is contagious and spreads throughout a group or organization.

- *Initiative:* Wanting and seeking opportunities. Emotionally intelligent leaders understand and take initiative. This means being assertive and seeking out opportunities. Emotionally intelligent leaders have to both see the opportunity for change and make it happen. Demonstrating initiative means that individuals take action and help the work of the group move forward.

Consciousness of Others

- *Empathy:* Understanding others from their perspective. Emotionally intelligent leadership and, more specifically, the capacity of empathy are about perceiving the emotions of others. When leaders display empathy, they have the opportunity to build healthier relationships, manage difficult situations, and develop trust more effectively. Being empathetic requires an individual to have a high level of self-awareness as well as awareness of others.

- *Citizenship:* Recognizing and fulfilling your responsibility for others or the group. Emotionally intelligent leaders must be aware of what it means to be a part of something bigger than themselves. An essential component is to fulfill the ethical and moral obligations inherent in the values of the community. As a result, emotionally intelligent leaders know when to give of themselves for the benefit of others and the larger group.

- *Inspiration:* Motivating and moving others toward a shared vision. Being perceived as an inspirational individual by others is an important capacity of emotionally intelligent leadership. Inspiration works through relationships. Effective leadership entails generating feelings of optimism and commitment to organizational goals through individual actions, words, and accomplishments.

• *Influence:* Demonstrating skills of persuasion. Emotionally intelligent leaders have the ability to persuade others with information, ideas, emotion, behavior, and a strong commitment to organizational values and purpose. They involve others to engage in a process of mutual exploration and action.

• *Coaching:* Helping others enhance their skills and abilities. Emotionally intelligent leaders know that they cannot do everything themselves. They need others to become a part of the endeavor. Coaching is about intentionally helping others demonstrate their talent and requires the emotionally intelligent leader to prioritize the time to foster the development of others in the group—not just themselves.

• *Change agent:* Seeking out and working with others toward new directions. As change agents, emotionally intelligent leaders look for opportunities for improvement or innovation—they think about possibilities and are future oriented. They see how change may benefit one person, an organization, or a whole community, and work to make this change happen.

• *Conflict management:* Identifying and resolving problems and issues with others. Emotionally intelligent leaders understand that conflict is part of any leadership experience. When managed effectively, conflict can foster great innovation. At times conflict is overt and may involve anger, raised voices, or high levels of frustration. Other times conflict is below the surface and shows itself only through cliques, side conversations, and apathy. Emotionally intelligent leaders are aware of these dynamics and work to manage them.

• *Developing relationships:* Creating connections between, among, and with people. Developing relationships is a skill as well as a mind-set. This capacity requires emotionally intelligent leaders to build relationships and create a sense of trust and mutual interest. Simply put, individuals, groups, and organizations are stronger, smarter, and more effective when they are rooted in and facilitate positive relationships.

• *Teamwork:* Working effectively with others in a group. Emotionally intelligent leaders know how to work with others to bring out the best in each team member. By facilitating good communication, creating shared purpose, clarifying roles, and facilitating results, emotionally intelligent leaders foster group cohesion and truly develop a sense of togetherness that leads to desired results.

• *Capitalizing on differences:* Building on assets that come from differences with others. Capitalizing on difference suggests that differences are seen as assets, not barriers. Difference may mean race, socio-economic status, religion, sexual orientation, or gender as well as ability, personality, or philosophy. When capitalized upon, these differences create a larger perspective—a more inclusive view. Emotionally intelligent leaders use these differences as an opportunity to help others grow, develop, and ultimately capitalize on them.

These modules are written as lesson plans; they can be used in either formal or informal learning environments. Whether presented in a class or a workshop at a retreat, three phases should be considered every time you plan to use your selected module(s).

← Preparation Phase

Have you looked through the entire selection of modules and identified those most appropriate to meet your learning objectives?

Each module begins with a description of the focus of the module, primary activities, and learning objectives. This information should guide your decision, but be sure you read through the entire module to get a feel for both the content that will be covered and the process you will facilitate. You will need to read through the module a few times to be comfortable with your role, the facilitation of the activities, and how to present the material in a way that is authentic. You will also want to be sure that you have access to the necessary supplies. The more specific your objectives, the more likely you are to facilitate a positive learning experience for your participants.

How much time will you have with the participants?

- Is this a one-time opportunity (for example, one class session or a workshop at a conference) or will you have the group over a series of days, weeks, or months (for example,

a full semester class, a quarterly leadership program, or a
multiday retreat)?

- How long do you have with participants? None of the
  modules can be fully experienced in less than forty-five
  minutes; a few even run for ninety minutes.

What have you done to create the desired learning environment?

The modules assume that an interactive learning experience
will unfold. For these modules to be successful, you will need
to create an environment where participants know from the outset that their voices will be heard and their active participation
is expected. We recommend following the 80/20 rule—the participants speak 80% of the time, the facilitator 20%.

Does the session fit?

Based on the many attributes of your participants (for example,
physical ability, purpose of coming together, year in school, gender) and your learning objectives, be sure the chosen modules
are appropriate. Is the tone of the module appropriate for your
participants? Will the activities of the module resonate
with your participants?

Have you practiced the module on a group prior to going "live" with the students?

Your participants will benefit greatly if they are not experiencing
your first pass at the module. We strongly recommend practicing
each module prior to conducting it with students. This can be
accomplished by approaching colleagues, friends, family
members, and co-facilitators to help you prepare. By doing so,
you will ensure that you and the participants have a better
experience with each of the activities.

✦ Facilitation Phase

How have you prepared the participants for the experience?

Most modules begin with the first statement that you should make or the instructions you should give for the activity. Prior to facilitating the module, you may want to give the participants an opportunity to quickly introduce themselves (if they don't already know one another). If you're new to the group, you should introduce yourself as well. Consider setting the tone for the learning by playing music as participants enter the room or displaying quotes posted for participants to see. An important first step for effectively facilitating the learning experience is to create a positive and safe learning environment, both physically (for example, room setup, temperature, and so on) and emotionally.

How well are you paying attention to the verbal and nonverbal cues of the participants?

Suggested time periods are indicated for each activity, short presentations of information, or discussion or debrief segment of the module. These are *recommended* times—equally important is your sense of the audience. If you engage the participants in a meaningful conversation and it runs a few minutes long because the energy of the group is there, be ready to adapt and cut short a subsequent section. *Remember*, your role is to facilitate, not to present or lecture. This means to pay particular attention to the learners and what their needs and interests are.

How are you encouraging participation from the participants?

As a facilitator, you've been given curriculum that strives to put the responsibility of learning in the hands of the participants. Your role is to guide them along the path and help them explore their own ideas. Share your own ideas (as relevant), but the focus should be on participants creating their own knowledge and understanding. Discussion questions are posed as open-ended questions; lecturettes offer chunks of information that participants then engage with through active learning, reflection, and/or dialogue. Your role as a facilitator is to stimulate, evoke, and encourage the participants so the focus is on the learning, not the teaching.

↢ Follow-up Phase

How will you evaluate the participants' learning experience?

- Use a simple evaluation form for participants to complete. Ask them at the end of the session to write their responses to the following questions:
  1. What was the best part of today's session?
  2. What do you wish had been done differently?
  3. What is one idea you want to remember from today's session?
- Develop a more complete assessment of the experience by connecting the learning with the stated learning objectives or your larger learning outcomes. Consider having participants complete the assessment at the end of the experience and again perhaps one week or one month later.
- Use an online assessment tool and send an email to all participants asking them to assess how much they learned in relation to the different content areas and/or learning objectives of the module.

How will you evaluate your own facilitation of the learning experience?

- Ask for written feedback from participants at the end of the session (for example, how well did the facilitator contribute to the learning experience?).

- Reflect on your experience as the facilitator. Consider the following questions:

  - How did you prepare for the session?
  - Did you practice with another group beforehand?
  - Was your preparation sufficient for facilitating the learning experience?
  - How well did you prepare the participants for the learning?
  - What did you do to contribute to a positive learning environment?
  - If you could do it again, what would you do in the same way? Differently?

Please provide us with feedback, observations, or additional resources to consider (shankman@mlsconsulting.net and sallen @jcu.edu). We would love to hear about your experiences with the sessions. Suggestions for improvement are welcomed.

These modules can be used in many different ways. Fundamentally, we see their utilization as stand-alone learning experiences, combined to create a retreat agenda, or used in a formal classroom environment. Consider the following program designs.

Workshop

- Match the goals of the workshop with the focus of the module and the learning objectives.
- Be sure the time you have available matches the total time stated for the module.
- Prepare participants with appropriate information before the learning experience—match the publicity or the written description with content from the module. Make it interesting so that it evokes curiosity and participants can see the relevance of the module to their role.
- The modules are not written specifically for a particular population—the depth of the material will depend on the experience of the participants and the comfort and familiarity of the facilitator with the content of the module itself.

One-Day Retreat or Conference

Consider the following possible outlines for a day-long learning experience.

Option A: Exploring Emotionally Intelligent Leadership

Welcome and Overview (thirty minutes)	General session to define emotionally intelligent leadership and why it matters—focus on the overall model and the three facets (consciousness of context, consciousness of self, consciousness of others).
Breakout: Consciousness of Self (sixty minutes)	Offer concurrent sessions so that no session has more than fifteen to twenty participants.
Break (fifteen minutes)	
Breakout: Consciousness of Self (sixty minutes)	Offer concurrent sessions so that no session has more than fifteen to twenty participants. Repeat the same set as before so that participants have the opportunity to learn about two different capacities in this facet.
Lunch (forty minutes)	Either have a speaker or allow for unstructured time.
Breakout: Consciousness of Others (sixty minutes)	Offer concurrent sessions so that no session has more than fifteen to twenty participants.
Break (fifteen minutes)	
Breakout: Consciousness of Others (sixty minutes)	Offer concurrent sessions so that no session has more than fifteen to twenty participants. Repeat the same set as before so that participants have the opportunity to learn about two different capacities in this facet.
Breakout: Consciousness of Context (sixty minutes)	Offer concurrent sessions so that no session has more than fifteen to twenty participants.
Conclusion and Wrap-up (twenty minutes)	Provide an opportunity for closure of the learning experience as well as evaluation.

Option B: Focus on Self

Welcome and Overview (fifteen minutes)	Create a positive learning environment and offer a brief overview of the day.
A Look Inward (ninety minutes)	Administer *Emotionally Intelligent Leadership for Students: Inventory.*
Break (fifteen minutes)	
Breakout: Consciousness of Self (sixty minutes)	Divide into small discussion groups (no more than fifteen) to review results of the assessment.
Lunch (forty minutes)	
Breakout: Honest Self-Understanding (sixty minutes)	Facilitate the module with the same small group to provide a greater level of trust and familiarity.
Break (fifteen minutes)	
Breakout: Consciousness of Others (sixty minutes)	Select which module(s) to facilitate to give participants an opportunity to look further into their capacities of consciousness of others. This could be done in either the same small group or different small groups. Multiple sessions could be offered concurrently on the same capacity or they could be on different capacities.
Breakout: Consciousness of Context (sixty minutes)	Determine which module(s) to offer to small groups to look further into a capacity of consciousness of context. Same options as above.
Conclusion and Wrap-up (twenty minutes)	

✦ General Course Syllabus

General Sixteen-Week Class

Class 1	Introductions	Review expectations
		Course overview
Class 2	Community Building	Create a positive learning environment
Class 3	What Is Theory/	Overview of theory
	What Is	Overview of relevant leadership theory
	Leadership?	Personal definitions of leadership
Class 4	What Is Emotional	Overview of emotional intelligence theory
	Intelligence?	Personal reflection on emotional intelligence
Class 5	My EIL	*Emotionally Intelligent Leadership for*
		Students: Inventory
Class 6	My EIL	Discuss results
Classes 7–8	Consciousness	Review facet and capacities
	of Context	Hands-on learning experiences
Classes 9–11	Consciousness	Review facet and capacities
	of Self	Hands-on learning experiences
Classes 12–14	Consciousness	Review facet and capacities
	of Others	Hands-on learning experiences
Class 15	Putting It All	Comprehensive learning experience of EIL
	Together	Developing an action plan
Class 16	Presentations	Present personal action plans
	and Feedback	Receive feedback

General Ten-Week Class

Class 1	Introductions	Review expectations
	Community Building	Course overview
		Create a positive learning environment
Class 2	What Is Theory/	Overview of theory
	What Is Leadership?	Overview of relevant leadership theory
		Personal definitions of leadership
Class 3	What Is Emotional	Overview of emotional intelligence theory
	Intelligence?	Personal reflection on emotional
		intelligence

General Ten-Week Class

Class 4	My EIL	*Emotionally Intelligent Leadership for Students: Inventory*
Classes 5–6	Consciousness of Context	Review facet and capacities Hands-on learning experiences
Classes 7–8	Consciousness of Self	Review facet and capacities Hands-on learning experiences
Class 9	Consciousness of Others	Review facet and capacities Hands-on learning experiences
Class 10	Presentations and Feedback	Present personal action plans Receive feedback

☇ Specific Course Syllabus

*Leadership Course—Sample Syllabus**

Course Description Emerging Leaders provides an introduction to leadership concepts relevant for being a student leader at the University of San Diego. It is designed to provide exposure to different involvement opportunities at USD, allow for opportunities to engage in leadership, and provide a basic understanding of leadership concepts and models.

Course Learning Objectives Through this course students will:

- Learn about leadership concepts and theories and apply these concepts and theories to their lives.
- Engage in critical thinking about leadership through assignments, activities, and discussions.
- Engage in large group and small group learning communities to learn about leadership.
- Learn about involvement opportunities and resources at USD.
- Form significant relationships with peers and facilitators.

*Thanks to Paige Haber, University of San Diego, for sharing the following excerpts.

- Engage in a service-learning project to enhance their understanding of meaningful service and to engage in a group leadership process.

Course Plan

Date	Topic	Assignment Due
Sept 3	Intro What is leadership?	
Sept 10	Involvement at USD	Attend Alcala Bazaar
Sept 17	Values	Read *EIL* pp. 1–9, 49–72
Sept 24	Consciousness of Self	Reflection #1—Consciousness of Self Complete MBTI
Oct 1	Group Development/Team Building	Read *EIL* pp. 25–47, 113–116 SERVE Project: Social issue and organization selected
Oct 8	Consciousness of Self	
Oct 2–14	*Social Issues Conference*	
Oct 15	Consciousness of Others	Read *EIL* pp. 73–92
Oct 22	Consciousness of Others	Reflection #2—Consciousness of Others Read *EIL* pp.117–120
Oct 29	Current Events & the Election	SERVE Project: Educate & Inform Briefing Due At-home activity: TV coverage & the election
Nov 5	Conflict & Decision Making	Read *EIL* pp. 93–113
Nov 12	Consciousness of Context Leadership Systems	Read *EIL* pp. 11–23
Nov 19	Ethics & Integrity	Reflection #3—Consciousness of Context SERVE Project—Direct Service Hours Due

Course Plan

Nov 26	Thanksgiving Break—No Class	
Dec 3	Closure Service Learning Project Prep	Turn in Copy of Student Development Transcript Read *EIL* pp. 121–124
Dec 10	Service Learning Project Presentations	SERVE Project—Group Presentations
Dec 15—No Class	***Final Paper Due***	

*University 101—Sample Syllabus**

Course Description University 101 is designed to help first-year students adjust to the University, develop an understanding of the learning process, and acquire the academic skills and knowledge to be successful in and out of the collegiate experiences.

Learning Outcomes of the Course

I. Foster Academic Success

As a result of this course, students will

a. Adapt and apply appropriate academic strategies to their courses and learning experiences.

b. Demonstrate how to effectively evaluate information sources and utilize University libraries and information systems for academic inquiry.

c. Recognize the purpose and value of academic integrity and describe the key themes related to the Honor Code at the University of South Carolina.

*Thanks to Amy Kautz, University of South Carolina, for sharing the following excerpts.

d. Use written and oral communication to discover, develop, and articulate ideas and viewpoints.

e. Identify and apply strategies to effectively manage time and priorities.

f. Identify relevant academic policies, processes, and procedures related to advising, course planning, and major exploration.

II. Help Students Discover and Connect with The University of South Carolina

As a result of this course, students will

a. Identify appropriate campus resources and opportunities that contribute to their educational experience, goals, and campus engagement.

b. Develop and apply skills that contribute to building positive relationships with peers, staff, and faculty.

c. Describe what it means to be a Carolinian in the context of the history, traditions, and culture of the University.

III. Prepare Students for Responsible Lives in a Diverse, Interconnected, and Changing World

As a result of this course, students will

a. Examine how their background and experiences impact their values and assumptions and explain the influence these have on their relationships with others.

b. Describe concepts of diversity and recognize diverse perspectives.

c. Describe and demonstrate principles of responsible citizenship within and beyond the campus community.

d. Describe processes, strategies, and resources, and explain the implications of their decisions, related to their overall wellness.

Date	Class Topic	Assignment for Today
8/20	Syllabus Overview and Class Expectations Carolinian Creed Signing	Create a blog
8/25	USC Jeopardy	Transitions Chapters 2 & 3
8/27	Lifelines, blogs and more	
9/1	Time Management and Academic Success, Academic Integrity, Out to Lunch Discussion	Transitions Chapters 5 & 6
9/3	It's Not a Game	Transitions Chapters 10 & 11
9/8	Emotional Intelligence discussion	EI overview article
9/10	Context and Big Picture EI discussion	Foreword, Chapters 1, 2 & 3, Overview of Parts 1, 2, 3, (pages xi–xiv, 1–26, 73, 75)
9/15	See the World	
9/17	Sex and the College Student	Transitions Chapter 9
9/22	Dinner at Amy's House	
9/24	USC Traditions	
9/29	USCPD (Kenny Adams)	
10/1	Research, Plagiarism, and Out to Lunch Discussion	Bring in ideas for Final exam
10/6	Groups We Are In	EIL Chapters 2 & 3
10/8	Fall Break	
10/13	Diversity Discussion	Midterm Paper due Transitions Chapter 4 EIL Chapter 22
10/15	Managing Emotions	EIL Chapters 4, 5, 13
10/20	Motivation and Managing Emotions	EIL Chapters 6, 7, 14, 15
10/22		EIL
10/27	Climbing Wall	Transitions Chapter 8
10/29	Interpersonal Skills	EIL Chapters 8, 9, 16, 17

(*Continued*)

Date	Class Topic	Assignment for Today
11/3	Intrapersonal Awareness	EIL Chapters 10, 11, 18
11/5	Activity	EIL
11/10	Career Center	Transitions Chapter 7
11/12	Working in a Team	EIL Chapters 12, 19, 20, 21, 23
11/17	Thinking Globally	
11/24	Horseshoe Activity	EIL
11/26	Thanksgiving Break	
12/1	Activity	EIL
12/3	Last Day of Class—Class wrap-up	

Session Supplies

1. Internet connection
2. Computer, projector, and screen
3. *EILS: Inventory* (one per participant)
4. Pens and pencils

← Introduction

Ten minutes

1. Welcome participants and begin by sharing the following quote from James McGregor Burns (1978): "Leadership is the most observed and least understood phenomenon on earth."
   a. In pairs or small groups, ask participants to discuss their thoughts on the quote for three minutes.
   b. After three minutes, ask for observations and thoughts from the group.
2. Share one of the following clips from YouTube:

   Test Your Awareness: Do The Test – http://www.youtube.com/watch?v=Ahg6qcgoay4

   Test Your Awareness: Whodunnit? – http://www.youtube.com/watch?v=ubNF9QNEQLA

   a. In pairs or small groups, ask participants to discuss their thoughts on the following question—why show this video prior to a discussion on leadership?

b. After three minutes, ask for observations and thoughts from the group. Potential answers:
We all see the world from a different place.
Not everyone can see everything.
If you agree with the quote from Burns, we all need to enter the dialogue with a certain level of humility.

c. A low-tech alternative to the preceding activity can be found in the Nine Dots Exercise:
Thinking Outside the Box—http://en.wikipedia .org/wiki/Thinking_outside_the_box

3. Conclude with the following assumptions about leadership:
Leadership can be learned (see FAQ for additional information).
You do not need a formal title or role to lead others.
We all step in and out of leadership roles. All of us are leaders *and* followers.

No one of us is as smart as all of us—the correct course of action often lies in the group.

Developing your ability to lead others is similar to other knowledge, skills, and abilities—it takes time, practice, feedback, and an internal desire to learn. *Intentionality is key.*

EIL is *one of many* ways to examine leadership.

✦ The EILS Inventory

Forty-five to ninety minutes

1. Introduction
   a. We will be exploring one model of leadership—there are many ways to view the phenomenon.

    b. The assessment is formative in nature. In other words, the EILS: Inventory is not designed to diagnose the student, predict effectiveness, or compare results with anyone else. It is an indicator based on self-reported information and meant to help illustrate a student's self-perception of leadership abilities and challenges (see FAQ for more information).

    c. Please read the directions carefully and pay close attention to the word *intentionally* in the directions. *Intentional* means "to do on purpose." In other words, it is conscious and a forethought, not simply a reaction or done by accident.

    d. Participants should feel free to ask questions throughout the exercise.

2. Ask participants to complete *Part I: The Three Facets of EIL*.

    a. Participants should answer the questions, score themselves, and read "What do your scores mean?" However, they should pause prior to moving on to *Part II: The Twenty-One EIL Capacities*.

    b. When participants are ready, pause and create space (ten minutes, if time allows) for students to discuss their responses to each of the questions with a partner. Participants should talk through each question and their corresponding score for each facet—consciousness of context, consciousness of self, and consciousness of others.

3. Ask participants to read *Part II: The Twenty-one EIL Capacities*.

    a. Participants should read the section introduction and pause after the handwriting exercise.

    b. In pairs or small groups, ask participants to discuss their thoughts on the following question—what did it feel like to write with your non-dominant hand? Potential answers: awkward, unnatural, OK, weird, uncomfortable.

    c. Ask participants to continue reading and complete Steps One through Three of Part II.

d. When participants are ready, pause and create space (twenty to thirty minutes, if time allows) for students to discuss their responses to each of the questions with a partner.

4. Ask participants to complete *Part III: Below the Surface* (*ten to thirty minutes*).

   a. Depending on the energy of the group and time available, it may be good to turn this activity into a twenty-minute "walk and talk" or "solo reflection" opportunity.

   b. Another option is for students to blog about their experience as it relates to the questions in Part III.

   c. To add a level of accountability, students could also be tasked with creating a short presentation about their responses that is shared in small groups (thirty minutes). Groups could be created based on self-identified strengths or interests around specific facets or capacities.

5. Ask participants to work alone through *Parts IV* through *VI: Synthesis, The Next Step, and The Development Plan*. Reinforce the notion that those items identified in Part IV should feel powerful and important; in other words, they are important areas for development.

   a. When participants are ready, pause and create space (fifteen to twenty minutes, if time allows) for students to discuss their responses to each of the questions with the group. Participants should talk through Parts IV through VI in the small group.

   b. If applicable, allow time for students to respond to each group member's observations and development plan.

6. *Optional:* Take participants through an action planning process. If desired, ask participants to design three Specific, Measurable, Attainable, Realistic, and Tangible (SMART) goals for their area for development.

✦ Conclusion

Ten minutes

1. Conclude the session by reiterating the following observations and points of emphasis from the Introduction:
   a. Leadership can be learned (see FAQ for additional information).
   b. You do not need a formal title or role to lead others.
   c. We all step in and out of leadership roles. All of us are leaders *and* followers.
   d. No one of us is as smart as all of us—the correct course of action often lies in the group.
   e. Developing your ability to lead others is similar to other knowledge, skills, and abilities—it takes time, practice, feedback, and an internal desire to learn. *Intentionality is key.*
   f. EIL is *one of many* ways to examine leadership. To learn more, read *Emotionally Intelligent Leadership: A Guide for College Students* (2008).
2. Choose one or more of the following:
   a. Open up to questions and observations from the group.
   b. A quote such as "Every system is perfectly designed to achieve the results that it gets."—David Beckwith, M.D. Rhetorical question: what system for development do you have in place?
3. Conclude with a personal story about your own development or success you have witnessed with the EIL model.

✦ Frequently Asked Questions

- *What kind of assessment is the EILS: Inventory?*
- *Can the twenty-one EIL capacities be learned?*

- *Is the assessment valid and reliable?*
- *What is Cronbach's alpha?*
- *What does Cronbach's alpha mean to the assessment's reliability?*
- *Is EIL the best way to think about leadership?*
- *How long does the assessment take to facilitate?*
- *How does the overall model work?*
- *Are there any cautions for use of the assessment?*
- *Who is the assessment designed for?*
- *Is the concept of EIL based on original research?*
- *Would I get different results if I thought about a different experience in Sections II and III?*
- *Do the authors conduct workshops, keynotes, and retreats?*

What kind of assessment is the EIL Inventory?

The *EILS: Inventory* is a formative assessment. According to Boston (2002), "Feedback given as part of formative assessment helps learners become aware of any gaps that exist between their desired goal and their current knowledge, understanding, or skill and guides them through actions necessary to obtain the goal" (para. 5). The *EILS: Inventory* is not summative in nature, "which generally takes place after a period of instruction and requires making a judgment about the learning that has occurred" (para. 1). In other words, the *EILS: Inventory* is not designed to diagnose or pigeonhole the student. It is simply an indicator based on their self-reported information.

Can the twenty-one EIL capacities be learned?

We would assert that leadership is a product of nature *and* nurture. So yes, we feel that not only can leadership be learned, but the specific capacities suggested in this model can be developed through intentional effort. Other scholars agree with this assertion (e.g., Avolio, 2005; Arvey, Rotundo, Johnson, Zhang, & McGue, 2006).

Is the assessment valid and reliable?

The assessment is valid in that we measure the concepts that we set out to measure (namely, consciousness of context, self, and others), and it is reliable in that when tested empirically with large numbers of respondents, we generate the same results time after time. Specifically, the questions that are used to build the constructs achieve strong levels of reliability as measured by Cronbach's (1951) alpha coefficient. Consciousness of Context α = .82, Consciousness of Others α = .83, Consciousness of Self α = .75.

What is Cronbach's alpha?

The goal of each scale (consciousness of context, consciousness of self, consciousness of others) is to use several questions that are consistent in measuring the construct, yet each must contribute unique information. The coefficient α is based on the number of items in the scale and the ratio of average inter-item covariance to the average item variance (Cronbach, 1951).

What does Cronbach's alpha mean to the assessment's reliability?

If we increase the number of items, or questions, in the scale, we increase Cronbach's alpha. If the average inter-item correlation is low, alpha will be low. As the average inter-item correlation increases, Cronbach's alpha increases as well. Typically, .60 to .80 indicates acceptable reliability, .80 or higher means good reliability, and coefficients greater than .95 may indicate redundancy in the questions. Garson (2009) suggests that the widely accepted cut-off in the social sciences is .70 with some researchers using .75 to .80. Others are as lenient as .60.

Garson notes that .70 is as low as one should go, because at that point the "standard error of measurement will be over half (.55) of a standard deviation" (Garson, 2009, Measures of Internal Consistency section, para. 5).

Is EIL the best way to think about leadership?

No. There are a number of valuable ways to examine leadership. We agree with Burns (1978) who suggested that "leadership is one of the most observed and least understood phenomenon on earth" (p. 2). This is why we have incorporated the thinking of so many scholars. Emotional intelligence and components of Fiedler's Contingency Theory (1972) simply form the container in which we choose to house our thinking.

How long does the assessment take to facilitate?

Depending on how you choose to facilitate the experience, it can take anywhere from forty-five to ninety minutes, plus twenty minutes for the introduction and conclusion. Of course, the more space you take for dialogue and discussion, the more time you will need. We recommend providing this space so students can focus on making meaning of their results and feedback. We have tried to provide specific time frames for each segment to help you plan for the time that you have available.

How does the overall model work?

In a nutshell, we assert that leadership is a relationship between the leader, the follower, and the context (Fiedler, 1972). As a result, demonstrating emotionally intelligent leadership requires consciousness of context, self, and others. Housed within these three facets are twenty-one capacities that contribute to leadership effectiveness. Some capacities come more naturally than others to each one of us. Thus we need to be mindful of not overusing some and/or minimizing others. Because each context calls for differing capacities, a person must be aware of this and be intentional in his or her choice of actions. For additional details, see *Emotionally Intelligent Leadership: A Guide for College Students* (Shankman & Allen, 2008).

Are there any cautions for use of the assessment?

The *EILS: Inventory* should not be used in the context of job selection or in a diagnostic manner. As mentioned previously, the *EILS: Inventory* is a formative assessment. According to Boston (2002), "Feedback given as part of formative assessment helps learners become aware of any gaps that exist between their desired goal and their current knowledge, understanding, or skill and guides them through actions necessary to obtain the goal" (para. 5). The *EILS: Inventory* is not summative in nature "which generally takes place after a period of instruction and requires making a judgment about the learning that has occurred" (Boston, 2002, para. 1). In other words, the *EILS: Inventory* is not designed to diagnose or pigeonhole the student. It is simply an indicator based on their self-reported information.

Who is the assessment designed for?

The assessment is designed to help individuals interested in developing their leadership capacity reflect on experience and plan for development.

Is the concept of emotionally intelligent leadership based on original research?

The authors developed the EIL model based on Ernest Boyer's (1990) notion of integrated scholarship. A former president of the Carnegie Foundation, Boyer suggested that "by integration, we mean making connections across the disciplines, placing the specialties in a larger context, illuminating data in a revealing way . . . serious, disciplined work that seeks to interpret, draw together, and bring new insight to bear on original research." The EIL model stems from the thinking of scholars in the following areas: transformational leadership (Bass, 1985; Burns, 1978); situational leadership (Blanchard, 1991); contingency theory (Fiedler, 1972); emotional intelligence (Bar-On, 1997; Goleman, 1998; Goleman, Boyatzis, & McKee, 2002; Salovey & Mayer, 1990; Segal, 1997; Weisinger, 1998); authentic leadership development (Avolio & Luthans, 2006); and others (Gardner, J., 1990; Gardner, H., 1999; Heifetz, 1994; Komives, Lucas, & McMahon, 2007; Kouzes & Posner, 2007; Higher Education Research Institute, 1996; and Rost, 1993).

Would I get different results if I thought about a different experience in Sections II and III?

We expect that the results could differ, though not necessarily in dramatic ways. Each of us uses a different set of capacities at different levels in different contexts. However, themes of use do emerge, and it is likely that individuals have natural ease or difficulty accessing certain capacities across contexts. With intentional practice, we believe students can develop and learn to use each of the twenty-one capacities at higher levels and to develop awareness for understanding when to use which capacities.

Do the authors conduct workshops, keynotes, and retreats?

Yes! Feel free to contact us and we would happy to discuss how we may partner: Dr. Marcy Levy Shankman (shankman@mlsconsulting.net) and Dr. Scott J. Allen (sallen@jcu.edu).

FAQ REFERENCES

Arvey, R. D., Rotundo, M., Johnson, W., Zhang, Z., & McGue, M. (2006). The determinants of leadership role occupancy: Genetic and personality factors. *Leadership Quarterly, 17,* 1–20.

Avolio, B. (2005). *Leadership development in balance.* Mahwah, NJ: Lawrence Erlbaum Associates.

Avolio, B., & Luthans, F. (2006). *The high impact leader.* New York: McGraw-Hill.

Bar-On, R. (1997). *The Bar-On emotional quotient inventory (EQ-i): A test of emotional intelligence.* Toronto, Canada: Multi-Health Systems.

Bass, B. (1985). *Leadership and performance beyond expectations.* New York: The Free Press.

Blanchard, K. (1991). Situational view of leadership. *Executive Excellence,* 8(6), 22– 23.

Boston, C. (2002). *The concept of formative assessment.* (ERIC Document Reproduction Service No. ED470206). Retrieved May 5, 2009, from ERIC database: http://www.ericdigests.org/2003–3/concept.htm.

Boyer, E. (1990). *Scholarship reconsidered: Priorities of the professoriate.* (Eric Document Reproduction Service No. ED326149. Retrieved May 5, 2009, from ERIC database: http://eric.ed.gov/ERICWebPortal/custom/portlets/recordDetails/detailmini.jsp?_nfpb=true&_&ERICExtSearch_SearchValue_0=ED326149&ERICExtSearch_SearchType_0=no&accno=ED326149.

Burns, J. M. (1978). *Leadership.* New York: Harper & Row.

Cronbach, L. J. (1951). Coefficient alpha and the internal structure of tests. *Psychometrika, 16,* 297–333.

Fiedler, F. (1972). The effects of leadership training and experience: A contingency model interpretation. *Administrative Science Quarterly,* 17(4), 453– 470.

Gardner, H. (1999). *Intelligence reframed: Multiple intelligences for the 21st century.* New York: Basic Books.

Gardner, J. (1990). *On leadership.* New York: The Free Press.

Garson, G. D. (2009). *Scales & standard measures.* Retrieved July 6, 2009, from http://faculty.chass.ncsu.edu/garson/PA765/standard.htm

Goleman, D. (1998). *Working with emotional intelligence*. New York: Bantam Books.

Goleman, D., Boyatzis, R., & McKee, A. (2002). *Primal leadership: Realizing the power of emotional intelligence*. Boston, MA: Harvard Business School Press.

Heifetz, R. A. (1994). *Leadership without easy answers*. Cambridge, MA: Harvard University Press.

Higher Education Research Institute. (1996). *A social change model of leadership development: Guidebook version III*. Los Angeles: University of California Los Angeles Higher Education Research Institute.

Komives, S. R., Lucas, N., & McMahon, T. R. (2007). *Exploring leadership: For college students who want to make a difference* (2nd ed.). San Francisco: Jossey-Bass.

Kouzes, J. M., & Posner, B. Z. (2007). *The leadership challenge: How to get extraordinary things done in organizations*. San Francisco: Jossey-Bass.

Rost, J. (1993). *Leadership for the 21st century*. Westport, CT: Praeger.

Salovey, P., & Mayer, J. D. (1990). Emotional intelligence. *Imagination, Cognition, and Personality, 9*(3), 185–211.

Segal, J. (1997). *Raising your emotional intelligence: A practical guide*. New York: Henry Holt.

Weisinger, H. (1998). *Emotional intelligence at work*. San Francisco: Jossey-Bass.

Where Emotional Intelligence and Student Leadership Unite

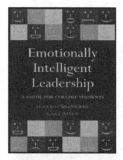

The book *Emotionally Intelligent Leadership* offers an in-depth explanation of the model and the tools for reflection on the concepts of leadership.

ISBN: 978-0-470-27713-3

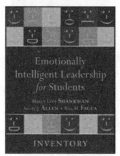

Emotionally Intelligent Leadership for Students—Inventory offers a formative learning experience. The *Inventory* is an opportunity for individuals to explore their experiences in leadership with a focus on learning one's strengths and limitations based on past behaviors.

ISBN: 978-0-470-61572-0

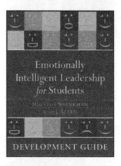

Emotionally Intelligent Leadership for Students—Development Guide offers further guidance for development for each of the 21 capacities, including: definitions, student quotes, suggested experiences and activities, further reading and films to watch, notable quotes, and reflection questions.

ISBN: 978-0-470-61573-7

Emotionally Intelligent Leadership for Students—Workbook brings further understanding and relevancy to the EILS model. It includes modularized learning activities for each capacity, as well as some case studies, and resources for additional learning. It can be used as part of a facilitated course or workshop, or as a stand-alone, follow-up experience that students can use on their own.

ISBN: 978-0-470-61574-4

Emotionally Intelligent Leadership for Students—Facilitation and Activity Guide uses step-by-step instructions to lead facilitators and instructors through modularized activities found in the *EILS Workbook*. The modularized, timed activities can be taught out of sequence and customized to fit the needs of a curricular or co-curricular program. The guide offers various options and scenarios for using activities in different settings with different time constraints.

ISBN: 978-0-470-61575-1

SAVE ON SETS

Sets tailored for facilitators and students are available at discounted prices.
Visit www.josseybass.com for more information